WARDS OF
THE STATE

Also by the author:

The Spider and the Fly: A Writer, a Murderer, and a Story of Obsession

Time Out

WARDS OF
THE STATE

THE LONG SHADOW
OF AMERICAN FOSTER CARE

CLAUDIA ROWE

ABRAMS PRESS, NEW YORK

Published in 2025 by Abrams Press, an imprint of ABRAMS.
All rights reserved. No portion of this book may be reproduced,
stored in a retrieval system, or transmitted in any form or by any
means, mechanical, electronic, photocopying, recording, or
otherwise, without written permission from the publisher.

Library of Congress Control Number: 2024951579

ISBN: 978-1-4197-6315-1
eISBN: 978-1-64700-748-5

Printed and bound in the United States
10 9 8 7 6 5 4 3 2 1

Abrams books are available at special discounts when purchased
in quantity for premiums and promotions as well as fundraising or
educational use. Special editions can also be created to specification.
For details, contact specialsales@abramsbooks.com or the address below.

Abrams Press® is a registered trademark of Harry N. Abrams, Inc.

ABRAMS The Art of Books
195 Broadway, New York, NY 10007
abramsbooks.com

For all the kids.

Contents

Author's Note

All of the characters in this book are real people. I have made every effort to verify the facts of their lives through court records, police reports, child welfare case files, and independent research, though certain experiences described here had no witnesses other than the young people who lived them. Those whose cases have come to public attention, or have become known through their work, appear in these pages under their real names. For the others, I have used pseudonyms to protect either their jobs or their chances for a better future.

Introduction

The question *why* hovers over every piece of writing I've ever done. Dissecting a person's motivation, especially for acts that appear incomprehensible, drew me into journalism and has powered my work for decades. Why had that man done this horrible thing? Why was this girl that way? What was in their heads? How did they understand themselves? These mysteries were rolling around the back of my mind on a February morning as I watched a pale nineteen-year-old escorted into a Scattle courtroom to be sentenced for murder.

Shortly before that snowy day in 2019, I'd been writing newspaper stories about kids who kept getting suspended from school. "Behavior is a language," a teacher had told me. Now her remark echoed. This girl in front of me had shot a young man in the head at sixteen years old—what was she trying to say? The handful of stories I'd read about the case portrayed her as utterly without conscience.

I'd written innumerable pieces about kids in trouble with the law and a few about kids who'd killed. But never in thirty years as a reporter had I heard a defense argument like the one this legal team was attempting to make. The girl's crime, they said, should be blamed on foster care.

America's child welfare system was part of my beat back in the early 2000s, when more than half a million kids in this country were being raised by strangers paid to house and feed them. But I had not thought much about the effects of this upbringing on a child's mindset, day-to-day. Conventional wisdom held that any behavior problems displayed by young people in foster care were the result of whatever family traumas had put them on the state's radar to begin with. Foster care was the net that had saved them. It existed in my mind as a sort of hazy parable about selfless people willing to provide for babies who needed stable homes until they were adopted. Foster care was not something newspapers monitored rigorously, like electoral politics or violent crime. We wrote about it only rarely, as an aberration, when horrific things happened to very young children. Once they were rescued, or buried, the story was over.

But ongoing, behind the curtain of confidentiality that shrouds foster care, kids endured more quotidian harms. The lawyers representing the teenage defendant sitting a few feet from me described her as the product of a failed child welfare system, the outcome of a government bureaucracy so poorly matched to the needs of its clients that thousands leave it in worse shape than when they are taken in. And our taxes pay for this, to the tune of $31.4 billion a year. In that sense, her legal team suggested, the teen facing decades in prison had been failed by all of us.

Though people often think of foster care as a short-term way station for babies born to drug-addicted parents, the fact is that about 40 percent of children under state guardianship are adolescents. These older foster youth, the ones least likely to be adopted, tend to attract far less attention. Before February 2019, that was true for me too.

I had, however, spent a great deal of time looking at juvenile crime. As I examined the case of this waifish teenager and thought back to so many others, I wondered at the enormous number who overlapped with the child welfare system. In 2021, while I was researching this book, two kids who'd fled a group home in Florida spent thirty-five minutes in a shoot-out with police. They'd broken into a neighbor's house, discovered his cache of guns, and as the officers closed in, began blasting. The fourteen-year-old girl ringleader was sentenced to twenty years. A few weeks earlier, a boy from the same group home had been convicted of manslaughter.

This was the same year that much of America read about sixteen-year-old Ma'Khia Bryant, a foster child shot to death by police in front of the home in Columbus, Ohio, where she'd been living with her younger sister. A cheerful girl with no prior record, Ma'Khia had been swinging a knife at two of the home's former residents, defending herself after days of their harassment. If she hadn't been gunned down, Ma'Khia surely would have been arrested. A study of nearly one thousand foster youth in the Midwest found that half left the system with criminal records, and more than 30 percent were imprisoned for violent crime within a year of leaving state care. At least 20 percent of prison inmates nationally are believed to be former foster children.

But why? Would these kids have been incarcerated if they'd never become wards of the state? Or was there something about the system itself that pushed children toward these ends?

The more I probed this question, the more pressing it became. Consider the numbers. About four hundred thousand kids in the U.S. today are growing up with the state as their legal guardian. Every year, upon turning eighteen, about twenty thousand of them "age out," many moving straight into homelessness. Yet, because they have been minors up to that point, their lives and the system shaping them remain largely shielded from public scrutiny—to protect children's privacy, the government says. It also renders them invisible. No obvious indicator identifies the child you see wandering the streets as someone removed from their parents in a police car. Nor that this child may have cycled through the homes of multiple strangers after that. Nor that they may not live in a home at all, but an institution where dinner arrives on a cafeteria tray.

Growing up this way has consequences. Research shows that foster youth suffer post-traumatic stress at nearly twice the rate of Iraq War veterans. The same nine-year study of foster care "alumni" from the Midwest that noted their frequency of incarceration also found that nearly half dropped out of high school. By their mid-twenties, more than half were living in poverty. Despite truly inspiring stories of individuals who surmount those odds, the pattern shows up in every locale, and it has for decades. In 2019, the National Academies of Sciences affirmed that the experience of foster care causes neurological damage to children's brains.

The questions became impossible to ignore. Was foster care creating kids we should fear? When the public assumes responsibility for a child, who is to blame if the child fails? Who answers for the system's results? At present, no federal law makes states liable for crimes committed by a foster kid on the run—that is, while a ward of the state but missing from their assigned placement. The converse is also true: No edict holds states responsible for anything that happens *to* foster children when they are "missing from care." The only people held accountable, it seems, are the kids.

For all of these reasons—from its abysmal outcomes, to the lack of accountability for them, to the fact that this system serves poor children almost exclusively—foster care is in the midst of a historic reassessment. Some experts advocate for its total abolition, insisting nearly all problems that lead to the removal of children from their families can be better addressed by connecting parents with mental health counseling, substance abuse treatment, or housing, and allowing them to keep their kids. On the other side are those who point out that this response, almost by definition, will leave some children in jeopardy. In the middle sits a tangle of more than 800 state- and county-run child welfare agencies staffed with low-paid, overburdened caseworkers whipsawed every decade or so by new legislation demanding a more aggressive approach in one direction or the other.

The backdrop for this debate is a brutal history of family separation in America, from auctions of enslaved people to Indian boarding schools to desperate immigrants at the border. On this point, there can be no dispute: The U.S. has repeatedly used the threat of child removal as a tool to control the disenfranchised. Legions of middle class and affluent kids grow up in homes convulsed with addiction, abuse, and neglect. But their families rarely face that risk.

The more I scrutinized the intersection between foster care and the criminal justice system, the clearer it became that there are specific experiences common to foster kids who end up in locked cells. Almost always, they are teenagers who have run from their foster parents or adoptive families. After some time on the street, they inevitably get hungry enough to shoplift or trade sex for shelter, which usually leads to a booking in juvenile detention. Now saddled with a criminal record, they are deemed "unadoptable." Any child not taken into a permanent family by thirteen is likely to land in a group home, where fights are common and police summoned routinely, which leads to more book-ings. Upon turning eighteen—or in some cases twenty-one—all foster youth neither adopted nor reunited with their families "age out" and are cut from the government system that has paid for their shelter, food, and clothing, to be cast abruptly into the world with minimal education and no money.

I began to wonder if foster care wasn't a crucible hidden in plain sight. I began to ask whether its failures might be an under-acknowl-edged factor driving mass homelessness, drug addiction, and prop-erty crimes, a major gear powering America's incarceration complex, pumping out kids so ill-equipped to function as adults that locked cells became the most logical outcome.

To test these ideas, I interviewed dozens of current and former foster youth. Most had spent at least a few nights homeless, hungry, or behind bars. How did they view their lives, their choices? How did they feel about the foster parents who had reared them and the government workers overseeing those placements? In the thousands of pages of research I read on foster care, its clients, the kids, appeared only as one-sentence pull-quotes, if at all. Mostly, they were numbers. I wanted to understand the experience through their eyes: What did it feel like to be a kid on the run? Did they think anything could have led them to a dif-ferent place? Exactly how had their broken adoptions, group homes, and aging out connected them with crime? And since these patterns were widely known—at least to those working in the system—was anyone, anywhere, doing something about them?

The people whose stories populate *Wards of the State* helped me to answer those questions. They ranged in age from eighteen to fifty-six when I began this project, representing more than four decades of American foster care and every region of the country. One had recently been sleeping on the New York City subways. Another was serving a life sentence in Washington state. A third was selling blood plasma to keep her cell phone service on in Houston. Others have become influential successes, ascending to positions in the justice system or navigating the halls of power in Washington, DC. Connected by a web of foster parents, social workers, judges, lawyers, activists, and state officials, each is a complex character with a survival story to tell. But every one of them carries a ghost inside. All believe foster care permanently twisted the trajectory of their lives.

Together, they form a portrait of a population that exists mostly below our radar, until it explodes into view.

CHAPTER 1

Under Question

SEATTLE, 2016

The gunfire cracked sharp and bright as a camera flash. But as she stumbled down the hill with High Price's gun in her hand, Maryanne didn't see anyone peering out from an apartment window. The street where she ran, past the back of the Holly Park development, was still so new it had no sidewalk, and the road was slick with February frost. Maryanne wore no coat, just a pink hoodie zipped tight around her narrow torso. She wouldn't notice the cold until much later. She could feel her feet thudding on the crumbly pavement but heard no sound. She tripped, pitched forward, kept running.

It worried her the way the gunshot kept ringing in her head, keening so high she couldn't hear the cars hissing past on the thoroughfare below. Maybe the blast had blown out her eardrums. A prickly panic clawed up her arms at the memory of High Price's head. It lolled backward and to the right when she shot him, blood draining straight down onto an orange t-shirt in the car's rear footwell. Not a drop on his tracksuit. Everything about that guy looked clean. No food wrappers or cigarette butts in his black Jaguar. Maryanne could hardly believe it when he'd let her drive it the night before. She was only six weeks past her sixteenth birthday. She'd barely ever held a gun, but High Price had let her play with his. He let her put the pistol in her purse and pose with it, snapping selfies. She loved the way the black metal looked next to her white skin, and she'd puckered up, kissing the air as she mugged for her phone. It was exciting—she couldn't deny it. And she got a ton of likes for those pictures on Facebook.

They'd had fun driving around. He was younger than a lot of guys she'd been with, just twenty-one. But he was obviously doing well, with his Jag and his gun and that stack of C-notes in his lap. He'd been so nice at first, asking about her life and all the places she slept. He said he knew how weird things could get. Maybe he really did know. He'd grown up in some war camp in Africa, and he told her his real name, Emmanuel Gondo, which sure sounded African. He said his father had died over there.

So Maryanne told him about all the foster families, and the bedbugs in her sister's apartment building, and the Friends of Youth shelter, and running from the cops. She told him about sleeping on buses and riding down the interstate to Oregon hidden in the trunk of a Cadillac. She even told him about the Atkinses and how they'd un-adopted her, dumped her back into the pool of unwanted kids like a Christmas puppy grown too big to be cute. Later, she wondered why she'd told him all that stuff. She never talked much about the Atkinses to other people.

Maryanne had been resigned to what was coming when High Price pulled into a clearing at the top of the hill and started touching her thighs. Such a fucking bore. Men were so predictable, the way they'd act all nice before making their stupid moves—grabbing at you, sitting in the bathroom while you were trying to take a shower, reaching over without asking when you were just trying to get warm. A bubble of panic rose in her stomach as High Price stroked her legs. But, really, what could she say? She didn't even know where she was, only that from the hill where they'd parked you could see past the city to the suburbs and all the way out to the snowy peaks of the Cascade Mountains fifty miles east. Was that where the Atkinses had taken her snowboarding?

Maryanne had lived all over western Washington. She knew every bus route and transit station inside and around Seattle. But she'd never seen this elbow-shaped patch of dirt where High Price had parked behind a clump of bramble and trees. There weren't many streets like it now that every sidewalk was clogged with scaffolding and construction cranes. You'd memorize a corner, try to find it a month later, and wander in circles looking at the plywood frames of a dozen new Lego-block houses.

By then, she and High Price had been cruising for hours but the sky was still velvet dark. She kept asking him to take her back to Montrell's house—didn't he care that she had a boyfriend?—but he kept refusing. She'd asked him to leave the heat on while they were talking—she was always so cold—but he'd snapped it off, keeping on in his smooth, steady voice about wanting to help her, saying he had a friend she could stay with who would pay her just to hang out. 'Trell talked like that all the time, telling her she could make racks, with her pretty blue eyes and long brown hair. She always told him to fuck off. But High Price made it sound like a legitimate business plan. Maryanne gazed straight ahead, making her eyes blur as he pulled her pants down and shoved himself inside, until the street lights in the distance turned to smears of color.

But then he changed, talking shit like she was a bitch, a ho, and she could feel her cold panic turn to hot rage. Afterward, she stared at the red condom he'd used. It lay crumpled in the dirt where he'd tossed it like a candy wrapper. Her stomach roiled. Fuck that guy.

***

Two months later, Maryanne plopped onto a swivel chair in a seventh-floor interview room at Seattle Police Department headquarters.

"What the fuck am I here for?" she said.

She was still bleary-eyed, rousted from sleep by a squadron of marshals who'd barged into Montrell's bedroom, guns drawn. "Maryanne Atkins! Maryanne Atkins!" they'd screamed. She and 'Trell stumbled to their feet. They'd fallen into bed only two hours before, and now his stuffy apartment was crowded with men in bulletproof vests, shouting her name. "Get on the fucking ground or we will kill you! Get on the fucking ground!" From the floor, she noticed a few of them were wearing cowboy boots. Then she heard another name. "Gondo! Emmanuel Gondo!" Maryanne couldn't figure out what they were talking about—it could have been so many things—until they yanked her upright, cuffed her hands behind her back, and marched her past the mirror in 'Trell's room, where she caught a glimpse of her face. It had been seven weeks since the night on Holly Street Hill, and she'd been jumpy every time 'Trell brought her downtown. Once, she'd even seen High Price's friend staring at her from across the street. She skittered around a corner and hid behind a car. 'Trell kept telling her to shut up and forget about it, which she'd halfway managed to do.

But now she was sitting in a small, airless room at police headquarters with a camera pointed at her face and a lady detective asking stupid questions, like did she want a glass of water.

"No," said Maryanne.

For nearly an hour they left her alone, spinning back and forth in her swivel chair, making half-circles in space. She leaned forward, put her head down on the desk, and choked out a few desultory sobs. The next minute she sat up, stared into the mirror lining the wall next to the detective's desk, and began smoothing her eyebrows. She hiked up the hem of her sweatshirt, picked some skin from her bellybutton, then flopped back down onto the swivel chair. She tested its wheels, pushing off the wall to give herself a four-foot ride across the floor. "Wheee!" She whispered, swinging her arms. "Wheee!" She spun one way, then the other. "It's so boring!" she cried, flinging her head down onto the desk.

Seconds trudged by. Maryanne turned her gaze toward the video camera bolted above the door and with the repetitive rhythm of a cat, set about grooming herself—chewing her cuticles, inspecting them, chewing again. She leaned backward, stretched, and spat out a piece of fingernail. From a room on the other side of the wall, she heard the rumble of voices. The words were muffled, but Maryanne could tell from their cadence that one of them was 'Trell.

"Babe?" she called out. "Is that my boyfriend? I want my boyfriend! Oh my god, let me fix my hair."

Maryanne clawed at the tangled topknot on her head. "What the fuck am I here for? This is crazy. I don't want to go to jail. I want my boyfriend! Oh my god, it's so boring in here. I can't be in this room!"

Then, an idea.

"Excuse me," Maryanne said, addressing herself to the camera above the door. "I have to go pee. Hello? Somebody? I gotta go pee."

Silence for two minutes. Three minutes. Five.

"I will pee on this fucking floor," Maryanne called out cheerfully.

Immediately, a male officer popped his head inside the door and let her out.

When she returned, Detective Dana Duffy was seated at the modular gray desk to read Maryanne her rights. Anything she said could be used against her in court, the detective explained, and she was entitled to a lawyer. Maryanne could stop answering questions at any time—did she understand all that?

"Mmm-hmmm," Maryanne said.

"Do you know why you're here?" the detective asked.

"Because I'm in foster care?" Maryanne buried her chin in the neck of 'Trell's gray hoodie. She was glad to be wearing something that smelled of him. "I don't know. They always make me go to court."

"That's not why we're here." Detective Duffy's voice was calm, though not warm.

"Okay."

"We're here to talk about an incident that happened back in February—ring any bells? Remember Gondo, Emmanuel Gondo? Someone you used to call High Price?"

Maryanne blew her nose on her sleeve.

"Yeah, I know him. That was my friend."

Duffy continued, matter-of-fact as a high school guidance counselor. She led Maryanne through the night in Gondo's car, the two of them driving for hours, first with his brother and friends, then alone. She asked about Gondo's gun, and Maryanne shook her head. No, she'd never touched one in her life. Duffy asked about sex. Gondo had wanted to, tried to, Maryanne said, but she'd refused. He kicked her out of his car for that, so she took the bus back to 'Trell's house.

"Okay. Did you shoot him?" Duffy asked.

"No! I've never—I don't know how to shoot a gun!" But Maryanne did realize, quite clearly, what was happening. "I need my lawyer," she said.

Detective Duffy kept probing. She told Maryanne that they'd seen her Facebook posts, the pictures with her and Gondo's gun. She pulled a photo printout from the stack of papers on her desk and placed it near Maryanne. It showed her in close-up, puckering her lips into a kissy face and pointing a handgun at the camera.

"You're trying to say that I did this?" Maryanne squealed. "Are you guys trying to say I did this to him?"

"Yeah," said Duffy softly.

"No! I would never do that. If my life depended on it, I wouldn't know how to shoot a gun!"

"Just tell us why this happened," the detective said. "Did you ever have sex with High Price?"

"I don't see why that even matters."

"So he never made you have sex with him or anything?" Maryanne shook her head, no. "Okay, well, that's good," said Duffy, rising to leave.

"I don't wanna be blamed for this."

"Well, you need to keep talking then."

Maryanne did. She repeated the story about High Price kicking her out of his car, whimpering a bit with her narration.

"Tears aren't gonna help."

"I'm not even capable of doing that! I'm not even that kind of person!"

"We'll let a jury decide," said Duffy, stepping out of the room.

Alone in the quiet, Maryanne screamed. "'Trell? Montrelllll! Please, somebody, I need my lawyer!" She was pacing now, wailing. "Somebody help me! I wanna kill myself!"

"Maryanne," said Duffy, opening the door. She spoke stiffly, as if trying to control her temper around an obstreperous child. "You need to be quiet. Sit down and gather yourself."

"Sorry. I've never been in this situation."

"Well, I should hope not. Is there anything else you want to tell us?"

"No. I think you just figured it all out."

Alone again, Maryanne shrieked. She walked straight toward the two-way mirror, collapsed down onto the swivel chair again, and began muttering to herself. "I'm such a good person. Why does this stuff have to happen? It has to be God telling me to go back to school. I'm gonna go back to school, God, okay? I promise. As long as you keep me away from jail, I'll stay in school for my whole life."

She stood up, holding her crotch, and knocked on the locked door. "Excuse me, if somebody's listening, I have to go to the bathroom. Oh, my gosh, I gotta take a shit. I'm about to go to the bathroom on the floor, okay? How about that? I got napkins and everything and I don't care." She caught a glimpse of herself in the two-way mirror. "What's going on with my face, though? I got a pimple! And I got a mustache!" She pulled at her cheeks, stretching them, peering at her pores. "I need my mommy. What is my mom gonna think when they put me in jail? If I really didn't do it, then I can't get in trouble, so I don't care."

She walked a few paces and turned to address the mirror again.

"They need to catch real criminals instead of little girls. Look at me!" she sobbed, unzipping her hoodie. "Look at me! How is this possible—I'm a fucking *girl*!"

She returned to grooming herself, removed her sneaker and bit off a toenail. Finally, with nothing more to pick at, Maryanne began to sing in a high, bluesy voice, as if crooning to a baby. "I suck," she whispered, cutting herself off. "I suck."

She tapped on the locked door once more. An affable detective poked his head inside, called her kiddo, asked what she needed.

"This shouldn't even be legal to happen."

"It is legal," he said. "I'm sorry."

At 5:23 P.M., after Maryanne had been in the police station well over three hours, the detective asked, "So, did you want to talk to a lawyer?"

***

Maryanne never left confinement again. After she had spoken by phone to a public defender, Detective Duffy returned and told Maryanne to put her hands behind her back for handcuffing. "Like you're praying," the detective said.

For the next few weeks, sixteen-year-old Maryanne sat in a jail cell, charged as an adult with first-degree murder. The Regional Justice Center held minors in a separate wing, and Maryanne, as one of only two girls there, was locked in solitary. For her protection, the guards said. For twenty-three hours a day, she sat on a cot, back against the concrete wall. More than once, she caught an eye blinking at her beneath the curtain pulled across the window of her unit. She had no books for distraction, no natural light. She told her lawyer that she wanted to kill herself.

During her first week, two visitors showed up: Maryanne's father, who looked like he was nodding off; and Tasha Smith, Maryanne's last foster parent. Talking to Tasha, she was wild-eyed. With her father, impatient. But on the phone to her mother, Maryanne betrayed herself again and again.

"I guess they're talking about the guy who died—his phone is missing," Maryanne said during their first conversation. She'd tracked news reports obsessively in the weeks before her arrest. "Obviously, I can't be the last person who was with him."

"Yeah, they said his wallet and his phone and gun," her mother answered in a dreamy voice. She was calling from a bathroom. What a drag that Maryanne had got herself locked up, her mom said. She'd been hoping they could catch a movie.

"Mom!" shrieked Maryanne. "I'm about to miss my summer—maybe next summer too! I don't know how many summers I'm gonna miss!"

She berated herself for posting pictures of Gondo's gun on Facebook. She confessed to "freaking out" on the guards when they told her she'd be in jail for two weeks before an arraignment. "That's so far from now—it's not fair!" she wailed. Then her voice turned soft, almost pleading. "Think you can come to my court date?"

Maryanne's mother said she would try. They'd get everything straightened out. Since Maryanne wasn't the person who'd shot Gondo, there was no need to worry, and surely her lawyers would be able to get the case moved down to juvenile court.

Maryanne sniffled.

"If it comes down to it, if it comes to the point where they really try to charge me with Murder 1, I'm going to have to, like, make up a good story—"

"No," her mom broke in sharply. "You can't make up anything. You need to be honest with them."

"But I don't want to be charged like twenty years or more for Murder 1! I need to make it shorter!"

"Honey, if you didn't do it, then you're going to be fine."

"I *really* want to get out of here," said Maryanne, starting to sob.

"I know it's hard, but it's going to be sunny for months and you have your whole life ahead of you—"

"I don't have my whole life ahead of me, Mom! If they give me twenty years, I'm not going to have no life, no more!"

"Why would you even worry about that?" said Maryanne's mother, who had spent time in prison and knew the call was being recorded.

"I'm worried about that 'cause it's possible!" shrieked Maryanne. "If I didn't have a Facebook, I wouldn't be in here!"

"Well, yeah. I told you the first time you did that," her mother chided. "But I don't get why you're so worried. You don't have any reason to be worried if you didn't do it."

"I'm only sixteen—they don't get it! I want to have a whole life! I don't want to be in jail for years!"

"They do get it," said her mother.

The following day, Maryanne asked her mom to print pictures of Montrell off Facebook and send them to her as a keepsake. She asked about sentencing ranges for first-degree murder, as her mother Googled for answers.

"Don't ever lie to them about anything 'cause that's the worst thing you could do," Maryanne's mother said with the calm assurance of experience. "Detectives are smart and they'll figure it out. If you're scared or whatever, just be honest with them. Tell them what happened, because right now it looks like you're just this cold-blooded killer."

"If I say self-defense, will that help?"

"Well, yeah, if it was," said her mother, question marks embedded in every word.

***

Maryanne's attorney took her talk of suicide seriously, and King County finally did too. After she'd spent forty days locked in isolation, Maryanne was cuffed and loaded into a van for the drive up Interstate 5 to Seattle's juvenile detention hall.

But there was little urgency in getting her case to trial. Before the miserable night on Holly Street Hill, Maryanne had been well known to the system as "a runner." She'd generated thousands of pages of caseworker notes, police reports, and warrants as a Child in Need of Services. Now that Maryanne was caught, no system appeared eager to claim her. Not foster care, which still held her files; nor juvenile detention, which now had to address her long-deferred dental care; nor prosecutor Jessica Berliner, who didn't mind Maryanne moving further away from sixteen with each passing day, her round face developing cheekbones. Birthdays were particularly fraught, since each one made any chance of serving time in a juvenile lockup less likely, and state prison more probable. Maryanne's eighteenth birthday, nearly two years after her arrest, was marked with a pair of handcuffs and a ride across town to the King County Jail, where her blue juvie scrubs were exchanged for scarlet. But she kept herself entertained. Read memoirs. Wrote in her journal. Found ways to get on Facebook and post selfies from her cell. Maryanne was a clever girl—no one but her math teachers had ever argued that.

Of much greater mystery was Maryanne's state of mind when she shot Emmanuel Gondo. Because she had been charged with felony first-degree murder—for killing Gondo in the course of robbing him—prosecutor Berliner argued that testimony about post-traumatic stress disorder, or the effects of being trafficked, or a lifetime of abuse was irrelevant. It would only "induce sympathy" for the girl, Berliner argued. "At some point, there is just a human inability to ignore it," she told Judge Marshall Ferguson. "I think that's a real risk in the context of this case."

Judge Ferguson agreed. At that, Maryanne's lawyers called a halt to the proceedings and urged their young client to plead guilty. A jury verdict could have locked her away for more than thirty years. This was when I first saw Maryanne, on a snowy February morning in 2019, almost three years to the day of Emmanuel Gondo's murder, when Judge Ferguson would decide how Washington state should punish the child it had raised.

***

I wasn't thinking about the number of foster kids who wind up in prison as I settled myself in the second row of benches in Judge Ferguson's courtroom for Maryanne's sentencing. I wasn't even thinking much about Maryanne. A forensic psychologist I knew had been hired to testify for the prosecution on an appropriate punishment, and because I'd been thinking about writing a book on youth crime, he suggested I listen in. Maryanne was "probably a budding sociopath," he'd told me after interviewing her at the King County Jail. He planned to recommend that Judge Ferguson lock her away for a quarter century.

I remembered hearing about Maryanne's arrest. I'd been an education reporter at the time, covering racial segregation in Seattle schools and debates over discipline for kindergarteners, but something about her story nagged me. Something about the tightness in the chief prosecutor's voice when he mentioned her as an example of surging youth violence. "Cold blooded," said the headline over Maryanne's photograph on one news site. The picture showed her in a car, eyes narrow and hard as she glared at the camera. This was the image I held in my mind as she walked into court.

"Hello," Maryanne grumbled at her state-appointed attorney Colleen O'Connor, before plopping into a chair at the defense table. She stretched her legs out straight, held them a few inches off the floor, and paddled her feet in the air like flippers. Though she'd spent three birthdays in juvenile detention and jail, Maryanne, now nineteen, still looked like a girl. Pallid and slight, she had tweezed her eyebrows into delicate bird's wings and twisted her long brown hair into two dainty braids like Dorothy from *The Wizard of Oz*. This persona was calculated, I thought, scribbling impressions in my notebook. Maryanne had clearly primped for her appearance. But she hadn't been able to hide the shadow surrounding her eyes. It did not look like sleeplessness so much as something that came from within. Nor had she tried to cover up a dollar sign tattooed on her neck, or the words *fuck love* inked across the back of her right hand.

The courtroom was packed with onlookers, its first row crowded with the family and friends of Maryanne's victim, many dressed in traditional African robes and headwraps. Behind them sat a dozen young women from a prostitution survivors' group, who'd come to support Maryanne. All of them wore purple. "The color of transformation," one whispered to me. No one from Maryanne's various families—biological, foster, or adoptive—was present.

The forensic psychologist who'd invited me never testified. Instead, I listened as prosecutor Jessica Berliner spent two hours arguing that the teenager in front of us should be locked away for twenty-four years. Maryanne rocked gently in her chair. An affectation, I told myself, a show of self-soothing to create sympathy. I'd spent much of my early adulthood trying to understand criminal violence, including five years conversing with a serial murderer, and my perceptions of Maryanne were filtered through that experience. I viewed everything about her through the prism of the budding child-sociopath I'd been warned about. Maryanne, showing little reaction to anything being said about her, fit neatly into my assumptions.

Only when Berliner described her as a remorseless manipulator did Maryanne's face betray emotion. Her nostrils flared. A tear trickled down her cheek. It was true, Berliner allowed, that this teenager had suffered years of neglect. She had come into the child welfare system as an abused nine-year-old. Even before neighbors' calls to the police finally got Maryanne taken away from her father, everyone in their small development knew something was wrong. They'd called Maryanne's school to report constant screaming inside her home. They'd passed food to her through a bedroom window because Maryanne was locked inside, alone and hungry. They'd knocked on her father's door, wondering about the sound of something being thrown against the walls, and peered inside to see a child's bedroom with no clothes in the closet, no pictures on the walls, no toys. Maryanne's dad thanked them for their concern. But he never introduced his daughter. "It was as if she was no one," a neighbor said.

When the police finally arrived on a December morning, they found the fourth-grader sobbing, her nose bruised, and her knees pulled up close to her chest. Her mother had "dumped her," Maryanne told an officer quietly interviewing her in the bedroom. She begged to be allowed to go to class. Records showed that her father had kept her home from school eight times since September. Whenever Maryanne heard his voice in the adjoining room, she flinched.

During her first years in foster care, Maryanne bit herself in sleep, weeping as she dreamed. At fifteen, rejected by the family who'd adopted her and returned to foster care, she had been trafficked for sex, her name added to the National Registry for Missing and Exploited Children. All of these things had happened while Maryanne was a ward of Washington state, the prosecutor acknowledged. But the responsibility for murder was hers alone. "Because we feel sorry for her, do we give her a pass?" Berliner demanded of Judge Ferguson. In the back of the courtroom a baby wailed. Maryanne swallowed hard, as if trying to push down a stone.

Berliner stopped short of using the word *monster* to describe Maryanne, but it seemed to hover, unspoken. What about the things her adoptive parents said about the ways she'd terrified them—how she hoarded food, kicked holes in walls, and hurt animals? What about her chronic dishonesty, documented in a foot-tall stack of reports from her years in foster care? Evidence from the crime scene suggested she'd shot Emmanuel Gondo as he slept, standing outside his car, not in the chaotic terror of a rape, as Maryanne's lawyers had tried to claim. "Her history has made her this way. But it's still who she is," the prosecutor concluded. "I fear she may be broken. I fear she may be this way forever."

Despite Berliner's zeal, many of her colleagues in the King County Prosecutor's Office felt squeamish about the case. Age of consent in Washington is sixteen, and Maryanne had crossed that line just six weeks before the shooting. If Emmanuel Gondo had been twenty-two, rather than twenty-one, the difference in their ages could have opened him to a statutory rape charge. But since he was dead, and twenty-one, those possibilities were moot.

The same could be said of Maryanne's childishness. Utterly performative, Berliner felt. Obsessing over a missed summer, fretting at her pimples and messy hair, threatening to pee on the interrogation room floor—to the prosecutor, these were the acts of a self-absorbed manipulator, a person willing to do whatever she considered necessary to get what she wanted. Particularly offensive to Berliner was the idea that a pretty white girl would attempt to claim rape and pin it on a Black man, after initially denying any such assault. The prosecutor's long red hair trembled with outrage as she described Maryanne's fabrications to Judge Ferguson, who also happened to be Black. "If it comes down to the point where they really try to charge me with Murder 1, I'm going to have to, like, make up a good story," said Berliner, quoting Maryanne's phone calls with her mother from jail.

Judge Ferguson had been on the bench for all of six months. Maryanne's case was his first murder trial. Weeks before her sentencing, he'd written about the "grossly different outcomes" for Black criminal suspects compared to whites. Could the judge have been thinking about Maryanne as he typed those words, assuming she expected to be treated differently than Gondo would have been, if their roles were reversed?

Maryanne's lies muddied everything. But the fact was, she had been sixteen, alone with an adult man, late on a winter night in a part of the city she did not know. It was not hard for me to imagine that she'd allowed it to happen but wanted it to stop. Nor was it difficult to envision a kid who'd been trafficked suddenly exploding with rage. "I don't think Maryanne really understands her own story," one of the prostitution-survivor advocates had testified. None of that mattered. Because Maryanne had pleaded guilty to murder in the course of a robbery, such nuances were beside the point. Detective Duffy had offered Maryanne a way to tell her story three years earlier in the interrogation room, when she'd asked if Gondo forced her to have sex. But humiliated and frightened, ashamed to explain all that led up to that moment, Maryanne said no, she had never been a victim.

Legally speaking, Berliner had a delicate line to walk. By the time Maryanne sat in court, it was settled law that kids' brains are physiologically different from adults' and that these differences make minors less culpable because, as children, they are neurologically wired for impulsivity. This was exactly the point, Berliner said. Maryanne's childhood had left her emotionally bruised, wildly reactive, and capable of enormous destruction. She was indeed a kid, self-involved and heedless. Those were the very qualities that made her dangerous, said the prosecutor, pushing for a sentence that would keep Maryanne locked away until middle age.

Berliner had called for similarly tough sentences on other minors who killed, exasperated by Seattle's drift toward what she considered naïve fads—restorative justice, peace circles, community service. The word she used most often to describe Maryanne was "manipulative," which also leads most every list of sociopathic hallmarks, though the other typical traits—frequent boredom, impulsivity, lack of empathy— could be applied to many teenagers. To people who worked with street kids, *manipulative* was just an ugly term for survivalism.

It wasn't as if Berliner had grown up oblivious to the ways being passed from one home to another could torque a kid's brain and twist their decisions. Her own mother was a prominent victims' advocate with special expertise on sexual assault. These topics had been dinner table conversation throughout Berliner's adolescence. But to her mind, juvenile brain science did not change the questions of justice or public safety. Maryanne's childhood had made her lethal. That was the only fact that mattered.

It was a canny legal strategy. Berliner conceded the teen's dishonesty once might have been a survival tactic, but it now appeared to be chronic. She was willing to do or say whatever she felt she needed to, regardless of who got hurt, and it was time to account.

"This is her responsibility," the prosecutor said. "She isn't the victim here."

But the crux of Colleen O'Connor's defense said Maryanne absolutely was a victim, not just in Gondo's car but throughout her entire life. It could have been a powerful argument. By the time Maryanne sat in court facing a future behind bars, more than thirty states had been sued for damage done to children raised in foster care. To control their behavior, foster kids grew up swallowing psychotropic drugs that had never been intended for children, and their rates of post-traumatic stress were off the charts. Maryanne herself had been diagnosed with PTSD in the sixth grade and medicated ever since with a cocktail of pills to treat anxiety, sleeplessness, and depression. Since the December morning in 2009 when police led her away from her dad's one-bedroom shack, Maryanne had lived in seven homes. Her behavior deteriorated with each new placement.

The neighbor who'd called authorities about Maryanne's father never forgot that little girl. Cherie Ferguson had often invited Maryanne to spend time at her home across the courtyard. She'd set the child down on the carpet with a pile of her own granddaughter's toys and watched Maryanne methodically destroy them. She wasn't a bad kid, Cherie believed, just starved and angry and lost. Cherie would make dinner and offer to bring Maryanne to school in the morning. But her father spurned every overture, pounding on Cherie's door at 2:30 A.M., demanding that Maryanne be sent home right that minute. Cherie, now in her eighties, had long wondered what ever happened to that little girl. "I'm not saying two wrongs make a right, but she was so ill, such a poor little mixed-up kid," Ferguson told me. "I always hoped some relative would take her, but no one came forward for Maryanne. Not one soul."

This was precisely the kind of information Berliner did not want introduced at trial. Even now that Maryanne had pleaded guilty, the prosecutor objected each time her lawyer tried to introduce sentencing witnesses who could speak about Maryanne's crime within the context of her life. O'Connor kept offering experts in trauma and trafficking, but Judge Ferguson would only allow testimony relevant to the charges

Maryanne had pled to. No one was arguing the miserable facts of her life, but what did they matter in the case of a robbery? To the judge it sounded like Maryanne's lawyer was still pressing her old story about self-defense during a rape. But Maryanne had stolen Gondo's phone and cash, so how could self-defense be an issue? The judge eventually grew so frustrated with O'Connor's approach that he adjourned court early and told her to get her story straight.

More than a few legal observers told me Maryanne's lawyers had let her down. O'Connor clearly felt protective of her teenage client, and she was an experienced attorney—head of the King County Department of Public Defense. Yet she'd failed to make an issue of the fact that Maryanne asked to speak with a lawyer hours before the police connected her with one. She'd considered requesting a different judge, knowing Ferguson's lack of experience would be a disadvantage, but let it go. She'd thought about driving down to Oregon to talk with the officers who'd picked up Maryanne in a juvenile prostitution sting only days before she shot Gondo—but never did. She'd allowed the case of a trafficked foster child to somehow get twisted into the story of an ice-cold temptress. Maryanne had not made things easy. She was horrified by the idea of talking in public about being sold for sex. At first, she didn't even understand that had happened to her.

By closing arguments, O'Connor conveyed the impression of a limp rag. She looked weary, depleted. She urged a nine-year sentence, making Maryanne eligible for release at twenty-five. Berliner argued that the teenager should be locked away until her forties. Judge Ferguson, fresh from a career in real estate law, appeared to be concerned mostly with maintaining order. He said he wanted to acknowledge the "really horrendous tragedy" this case represented, clearly referring to both Gondo's murder and Maryanne's shredded childhood leading up to it. He noted Maryanne's "otherwise nonviolent life," and acknowledged that her crime touched on difficult topics—not least, sex between a minor and an adult. The judge spoke about the "evolution of juvenile jurisprudence" regarding kids. A young person's brain and character were "less formed," making them "less culpable," Judge Ferguson affirmed, sounding almost as if he were explaining the concept to himself. And Maryanne's capacity for decision-making was "certainly not the same as an adult's," he added, conceding that she showed potential for rehabilitation, "maybe even redemption."

These were careful words, a checklist to ensure Judge Ferguson wouldn't have his decision reversed on appeal for failing to recognize Maryanne's youth. When he invited the Gondos to speak, their family pastor rose. George Everett described the Gondos' suffering during the Liberian Civil War, where they had survived in a refugee camp, arriving in Seattle in 2005, when Emmanuel was ten. The judge's decision would show whether the life of a Black man had as much value in America as any other, Everett added in a resonant voice. "What will our children learn from what has happened to one of them?" he asked. Would it be that because you're from Africa, "your life does not matter?"

When Judge Ferguson turned toward Maryanne, she sprang to her feet.

"I did not mean for this to happen," she sobbed, her face blotchy and red. "If I could take it all back, I would. I wish I could do anything to take it all back. I pray for forgiveness every single day." Then suddenly, her tears vanished, and Maryanne spoke with great control. "No matter how much the prosecutor calls me a liar, I am not a bad person." Despite affecting disinterest throughout the three-day proceeding, Maryanne had been listening to every word.

Judge Ferguson nodded. If Maryanne had been fifteen when she shot Gondo, there would have been a hearing to debate whether adult prison was the right place for her. Because she was six weeks into sixteen, that question had been taken off the table. An arbitrary deadline, the judge acknowledged, but he felt that Maryanne's crime was due neither to her youth, nor her "harrowing" personal history. Lots of teenagers lie when backed into a corner, Ferguson understood. But the "scale and cruelty" of Maryanne's dishonesty was not attributable to mere immaturity. "These were particularly ugly and pernicious lies," the judge said. "They were, in the court's opinion, opportunistic."

As Maryanne buried her face in O'Connor's shoulder, Judge Ferguson handed down his decision: nineteen years and three months in prison—a few weeks longer than Maryanne had been alive.

"The court is hesitant to indict, wholesale, the foster care system," Judge Ferguson concluded. "But opportunities were missed."

***

Two guards led Maryanne away, but I could not stop thinking about her. Before writing about education, I'd spent a few years covering child welfare in Washington state. All that time, Maryanne had been my unseen subject. She was a four-year-old living with a dad she barely knew when I started the beat in 2004. She was standing on a table, shrieking in her second-grade classroom when I wrote about the mental health needs of foster youth in 2007. She was one of 52,000 American children adopted from foster care in 2012, when I wrote about new laws aimed at helping teens who age out of the system. And she was among the thousands of adoptees who are sent back to foster care when their adoptions fall apart.

But behind all the reports and evaluations, who exactly was this girl—a desperate and misunderstood child? Or something more menacing? There was a quality about her that clawed like a guilty conscience. Even those who despised Maryanne could not conceal a grudging admiration for the waif who ran from youth shelters in her stocking feet and somehow found shoes. And in our evolving understanding of consent, it would not be such a stretch for a sixteen-year-old girl—late at night, with an adult, in a part of the city she did not know—to feel she had, in fact, been raped, whether she said the word "no" or not. She shaped herself to please whoever was looking. French braids for the courthouse. Bare shoulders for online escort sites. Black slang when she ran with street kids. Yet these signifiers of identity seemed less like billboards than masks. And behind them, was Maryanne just a traumatized child doing whatever she could to survive? Or had there been someone more sinister sitting before Judge Ferguson, nervously tapping her foot?

Six days later, I visited Maryanne at the King County Jail. She had not yet been transferred to state prison, and I wanted to catch her before she disappeared into the maw of another government system. Mainly, I wanted to convince her to let me look more deeply. Maryanne was a cipher, but I wondered how much of her path had been set by larger forces. In court, Maryanne's lawyers had attempted to document her development through the years by presenting a timeline of photographs. They'd found just a handful of images. There was Maryanne, buck-toothed and dorky at ten, entering her second foster placement. She'd clung so ferociously to her new mom that the woman called the state, insisting Maryanne had to go; Maryanne, at eleven, standing next to a community center Santa Claus, her shoulders hunched inward, as if trying to take up less space. There she was two years later, after the adoption, with makeup sparkling her eyes. The last shot showed Maryanne at eighteen in a mortarboard and silky blue gown, receiving her high school diploma at the King County Jail. From her seat at the defense table, Maryanne had glanced up at that frozen moment of achievement, then averted her eyes. Other than these four portraits, she was an empty silhouette—no first-day-of-school pictures, no snapshots from babyhood. The years signified by blank squares felt like the most accurate depiction of all.

The jail was a grimy, putty-colored building at the edge of Seattle's glass-and-chrome downtown. Everything about it felt old, dirty, and worn out, except for the metal detector and video screener that scanned my bag. I used one of the golf pencils provided to write the name of the inmate I wanted to see on a small sheet of pink paper, which struck me as strangely old-fashioned for this city built on technology. A creaky elevator brought me to the ninth floor. There, I handed my paper to the guard and seated myself inside a booth where a sticky handset would allow me to speak with Maryanne through smudged glass. I was a middle-aged woman with children of my own, strangely intimidated by what I imagined to be the judgment of this teenage girl. She sat down and lifted the receiver on her side of the window. The *fuck love* tattoo on her hand was impossible to miss.

Maryanne's lawyer had wondered about the prosecution's portrayal of her client as the coldest kind of villain. As a public defender, Colleen O'Connor had known far scarier people, true sociopaths who were easy to work with—well-mannered and -behaved—precisely because they could control their emotions. Unlike Maryanne. The first time they'd met, when Maryanne was sixteen, she'd paced their locked conference room at juvenile detention like a wild creature, shrieking, hysterical, unable to sit still. "She was off the walls," O'Connor said. "She'd never been any place she couldn't leave."

Through the protective divider between us, Maryanne nodded hello and offered a tentative smile. She said she recognized me from court. I had not planned to conduct an interview, just an introduction. But Maryanne seemed eager to talk. The first thing she wanted to discuss was love. The older women in jail, who'd taught her to make tattoo ink from baby shampoo and crushed-up pencil lead, had explained what it was to be a mother with addictions. All of them had children in foster care, and they'd helped Maryanne understand how her own mother could have put heroin first. "They miss their kids, but the addiction takes over everything," Maryanne said wearily. "So, I forgive my mom."

Recordings of their jailhouse phone calls after Maryanne's arrest had left me confused. They'd spoken on Mother's Day, with frequent "I love yous" batted back and forth over the line, and when their allotted twenty minutes were up, Maryanne said she'd be able to call right back. Which she had done. But her mother never picked up. Maryanne called, and waited, and called again. Her mother was gone. This was standard, she told me with a shrug. Yearning for her mom had gotten Maryanne into trouble over and over. It had driven her to run from foster homes in hopes of finding her mother on the streets. It had left her waiting in bus stations for hours, because her mother had promised to be there. "She's kind of like a celebrity that way," Maryanne said.

Despite her tattoos and jail scrubs and the fact that she'd murdered a man, there was a gentleness to Maryanne I had not anticipated, a certain naivete. I distrusted this impression and kept offering her off ramps, reasons to back away. A book would take years, I said. There would be endless questions. And they would be intrusive. And I would be checking everything she said against her records, which I would also need to see.

"That's okay," said Maryanne. "I'm used to it."

CHAPTER 2
Hiding in Plain Sight

To those of us who learned Maryanne's story in a courtroom, her slide from foster child to convicted murderer looked like a freefall. It was just eight months between the Friday in June when child welfare workers confirmed she was being trafficked and the February night Maryanne shot Emmanuel Gondo in the head, a rapid tumble from soccer kid to street urchin. But Maryanne's transformation was sudden only in the way of a flipped calendar page on New Year's Eve, when the crossover from one decade to the next has been building, minute by minute, for years.

Some might peg the start of Maryanne's countdown to detonation to May 2014, when she walked out of the Friends of Youth shelter in suburban Kirkland and felt a freedom she'd never known, the dawning realization that no one could hold her. Maryanne's mother and father had lost their parental rights years before, her adoptive family was actively trying to sever its legal responsibility, and Washington's unusually liberal laws allowed kids as young as thirteen to refuse counseling. All of which left Maryanne, at fourteen, completely untethered.

Others might set the clock back further, to the weeks before Christmas 2012, when Maryanne, then twelve, sat in a King County courtroom and told the judge she wanted to be the Atkinses' daughter. She had fantasized about this day, sitting through one adoption fair after another as prospective families looked her over. Maryanne was the oldest kid in the room. Almost all parents adopting from foster care want babies or very young children—Maryanne had an infant half-brother who'd been immediately taken by a single mom in Olympia—so she was thrilled when the Atkinses sat down at the table where she was making friendship bracelets. The state moved quickly. After two lunch dates and a sleepover at their home, Maryanne climbed into the back of a social worker's car for the drive from her fourth foster home, in a suburb north of Seattle, to the Atkinses' place in the country.

The honeymoon lasted just a few months. Everything about family life grated on Maryanne: the way her new parents looked so disappointed when she didn't want to watch movies with them on the couch or asked to eat dinner in her room, as if they thought you could create a family just by acting like one. Their wholesomeness made her squirm—all granola and the Grateful Dead and horseback riding. Sometimes Maryanne wanted to fit in; sometimes she didn't. At all times she felt like a fraud. But on adoption day, these warning signs were pushed aside. The Atkinses invited a bunch of their friends to court, the judge rapped his gavel, and Maryanne's social workers applauded. Her new mom wept. Afterward, they walked through downtown Seattle, gazing at the holiday lights and children lined up outside Nordstrom's for a moment on Santa's lap. It had taken all of fifteen minutes to rule that Maryanne Hageage was now Maryanne Atkins. Less than two years later, her adoptive mom would serve Maryanne with legal papers severing all connection.

But perhaps the moment that led to Emmanuel Gondo's death can be traced back still further, to the December morning in 2009 when the police banged on Maryanne's front door, arrested her father for assault, and took custody of the fourth-grader. There had been dozens of calls to Washington's child abuse hotline by that point, neighbors reporting that Maryanne, at six or seven, was shrieking "get off me!" Nights when the future murderer, age eight, was left alone and hungry while her dad worked the soundboard at an Everett bar.

Or maybe the precipitating event was the day Maryanne's aunt found her dad sitting on a barstool and thrust his four-year-old daughter at him because her mother was in prison on drug charges. Plenty of people would say it began the day Maryanne was born.

***

Fifteen years later, almost to the day, Maryanne stood against a building in downtown Seattle, smoking a cigarette as she watched women spin out the front doors of Macy's department store with their oversized shopping bags. Maryanne couldn't believe how different this stretch of sidewalk looked to her now, compared to the adoption-day walk through downtown with the Atkinses, when she'd been so dazzled by the holiday lights. Now all she saw were other kids like her, loitering in the shadows.

"Excuse me, you need to put that out," an officer on a bike said, pointing at Maryanne's cigarette, though this appeared to be only a pretext. As Sheriff's Deputy James Mitchell and his partner rolled toward her, Maryanne's two companions dissolved into the human tide, and she was alone.

"Sorry," Maryanne said, stubbing out her butt and trying to skitter away. Deputy Mitchell blocked her path.

"You are in violation of RCW 70.160.070, which prohibits smoking in a public place," he said. "Please step back. I need to ask you a few questions."

Deputy Mitchell had been watching Maryanne for a good twenty minutes. He'd noted her braces and slight build. He guessed she was about the same age as his son, who was in middle school.

"Can I see some identification, please?" Deputy Mitchell said.

"I don't have any."

"How old are you?"

"Fifteen."

"And what is your name?"

"Mariana M. Rogers."

"Where do you live—with your parents?"

"I live with my mom."

"Name and phone number?" the officer pressed.

Maryanne's cool demeanor rippled.

"Her name is Robin Rogers, but I'm not living with her right now. She's on drugs."

Deputy Mitchell was unmoved. "I think you're a runaway," he said.

While Deputy Mitchell kept his gaze on Maryanne, his partner rifled her purse, digging through condom packets and phone numbers on crumpled scraps of paper.

"Are you a prostitute?" Deputy Mitchell asked.

"Why would you ask me that!" Maryanne could feel her face growing hot.

"It's a fairly standard question to ask of a young lady out on the street after dark in an area known for prostitution," Deputy Mitchell said, noting how hard Maryanne was working to remain calm. "You can't tell me what you're doing here, or where you live. You are unable to produce any identification, and you are holding paraphernalia consistent with someone who prostitutes. What about the two with you before, the girl—does she work with you? And the guy, do you work for him?"

"No!" said Maryanne, trying to squelch the anxiety rising in her chest like a fluttering bird.

"Look who's lying about their name!" Mitchell's partner smirked, fishing an ID bracelet from juvenile detention out of Maryanne's purse.

The deputies conferred for a moment, and Maryanne bolted. She tore down Third Avenue in the twilight, weaving and dodging the obstacle course of pedestrians.

"Runner!" Deputy Mitchell barked into his radio.

A female officer stepped into Maryanne's path, crouching down like a linebacker ready to block. Maryanne barely registered her presence. She did not recognize that it was a woman in front of her, nor that the woman was a cop. Not that it would have mattered. The officer was just an impediment. Maryanne lowered her left shoulder, leaned into her sprint, and powered forward with enough force to fling both of them backward into a tree. One of the officer's ribs was cracked, but Maryanne's feet never stopped moving. Like a cornered deer, she changed direction and tore across the street, straight into Third Avenue traffic. When she stumbled, Deputy Mitchell leaped on her, pinning Maryanne's hundred-pound frame to the street, her face smashed into the asphalt.

"You're hurting me!" she screamed.

Later, after he had arrested Maryanne and driven her to juvenile detention, Deputy Mitchell began making calls. He phoned the police in neighboring SeaTac, just south of Seattle, with its international airport and highway motels. "We know her," a detective sighed. "She's a child prostitute." The young woman who'd been at Maryanne's side was her recruiter.

***

Everyone has a private logic for their decisions, even if it is impossible for an outsider to decipher. I wanted to understand Maryanne's life on the street through her own eyes, but I wasn't going to be able to do that until I could visit her in prison. In the meantime, I needed to figure out whether she was unusual, some sort of aberration. What I kept hearing was how common her path had been. Especially the running. The federal Children's Bureau estimates that at any given moment between 5,000 and 10,000 wards of the state are on the run. That's just a point-in-time snapshot. It provides no sense of scale. In West Virginia, about 12 percent of foster kids ran in 2018; in Washington state, more than 13 percent. A Florida study of 37,000 foster kids over six years found that nearly 20 percent ran from their placements. When interviewed, about half of all foster kids report having run at least once, though not for the reasons commonly imagined. As a result of media horror stories, a few of which I'd written, there is a widespread belief that foster care is rife with child abusers. They exist in the system, of course. But most of the time, kids take off for the reasons any teenager might: resistance to authority and a hunger to connect with people who understand them, like Maryanne loitering at an Everett bus station for hours waiting for her mother to show up. And while on the run—searching, wandering, wondering how this had come to be her life—it was not such a big deal to let some old guy buy her food in exchange for a few minutes of lying beneath him. She didn't see it as "trafficking," more like a trade.

The federal government didn't require states to keep count of foster kids being sexually exploited until 2014. But the reality became obvious to me well before that. I'd spent the summer of 2006 trudging up and down Seattle's Aurora Avenue, an infamous stretch of motels and blighted highway, talking to young girls about walking the track. One of them was just thirteen. "I am the Next American Idol," she'd scrawled in loopy magic marker on the front of her pink backpack.

The head of Seattle's Department of Human Services Division of Sexual Assault Prevention was so alarmed by my stories she commissioned a study of girls on the street. The researcher, a cultural anthropologist named Debra Boyer, examined the case files of two hundred and thirty-eight children arrested or detained for sex work on Seattle's streets in 2007. She listed their "modes of sexual exploitation" (internet, escort, massage, gangs, dance clubs, personal ads, brothel, street), estimated that they represented up to five hundred young people trafficked annually in the city, and interviewed their case managers. Everyone she talked to, from defense lawyers and probation officers to prosecutors and social workers, told Boyer they felt "powerless" to change the behavior of youth in prostitution. The inadequacy of services for them was, she wrote, "nothing less than shocking."

Yet, oddly, while Boyer described many of these kids as runaways, she ignored almost entirely the places from which they were running. The term "foster care" appears only once in her forty-four-page report.

As Maryanne remembers it, the first person to pay her for sex was a Mexican man she met downtown, a few blocks from the courthouse where the Atkinses had adopted her two years before. The next guy was sixtyish and married. He promised $800 if she'd ride with him to ritzy Bellevue and have sex there. When he offered half of the money upfront, she snatched the cash and ran. She'd lost her virginity only a few months before, to a teenage boy named Romeo, who she still kind of liked. These men on the street were ugly and old, but it was surprisingly easy to set up the dates. You didn't even need to dress "womanly" to attract them, Maryanne marveled. Most of the time she had friends nudging her forward, egging her on. It was like a dare, kind of a game. They'd stand downtown at Third Avenue and Pine Street, smoking weed and waiting for customers. They never had to wait long.

Eleven years after Boyer's initial report, she completed a followup. In the intervening decade, Washington state had been hailed as a national leader for its focus on runaways and sexually exploited youth. But on the street, the picture was virtually unchanged. Most of the kids out there were fifteen- and sixteen-year-old girls, just like Maryanne standing in front of Macy's. Several were younger than twelve. This time, Boyer noted that a plurality were foster kids, taken from their families in the name of safety.

In the newsroom, we'd reported on foster care as an intervention designed to rescue babies from abusive or neglectful parents. We interrogated the child welfare system only when it failed spectacularly. I wrote about an alcoholic mother whose infant and toddler starved to death foraging for dried ramen in the kitchen cupboards while she lay passed out, surrounded by empty beer cans; a foster dad who made and shared pornography of the boys he was being paid to care for. I followed caseworkers as they decided whether to remove children from their parents' homes, trying to understand the factors they weighed. All of these stories involved children under ten. Aside from a quick piece in 2004 about the then-novel idea of financially supporting older foster youth after they aged out at eighteen, the lives of adolescents in state care went mostly ignored by the newspaper, politicians, and the system itself. But the carceral complex knew them well. By conservative estimates, a fifth of America's prison population is comprised of former foster kids.

In 2020, a team of Washington social workers attempted to zero in on the characteristics common to those trafficked from foster care (Maryanne was among the eighty-three children in their sample). Almost 90 percent had run away at least once. All had been shuffled through multiple placements, and three-quarters had spent time in juvenile detention, usually for truancy or running, rather than actual crimes. Yet, just as Debra Boyer had found thirteen years earlier, it was difficult for adults to stop the cycle. Running from a placement left kids vulnerable as soon as they got hungry. And there was a camaraderie to it, a sense of bonding. Those who worked with pimps felt, for a time, that they were special. Then there was the money—even $40 seemed like power to kids who had none. Some girls were getting flown to California and Las Vegas, which sounded glamorous when you were hustling on the streets of downtown Seattle. Inevitably, the darker realities became clear. But when kids felt lost or frightened and wanted to return to their foster homes, they found the doors closed, their beds given away to other children. They'd call their caseworkers and say, okay, I'm ready to come in now. Only to be placed somewhere they knew no one. And the street became alluring again.

***

Tasha Smith rolled her eyes when a social worker called on a February afternoon in 2015, asking if she'd take a runaway just released from juvenile detention after breaking a police officer's rib. Typical overreaction, thought Tasha. As if they expected her to be afraid of a child. Sure, she sighed, she'd take the girl. When the government car pulled up with Maryanne in the back seat, Tasha had to turn away to hide her laughter. *This* kid? This skinny white girl had broken a police officer's rib? Preposterous, Tasha chuckled. Maryanne looked like she hadn't eaten a meal in weeks.

For twenty years Tasha had sheltered kids with behavior problems, and she was accustomed to exaggeration from the state. They investigated if a kid wanted to turn her closet into a sleeping den. Or if two girls wanted to cuddle in the same bed—romantic relationships between foster kids were prohibited. They questioned Tasha's brusque style and loud voice and every dime of government money that went into her bank account. Yet foster care depended on people like Tasha, unfazed by kids who were willing to charge a cop. She was forty-six years old, with a broad bust and stout gut that she tried to keep in check by marching around with a Fitbit every day. She'd become a single mom at fifteen and began taking in kids at twenty-three, starting with overnight emergency cases just like Maryanne. "I like children, and I like money," she shrugged.

In Washington of the 2010s, there were few alternatives. The Atkinses wanted nothing to do with their adopted daughter, two other foster homes had already refused to take Maryanne, and the facilities for "challenging" teens were full. So Tasha became the go-to. Otherwise, the state would have to put Maryanne up in a motel for the night, along with dozens of other "hard to place" kids for whom Washington had no answers. Kids who heard voices and kicked walls; kids released from detention who were unwelcome back home. Traditional foster parents, who saw their job as providing hot meals and a warm bed, felt utterly unqualified. Though conceived as a short-term custodial system, foster care was now processing scores of young people with profound psychological wounds. Washington, like most other states, had responsibility for a population it was entirely unprepared to handle. Some kids lived in motels for months.

Dumped in anonymous rooms they had to leave each morning, the kids often assaulted staff, or the furniture, or each other, which resulted in criminal charges. When social workers couldn't find a motel, children slept in their offices or, in a handful of cases, a caseworker's car. By the time Maryanne was facing prison, the number of Washington kids in these unofficial placements, fed with McDonald's and almost never going to school, had skyrocketed to nearly three hundred. For all the platitudes they heard about holding on to hope, every kid lugging their sack of belongings from government offices to motels knew the truth: They were wanted nowhere.

And because children are adaptable, they adjusted, throwing off memories of home life or lingering desires to be part of a family. As far as Washington's youth lawyers were concerned, the motel stays were just another rung on the ladder from foster care to prison. "We may represent them now as children, but we will see them again in the criminal legal system when they are older—when the harm they experienced during their time in foster care will not persuade a judge that they should be shown leniency as adults," said public defender Tara Urs. "Instead, they will face long sentences in the prison system, another form of state care rife with trauma."

Washington was hardly the only state placing foster children in motels. West Virginia, Texas, Maine, California, and Oregon were doing the same. Nevada put kids up in casinos. Georgia offered a $5,000 bonus to any foster parent who would house a child living in a hotel or office.

Against that backdrop, Tasha's place—with its upstairs balconies, sunken living room, and huge master suite with private fireplace— looked like a palace. Her girls stayed in six rooms off a narrow hall decorated with portraits of Billie Holiday. They slept on wood-frame bunk beds instead of institutional metal. The shag carpeting was worn, but Tasha thought nothing of dropping $200 or $300 on hair weaves or makeup for a new resident who felt ugly without them. Girls arrived trailing alphabet strings of diagnoses and medication regimes; girls who had been homeless or run from group homes; girls with scarred arms and pierced tongues. Tasha was happy to provide every one of them a hot meal and a warm bed—at least until midnight on their eighteenth birthday, when the state support stopped.

All foster kids know they represent money. Maryanne knew her dollar figure by age ten. But Tasha, who sometimes took in $15,000 a month, never made her girls feel like a paycheck. Her specialty was food. "When was the last time you ate something?" she'd ask if a girl was screaming or cutting herself. Tasha would fix the child a plate of fried fish and watch her wolf it down at the antique dining room table.

She had always liked *objets d'art*, and she had a thing for angels. When a neighbor gave her a ceramic cherub, the kind you might see at a garden shop, Tasha couldn't hide her delight. She installed her new guardian angel in a place of honor, the back steps leading to her kitchen door.

By the time Maryanne landed there, at fifteen, she hadn't been to school in a year. The Atkinses, desperate for a break, had sent Maryanne to live with her older half-sister just south of Seattle. When her sister moved out of state, Maryanne was left alone in a bug-infested apartment. School never crossed her mind.

No problem, said Kaaren Andrews, principal at Seattle's Interagency Academy. Interagency was full of kids on house arrest, and teenagers with gang ties, and girls like Maryanne who had passed through so many districts that their transcripts showed nothing but question marks and holes. Other than Tasha's address at the top of the page, Maryanne's high school record was blank. Andrews, a former college basketball player who still favored Converse high-tops, seated Maryanne in her cozy office to work through Interagency's "Getting to Know You" survey.

What do you like about school?

Nothing, wrote Maryanne in neat, rounded letters.

Do you have a job or career you think you would like?

Juvenile detention guard, 'cause I'm there a lot.

What is your plan to work toward your career goals this school year?

I'm not gonna work.

How will you know that you are making progress?

I'm not gonna.

Who is the adult who knows you best at your old school?

N/A

In all her years working with foster youth and gang-involved kids, Andrews had never met a teenager so hard to reach. The girl seemed unable to focus on anything. She whirled around constantly, as if expecting an ambush from behind. But Maryanne had immediately noted the framed picture of two little girls on the principal's desk, both adopted from foster care. She adored children.

The intake interview continued: What areas of the city are unsafe for you to go?

Pac Highway, wrote Maryanne.

The principal nodded. Lots of Andrews's students walked the strip of highway hotels between Seattle and the airport. It was infamous for drivers looking to buy underage girls.

So crazy, thought Maryanne, the way her life had changed in such a short time. Three years before, she'd been playing soccer on a country field, white-water rafting with the Atkinses, and riding horses. Now she ran with Black girls who lived on the street or in Pac Highway hotels. All of them worked as prostitutes. None was older than sixteen. They taught Maryanne how to cornrow her hair, and they let her say she was part Black, too. Maryanne's old friends from the soccer team would have called them skanks—and maybe she would have too, back when she lived with the Atkinses—but they always shared food when they had it.

They didn't kick her out, or drop her off somewhere and vanish without saying goodbye like adoptive parents and social workers. They picked up men together, watched each other's backs, and called her "sister." Maryanne knew it was wrong what they did, the robbing and tricking, but how else were they going to pay for a hotel when it was cold out? It was better than sleeping in the back of a bus, which had been her bedroom for a while after the Atkinses un-adopted her. She didn't even know you could do that, un-adopt a kid. And it was exhausting to steal all the time, always looking out for security guards, always running unless you wanted to end up in juvie. She'd grown so tired of it that sleeping with an old guy for money didn't seem so bad, really.

"I'm willing to do whatever you like. $80-$100 I'm the best," read her ad on Backpage.com, a year after moving into Tasha's. A friend had posted it along with her picture, Maryanne insisted. The following day another ad appeared, more urgent than the first. "Text me now. Very talented skilled soft ready to satisfie you. ☺" Two days after that, Maryanne's prices had been cut and the ad suggested she was part of a tag-team. "60–80$ I come to you. ☺ very lovely and talented. You want one of us you can chose ☺ ☺ text/call us now baby. Available whenever."

Maryanne's social worker knew all about it. Sihnae Moore documented each time and place the police found her teenage client. She'd alerted Washington's team of Missing from Care Locators and given Maryanne's name to the National Registry for Missing and Exploited Children. No one could claim this girl had fallen through the cracks, unseen. She was more like a red flag, snapping in the wind.

***

Tasha knew her girls showed up in escort ads more often than school. But she had limited ability to stop them. Like most states, Washington requires foster parents to maintain a source of income other than foster care stipends, and for Tasha that was her restaurant, The Soul Scene. Social workers might dismiss Tasha as opportunistic and lenient with supervision, but the girls loved her. After aging out, many went to work at The Scene.

Tasha was a realist. She sneered at advanced degrees that suggested forty-year-old white women who had studied in university classrooms knew how to handle the kids she was trying to save. She snorted when they told her "the professionals are going to talk." Tasha understood this was her cue to leave the room. But she often ignored it, standing at her kitchen sink and lobbing tart bombs of common sense into the conversation while social workers met with their clients at her dining room table. With her booming voice and deep dimples, long braids and a ready bellow, Tasha happily told anyone who annoyed her that she was "not going to be treated like hot buttered shit." To foster care's mostly white investigators it sounded like she was constantly shouting. So Tasha learned to modulate her tone, to sit on the floor so she might appear less intimidating, to stop being who she was: a tornado of love.

Tasha didn't care if people said she was in it for the money. Every New Year's Day and Christmas morning, dozens of families crowded her home—current and former foster kids, her own grown children and their kids—all considered by Tasha to be "part of the circle."

At her house the girls were expected to gather for dinner. But that was one of the only rules. They needed to be present by 6 P.M., and out the door for school by 7 A.M. No boyfriends allowed and no guests. Maryanne loved it there. In picture after picture, she is smiling, goofing, often beaming. Sometimes, she'd curl up on the formal living room couch and lay her head on "Auntie's" lap. Such a survivor, thought Tasha, stroking Maryanne's hair. With foster kids, your job was to love them with everything you had, knowing that at any point you might never see them again. You had to keep a leash on your heart, make sure you were able to cut yourself off. Tasha, with her houseful of tough girls, trans girls, runaway girls, never tried to hold any of them, and she always opened the door again—if only to offer a hot meal. For these reasons, Tasha no longer allowed the kids to call her "mom." But she'd noted the day Maryanne switched from calling her "Ms. Smith" to "Auntie." She couldn't help it—she'd warmed to this skinny, scrappy girl, despite her rules.

Within a month, Tasha adjusted her thinking. Maryanne made friends easily, but she fought them too, swinging hardest at those she liked most. Her best friend, Regine, was a year older than Maryanne, and Tasha considered them a pair, a matched set. Both slight and pretty, one Black, one white. Regine, who also had been thrown back to foster care after a dissolved adoption, learned her physical worth in middle school, when she first began earning money for sex. But with Maryanne the game, initially, was auto theft. All summer long, Regine and Maryanne would message men on Facebook, then shimmy out the window at Tasha's to jump into their waiting cars. "Could you buy us something to eat?" they'd ask. When the men obliged by pulling into a convenience store parking lot and stepped out to grab a few snacks, the girls would hotwire their cars and take off to party with friends. Regine was practiced at these maneuvers. Maryanne was not. At least once, the partying friends tossed her from a moving vehicle she'd helped steal.

"If someone don't want you, they don't want you," Regine would sneer, homing in on the most bruised part of her friend's heart. Lots of foster kids had a sixth sense for that, Tasha noticed.

Regine and Maryanne grew so close they often slept in the same bed. But when Regine grabbed Maryanne's sixth-grade yearbook and flung it across the room during a fight about turning out the lights, Maryanne erupted—screaming, punching, kicking. The yearbook was the only thing she'd kept from her time with the Atkinses, and she treasured it—even if they had kicked her out.

"Stop!" bellowed Tasha, rushing in to grab Maryanne from behind and hoist her clear off the floor.

"I can't!" Maryanne cried, clawing at the air.

This was when Tasha understood who was living beneath her roof: The girl was either suicidal, or homicidal, all the time.

"You really did break that cop's rib, didn't you?" she asked after Maryanne had finally calmed.

A girlish giggle.

"How'd you do that, a little thing like you?"

"I was mad," said Maryanne.

Bossy and brassy and ready to battle the state at a moment's notice, Tasha would never use the word "fear" to describe her feelings about Maryanne. But this girl worried her like none before. After Maryanne was thrown from a car and limped back home, scraped and broken, Tasha called 911. A different child in the same circumstance might have nursed her injuries, felt for the shattered places on an arm or ankle. Not Maryanne. She barely seemed to notice these externals. There had to be pain—Tasha could see the bruises and blood—but Maryanne appeared unconscious of it. She was hurt, clearly. But it was the injury to her feelings that consumed her. She kept wailing about the men who'd tossed her from the car, how she'd thought they were her friends. She was raging so wildly that the medics had to call police to get her safely into their ambulance.

The next morning, after doctors at Highline Medical Center had bandaged Maryanne and prepared her for release, Tasha refused to pick her up. The girl needed help, real help, Tasha kept saying, something far more intensive than her home could provide. "She's either going to hurt herself, or someone else," Tasha kept telling the doctors, before hanging up.

Two days later, Maryanne was standing on her back porch, knocking at the door. Yes, okay, she could stay the night on a couch, Tasha grumbled, fixing Maryanne a plate of fried chicken and mashed potatoes. But a social worker would be there in the morning.

"You're going to have me picked up?" cried Maryanne, incredulous.

At those words, Tasha knew it would be just a matter of hours before her problem child was gone again. When the state car pulled up at 8 A.M., the only evidence that Maryanne had been there was Tasha's treasured guardian angel, now decapitated, its smiling head knocked clear off.

***

Washington's protocol for such "run events" was clear. If Tasha's girls weren't home by 6 P.M., they were officially considered to be "on the run," though they were rarely running anywhere. Usually, they were holed up at a friend's place. Maryanne liked to stay in an abandoned RV parked in a backyard in South Seattle. It was filthy inside, but it was shelter. When she couldn't get to the RV, she rode Seattle's light rail back and forth between downtown and the airport, or curled up in the warm back seat of a Metro bus.

That hundreds of children were living this way was not news to anyone looking at child welfare in Washington. Twenty years before Maryanne was running the streets, the state had passed a law to address the problem presented by kids like her. Named for Rebecca Hedman—who'd been adopted from foster care, repeatedly ran, and was murdered by a john at thirteen—the Becca Bill of 1995 allowed police to hold runaways in juvenile detention, whether or not they'd been charged with a crime. The idea, again, was safety. The rationale, a vague notion that children, once confined, could get counseling or drug treatment. But the Becca Bill also made Washington the country's top jailer of children for non-criminal offenses. By the time Maryanne was on the run two decades later, the Becca Bill had become so controversial that in liberal Seattle, it was barely enforced at all.

The only other option was crisis centers. Washington had a loose network of these non-secure facilities, where kids could stay for up to a month but not a day longer. Maryanne took off quicker each time, because the thought of yet another social worker plunking her down in whatever home had an open bed felt worse than making her own way.

Eventually, the police would pick her up. But the Atkinses refused to take Maryanne back, and she had worn out her welcome at most of the nicer shelters. On to Spruce Street, a short-term crisis center that became the last resort for Maryanne, time and again. A drab building across the street from juvenile detention, Spruce Street forced its residents to hand over their shoes and pad around in state-issued sweats. There was nothing to do. Every girl was just marking time, waiting for the state to figure out her next stop. To Maryanne, it felt like purgatory, even worse than living in one of the locked cells across the way, so she'd wriggle out a first-floor window in her stocking feet, drop to the ground, and hop a bus to downtown. (Seattle's mass transit operates largely on the honor system, allowing passengers to board through doors in the middle of the bus, which made it easy for Maryanne to scoot to the back without paying.) The hardest thing about living on the street was never transportation or even finding a warm corner. It was food.

The need for cash to feed herself revealed Maryanne's talent for shoplifting. As in most cities, even those like Seattle that are predominantly white, youth of color comprise an outsize portion of kids in foster care and on the street. The first time Maryanne landed downtown, she was the lone white girl among throngs of Black youth. People laughed, called her a cracker, called her a ho. But Maryanne's willingness to scrap eventually endeared her to a pack of young thieves, and they soon realized her usefulness. Any Black kid walking through Nordstrom or Macy's would be watched, but Maryanne escaped notice. She became expert at lifting North Face jackets and flirty summer dresses for her new friends. Rarely was she afraid, though her sense of anxiety was constant. When she had a working cell phone, Maryanne enjoyed narrating her travels, walking through Seattle's Central District and talking to the world on Facebook Live.

Tasha, like all foster parents, was expected to report these disappearances immediately. She had the runaway call center on speed dial. But often, she delayed. As long as her girls got in touch by midnight, Tasha wouldn't hassle them. This put her at considerable risk, since anything a foster child did while under her authority was Tasha's problem, and the moment she called in a run report, that liability was lifted. Once listed as missing—whether for an hour, a week, or a month—the girls were officially no longer Tasha's concern. Nor were they explicitly the responsibility of the state. All of a sudden, they were no one's.

Later, after Maryanne had been arrested for murder, the realization blared like a car alarm in Tasha's mind: Had the girl been held in detention after cracking that police officer's rib—as Tasha believed a Black foster child would—or at the hospital, as she had urged, Maryanne never would have been in the car with Emmanuel Gondo. It was a question of consequences and when you faced them. "You can have your bowl of shit now, or you can have it later," Tasha told her friends. "But if you're a foster kid, you're gonna have it."

***

In September 2015, Martin Dietz, a Missing from Care Locator, was assigned to find Maryanne. Over five months, as she slept in stairwells and posted videos of herself online, Dietz could never bring her in. The first time he laid eyes on Maryanne was at her arraignment for murder.

Dietz enjoyed his work finding runaways from foster care, mainly because it was out of the office, and the paperwork was minimal. He spent most days in his Acura, slowly cruising alleys and underpasses, handing his business card to street kids and stapling missing person pictures on telephone poles. Running away was no crime, and Dietz didn't think it should be viewed that way. He sure didn't want kids arrested for it. But the sight of fourteen-year-old girls living in tents with men more than twice their age left him queasy. He saw it all the time. What Dietz wished for was the ability to "press pause" and take kids away from people who might use or hurt them. If that meant a night or two in juvie, okay—even if the police had to issue a warrant and, technically, criminalize kids to do it.

No other state had a team of runaway locators. The job had been created as part of the settlement to a groundbreaking lawsuit filed on behalf of thirteen foster kids in 1998. The lead plaintiff, fifteen-year-old Jessica Braam, accused Washington's child welfare system of being so derelict as a parent that it was violating children's constitutional rights. During her decade in foster care, Jessica had been moved fifteen times, and her case was by no means extreme. Many of Jessica's fellow plaintiffs had lived in twenty or thirty homes. One boy endured ninety placement changes.

Their lawyer, Tim Farris, knew almost nothing about child welfare when he answered a phone call from Dale and Vicki Braam. They were furious with the state for failing to warn them about the mental health needs of their adoptive daughter, Jessica. Reading through Farris's papers gave me a nauseating sense of déjà vu. It was Maryanne Atkins, fifteen years earlier.

Farris had never been a crusader. He'd built a solid, unflashy career in corporate and labor law, and found himself thrust into the murky waters of foster care only because he'd agreed to pick up a wrongful-adoption case for an overloaded colleague several years before. Washington had provided little more than a half-page narrative to the boy's would-be parents. "It said, basically, 'with a little love he'll be fine,'" Farris told me.

The boy was not fine. He terrified his new mom and dad. When Farris finally got his hands on the child's medical file, he found it was twelve inches thick and included a psychiatrist's note saying he had "never in his career seen a more disturbed child."

Farris won a seven-figure verdict against Washington for its failures with this adoption, and word spread fast. Parents across the state began calling with similar stories. In their cases Farris gleaned the same combination of blankness and rage I'd felt in Maryanne, the psychic wasteland created in children moved from place to place without warning or explanation. The expectation that they would be happy and grateful at each new home; the rejection that followed if they were not. Living like that, any kid would be lonely and confused, Farris thought. But laying this experience over whatever trauma had brought them into foster care to begin with—well, it was no wonder they had problems.

Like foster kids themselves, those working in the system develop a certain numbness to its realities. Farris was an outsider, and he was shocked. He'd always thought of himself as a guy who cared about kids— coached his son's soccer team, doted on his children—but the Jessica Braams of this world had been invisible to him. No more, he told the jury. By the time Farris was done, the Braam case had become a class action on behalf of all Washington foster youth in perpetuity. Farris's three-hour closing argument had passages that read like poetry, laid out in verse:

When I go places,
I see children.

Not the ones who play on my soccer teams.

Or at my children's school events.

I see the children in the distance.

Far away.

Withdrawn.

Quiet.

In the shadow.

Emotionally vacant.

That look in their eye.

For six years, Washington state attacked Farris's arguments, first insisting that children in foster care had no constitutional rights, then allowing that if they did, their rights were no greater than those of convicted criminals serving time. It was an illuminating perspective.

In 2004, Washington finally agreed to settle *Braam v. Washington* by paying each of the thirteen original plaintiffs $100,000 and submitting to a top-to-bottom overhaul of its foster care system. The ambitious plan laid out thirty-three new benchmarks for how often caseworkers would check on kids, how frequently those children would be seen by therapists, how regularly they'd get to visit their siblings, and how much background information would be provided to their foster parents.

To ensure this happened, Farris and the public interest lawyers he'd teamed up with asked five experts to monitor Washington's progress. For nine years, they did, meeting quarterly at a hotel near SeaTac Airport to slog through foster care data and hold the state to its promises. The panel included a former state senator; the onetime head of Illinois' Department of Children and Family Services; a children's mental health expert from Georgetown University; the director of a child-welfare research center in San Diego; and sociologist Dorothy Roberts, whose recently published book, *Shattered Bonds: The Color of Child Welfare*, decried foster care as a racist and classist response to the problem of child poverty.

In addition to making kids' time in care less tumultuous, the Braam Oversight Panel was also tasked with helping Washington cut the number who ran from placements. Hence, the locators. In other states, when foster kids took off, nobody was assigned to find them. Most caseworkers had little time to call a kid's friends or scour their social media. No one was going to drive around, putting up flyers and phoning hospitals. But in Washington, that work would now be done by ten locators, who fanned out across the state. Martin Dietz had half of the west side, from Bellingham to Seattle, an area of nearly one hundred miles.

He stood a gangly six feet tall, his reddish hair going gently gray, his eyes a milky blue. Dietz had grown up in a stable Midwestern home, majored in English, and imagined that he might become a writer. But his stories lay inert on the page. He went back to school for a degree in social work. Dietz had been with Washington's child welfare agency for twenty years before the Missing from Care job was created. He was glad for the assignment. A typical day began before 8 A.M., at a Starbucks in Everett, forty minutes north of Seattle. He'd suck down a triple tall coffee and hit the road, knocking on the front doors of drab homes where bedsheets covered the windows. He'd step back a good four paces, unassuming in his blue windbreaker and baseball cap. No overbearing body language, no sudden moves. Dietz was not law enforcement, and he never wanted to be perceived that way. He'd wait a few long minutes to see if anyone answered, and stand there as they lied to him.

"I haven't seen that kid for months," a meth dealer might say as Dietz tucked his business card into the doorframe and walked away, knowing the child might be sitting just beyond his view, laughing as he trudged back to his car.

Dietz didn't take offense. To him, it was a numbers game, like being a salesman. You knocked on twenty doors trying to sell your steak knives, and maybe one person would buy. That made the day. Either way, Dietz got paid. Most of the time, he could do nothing more than hand out his card and re-tread the same streets, the same ground, hoping to become familiar enough that one day a kid in trouble would step forward. It was up to them, though. Even if he found a runaway, Dietz had no power to make any minor go anywhere. The best he could do was give them coupons for free food and try to convince a few to come in out of the cold. His efforts were more successful during fall and winter, when western Washington's perpetual drizzle helped nudge kids toward shelter, though they rarely stayed. Once a kid started running, they were likely to continue until something happened—either they ended up in juvenile detention, or they were picked up for sex trafficking and brought to Spruce Street. Between 2013 and 2015, the state identified 1,084 children who had run, including Maryanne.

Dietz hadn't known many who wound up headed for state prison, but he wasn't surprised by the way her time in foster care ended. And he was eager to get a look at the girl after posting her picture all over King County. At Maryanne's arraignment, he squeezed himself into a back bench next to her social worker and watched the kid he'd been chasing for five months plead "not guilty."

Dietz told me that he saw himself as the physical embodiment of the state *in loco parentis*. "If you were a parent and your kid had run away, you'd talk to their friends. You'd put posters up on poles. You'd go everywhere they might be. That's what we do, what a parent would do, because they love you."

CHAPTER 3
Nobody from Nowhere

From outside, the Washington Corrections Center for Women looked like a public school, circa 1970. Its main building was long and low, with a cement portico that shielded visitors from the weather. The families clustered beneath it seemed jollier than those I'd noticed at other prisons. They joked among themselves. When a guard said I'd have to take off my khaki pants and change into sweats, he was cheery about it. Too close to his own uniform, he explained, handing me a pair of gray sweats like the inmates wore.

I had waited months to visit Maryanne. Four days after our conversation in the King County Jail, she was hustled into a van that took her fifty miles south to the state's only facility with a maximum-security wing for women. But state prison was nothing like the county jail. A week after she'd cleared the reception protocol—a month-long limbo where inmates waited in a holding pen for the next available cell—Maryanne told a guard to go fuck himself. That landed her in segregation, locked up alone for twenty-three hours a day. In response, she plugged her commode with bedsheets and flushed it until shit and urine flooded into the hall outside, watching smugly as staff cleaned up her mess.

"Just acting her age," sighed Maryanne's supervising caseworker.

Before a month had passed, Maryanne was romantically entangled with a woman eleven years older, whose segregation cell was within earshot of her own. They'd talk all night. Back in general population, Maryanne had the woman's name tattooed beside her right eye. "I love her," she told me as we got settled at a small card table in the visiting room.

Maryanne's hair was twisted into the same French braids she'd worn in court, and her eyelashes were fluted with mascara. She gave me a perfunctory hug hello and led me through a verbal tour of the prison campus as if I were an aunt visiting her niece at college. There was her "dorm," Maryanne said, pointing through a barred window toward an angular building that looked like a dystopian space station. Every other structure at the prison was nondescript cinderblock or prefab farmhouse. Maryanne's looked like an architect's rendering of punishment.

But she had not a bad word to say about any of it. She spoke of Friday night chapel, where inmates could socialize and sink into the music. She talked about her "roommate," who had a television set, and how they watched reality-TV shows together. She pointed out the wing where young mothers with fewer than five years to serve were allowed to live with their babies. As she spoke the word *baby,* Maryanne's entire affect changed. She was sitting opposite me, watching inmate-moms visit with their toddlers in an adjacent playroom, and her gaze did not waver. "Adorable," she murmured, following the children as they tumbled and ran. "Absolutely adorable."

I had interviewed sociopaths before and never known one to talk of love or little children. That was the question I was stuck on: Was Maryanne, as her prosecutor suggested, sociopathic? So deeply disordered at nineteen that she'd become incapable of honesty, or even genuine feeling for another person? Jessica Berliner had argued that putting Maryanne away for two decades was the only reliable way to keep Seattle safe from her. But other prosecutors in Berliner's office wondered at her interpretation of justice. One confided his dismay that Maryanne, at sixteen, had been charged as an adult. Another said she seemed emotionally barren, like a child raised on a pile of rocks.

Berliner needn't have worried about Seattle leaping to the defense of a traumatized waif. There was minimal press coverage of Maryanne's case, and almost all of it cast her as an icy predator. But to me, she was still a mystery. In the prison visiting room, she declared "I love dogs!" and "I hate beer!" like a kid in junior high. When I offered to buy her a snack from the vending machines, she chose chocolate chip cookies. She jiggled her foot incessantly, eyes darting from corner to corner, noting who was near, who was moving toward her, who was heading for the door. She rolled her eyes when I said I liked her name.

"It sounds like an old lady. I always wanted to be an Annabella or Isabella, something pretty."

We made small talk, chatting about her various foster parents and how she'd felt living in their homes. Maryanne was polite about all of them and had kind words for most. She struck me as wily but unsophisticated. Hard yet fragile. She yearned—for children, for connection, for her mother—but she also appeared chillingly self-possessed for someone still too young to buy a cocktail. She was Dorothy-in-French-braids, branded with tattoos that marked her as property. She was the child raised on a pile of rocks who wanted to hold a baby on her lap.

"What's your happiest memory?" I asked after she had recited her journey through seven foster homes and youth shelters.

For the first time since sitting down, Maryanne was tongue-tied. She could not come up with an answer, and she seemed flummoxed by this, embarrassed. There were happy times, she assured me. But she couldn't put her finger on a specific memory.

We connected most easily when talking about books—writing and reading them. Maryanne loved writing, she admitted shyly, and she knew she had a story to tell. She asked for prompts to get focused. I'd spent hours trying to imagine Maryanne's life on the streets, what it felt like to be fifteen and walking a highway at two o'clock in the morning. Exhilarating? Terrifying? Lonely?

"Write about what nighttime means to you," I said.

After we'd talked for two hours, I rose to leave. Maryanne had been consistently cheerful, even bubbly, and she gave me a light hug goodbye. I thought of the pictures Berliner had shown me of a girl beaten bloody by Maryanne in jail. I thought of her swinging and kicking at Regine, from Tasha's group home, though she'd known her friend was pregnant. I thought of her best buddy from the years with the Atkinses, who said trying to understand Maryanne was like following a dead-end road.

At the door of the visiting room, I turned back to wave goodbye. Maryanne had moved across the room to the guards' station, waiting for permission to return to her cell. She sat with her head against a window covered in wire mesh, staring out at the afternoon sun. But she looked altogether different from the animated young woman who'd been talking to me moments before. Her skin was somehow paler, and the shadowy gaze I'd noticed in court was back. Maryanne glanced up and caught me watching. She flashed a smile, but it did not reach her eyes.

***

I began wondering about the connection between these two systems—child welfare and corrections—in 2004, when the Chapin Hall Center for Children at the University of Chicago released the first in a series of landmark studies known as the Midwest Evaluations, which followed kids from foster care into adulthood. Researchers tracked 732 seventeen- and eighteen-year-olds from Illinois, Wisconsin, and Iowa. Even before leaving foster care, 60 percent had spent time in the criminal justice system, mostly with short stays in juvenile detention. Nearly half would land on the streets at eighteen having nowhere to live, no job training, not even a high school diploma.

It was no surprise when the researchers checked back two years later and found that 40 percent of their original cohort were neither employed nor in school. Now nineteen years old, 34 percent had been arrested since leaving state care. By the time they turned twenty-one, 43 percent were surviving on food stamps, and a quarter had been convicted of violent crimes. "Our findings call into question the wisdom of federal and state policies that result in foster youth being discharged from care at or shortly after their eighteenth birthday," the researchers wrote in academic deadpan.

Researchers are careful people. They stick to data and tend to avoid sweeping statements. So it struck me when the Chapin Hall team characterized their findings as "sobering." The state, as parent, had been a negligent one at best.

It wasn't that all of these foster children had been directly victimized while wards of the state. Rather, the Midwest Evaluations seemed to imply that the system itself perpetuated a kind of unconscious, mechanized abuse. The last chapter of the Chapin Hall study, released in 2011, looked at former foster youth when they were in their mid-twenties. By that point, fewer than half of the original group were employed, and those who had jobs were earning about $14,000 annually. In the eight years since they'd first spoken with Chapin Hall's researchers, 30 percent had spent time homeless. Forty-eight percent had been incarcerated. They were floundering and alone, painfully aware of their diminished existence. More than 20 percent said they saw "no point in thinking about the future." Almost a third had "difficulty experiencing normal feelings." Nearly half had seriously considered suicide.

"Disquieting," concluded the researchers. "Former foster youth are faring poorly as a group."

But did foster care actually *cause* these outcomes? Or would this group of young people have ended up in the same place if they'd never entered the child welfare system? The question is difficult to nail because devising a true control group would be impossible. But in 2008, MIT economist Joseph Doyle published the first authoritative study to take a stab at it. He looked at children whose families had been investigated for alleged maltreatment in Illinois. Some were visited by "strict" investigators—people whose caseloads showed they removed children at higher-than-average rates. Others landed in front of "lenient" workers who tended to give parents and guardians a second chance. They became Doyle's alternative scenario, his de facto control group. Then he tabulated the life outcomes for each.

Doyle's conclusion: Children placed in foster care were three times more likely to end up in prison than kids who had been allowed to remain at home—even when those homes were deeply troubled. Despite my job covering child welfare in Washington state, I heard nothing about Doyle's study until years later. The connection between foster care and prison, while well known to those within these systems, went largely unacknowledged outside of academia. The year Doyle's study was released, I'd asked a child welfare advocate if anyone had data on the overlap between foster care and the criminal justice system, and I could almost hear her mentally scrolling her contact list. "Maybe Joseph Doyle?" she said hesitantly, as if I'd posed a bizarrely obscure question and the work of an MIT economist was pushing the limits.

But people were beginning to call out the obvious. In 2018, reporters at the *Kansas City Star* surveyed almost 6,000 prison inmates across the country and found that 25 percent said they'd grown up as wards of the state. The National Academies of Sciences weighed in a year later with a four-hundred-page report that endorsed Doyle's claim. Time spent in foster care was clearly correlated with an increased likelihood of incarceration, the distinguished panel said, and there were biology-based reasons. Put simply, foster care seemed to rewire kids' brains. The National Academies' scientists and lawyers scrutinized records from 6,000 former foster youth and found "compelling evidence" that their subjects' "elevated mental health symptoms" were due at least partly to the trauma of being constantly uprooted and thrust into strangers' homes, where there was no pretense of creating a lasting connection or deep attachment. The kids were just visitors. Everyone knew that those not adopted would be moving on.

The question of adoption had loomed over Maryanne's early years in foster care. She'd loved the first family to take her in, an elderly couple with a houseful of puppies. But the state yanked her away after a few weeks. A friend of her father's was the preferred choice, as she was more closely connected to Maryanne's family. But Maryanne required so much attention that after a few months the woman insisted she be removed. Maryanne was informed of this decision by a social worker who picked her up at school and told the confused eleven-year-old that she would be sleeping in a new home that night.

"She never even said goodbye," Maryanne, still wounded, said of her would-be foster mom, a decade later.

Even without abuse, this kind of instability triggered chronically elevated stress hormones in children that could "disrupt the brain's developing architecture" and lead to "hypertrophic growth of the amygdala," the National Academies panel said. With that neurological setup, it was difficult for former foster kids to handle adult life.

Even those who disputed a causal link between foster care and incarceration could not argue with numbers showing that this intervention intended to save children appeared to be failing huge numbers of them. The top child welfare official in Washington described the system to me as a poison, like chemotherapy—a cure that damaged the body anew.

**

Maryanne herself was in no position to explain how this happened. She had been quizzed and studied by so many adults in the decade before we met that when I asked questions, she batted back bite-sized answers by rote, offering minimal insight. I wanted to understand what it felt like to be in Maryanne's head. But that required a capacity for self-reflection possessed by few nineteen-year-olds, let alone one who had spent much her childhood nearly feral. To get a better feel for life on the run—and to test my ideas about the way a kid could slide from the government's care into its prisons—I wrote to an inmate who was puzzling over the same question. By the time I emailed him, in June 2020, Arthur Longworth had become something of an unofficial dean for this line of inquiry.

A former foster kid, Longworth had murdered a woman in Seattle shortly after being cut from Washington's child welfare system in 1981, when he was sixteen. He had spent the four decades since locked away from the world. Sentenced to life without possibility of parole, Longworth expected to die in prison. But he'd begun to write about his experiences, publishing a roman à clef called *Zek* and several award-winning essays. I'd heard of him long before I typed my first letter. Could a man in his fifties tell me anything about what it felt like to be a teenage girl on the streets of Seattle? I was skeptical.

But a former inmate who'd done time with Longworth insisted he was exactly the person I needed. In prison, Longworth had convened a group of inmates, all of them former foster children, who spent their meetings trying to figure out how to explain the ways foster care channeled young people into locked cells.

I introduced myself over the Department of Corrections email system, explaining that I was looking into the case of a teenage girl who also had grown up as a ward of the state and was now incarcerated, sentenced to nineteen years. I did not mention Maryanne's name or her crime. I asked only if Longworth would consider sharing his perspective on foster care and its connection, if any, with where he sat now.

I'd uncorked a geyser. Longworth replied within hours, displaying an effusiveness I had not anticipated. In his view, the biggest misconception people had about foster care was the word *care*, which implied a home, a family, the possibility of love. "It doesn't work like that very often," he wrote. The reality was that foster care trained kids not for productive adult lives, but for success in carceral settings. "When your young woman makes it to prison, she'll find that former foster youth are a grossly outsized demographic in here. In fact, I believe they are the prison system's most disproportionately represented demographic. If she was raised in the foster care system in Washington, she'll be in the company of other state kids she grew up with."

Longworth pointed me toward a half-dozen other imprisoned foster youth as well as a battalion of lawyers, researchers, and advocates who could back up his assertions. But it was Longworth's writing that intrigued me most. He could still taste his adolescent rage, and he'd matured into an essayist with the skills to explain it.

The anger didn't stem from any logical source, he'd written in an essay called "How to Kill Someone." The title appeared to refer to its author as much as his victim. "It isn't constructed from conscious thought. Rather, the anger is the confluence of all you've pushed down inside yourself, the memories and unbearable truths you suppress and do all you can not to think about. Like the State itself, this anger is an amorphous entity, a hydra to whom an infinite number of faces, or images, are attributable, yet whose authority issues from a single omnipotent body. The anger is your subconscious reacting to everything you don't allow yourself to see."

Lying on his bunk at juvenile hall, staring at the ceiling, the rage would rise up and clog Longworth's throat like a brick wedged sideways. It felt like a wave he couldn't stop, a propulsion. But its connection to foster care became clear to him only much later. At first, this link was just a shapeless feeling, a sense more than a thought he could articulate.

"Maybe the most harmful, yet almost inescapable, element of experience in the foster care system is the lack of anything to hold onto," Longworth wrote to me in June 2021, some forty years later. "You have no stability in anything: you're moved from placement to placement, school to school, and your caseworker's face changes constantly. With each change, you're expected to tell your story over again, and again, and again, until you get to the point where you just can't do it anymore—you can't bring yourself to step foot in another new classroom full of faces to explain yourself to, so you don't go to school—and when you're moved to a new placement, you're just numb. As far as anyone knows, you're nobody, from nowhere, and that's just fine with you. Would it surprise you to know that foster youth in group homes almost never talk about where they're from, even with each other? Yet, with normal kids, where they're from is probably the biggest part of their identity."

The root of his anger and how it might have been addressed, rather than fueled, by the system became clear to Longworth slowly, over decades of watching other foster kids walking alongside him in the halls of Clallam Bay prison, and then Walla Walla, and now the Washington State Reformatory at Monroe.

"If you could feel the conflagration of rage born out of powerlessness and the feeling of worthlessness that is cultivated inside a young person raised by the State, you might begin to understand the problem—why raising young people in this way, then throwing them out onto the street makes them incompatible with society," he'd written in "How to Kill Someone."

Was this Maryanne? I wondered. Longworth was certain of it.

"I can assure you that it's easy to hurt someone when 1) you're a foster youth who's trying to survive, 2) you feel like your own life has never mattered, 3) and parts of you, like empathy and other human qualities, haven't been allowed to blossom because of your circumstance of perpetual crisis and survival," he wrote me. Foster girls showed these effects differently than boys, he felt, with the harm frequently turned inward, rather than out. But the link that united virtually all wards of the state was the feeling that they mattered to no one. No particular caseworker or foster parent or bureaucrat was to blame; the structure of the system itself guaranteed this experience.

But surely, foster care had changed since Longworth's tour through the system in the late-1970s and Maryanne's thirty years later? He didn't think so. Through the 1980s, '90s, 2000s, and 2010s, Longworth watched hundreds of young people file into the prisons where he now presided as an elder, and he kept recognizing them. First came men of his own generation in Washington's group homes, kids he'd known. Later, their sons arrived, youth who'd grown up in foster care because their parents were in prison, or dead. They now joined the long line of kids trudging from one system into the other.

***

Finding a source who was not only willing to talk about the ugliest moments of his life, but able to express the emotions framing them was unusual. Also unusual in my experience of prison inmates was Longworth's willingness to confront his shortcomings. He described himself in youth as a "complete failure of a human being," which was more naked self-reflection than I'd ever heard from a convicted murderer, though it flickered in and out, tangled in a constant sense of injustice.

The second eldest of five children born to a carpenter and a mail carrier, Longworth had grown up in Federal Way, a small, then-rural community south of Seattle. To escape childhood beatings, young Arthur began running away in elementary school, often camping in the woods behind his family's home. He led his siblings through the forest, teaching the younger kids about the trees, the land, the creatures. Longworth lived a whole summer out there on the riverbank, learning survival skills from "the hoboes," before returning for school in the fall of 1975. His parents, to hear him tell it, were glad to be rid of him.

Worse than any punishment Longworth received from his mother or father was witnessing their treatment of his little sister Dawn. The Longworths believed she was mentally ill, and they beat her bloody for it. Often, they starved her. More than once they locked Dawn in a tiny bathroom at the back of the house, where she drank from the toilet bowl because there was no sink. By age nine, Dawn stopped speaking. She pulled her hair out compulsively. Longworth's parents finally drove her into Tacoma and abandoned her outside juvenile hall.

Young Arthur vowed never to live with them again. He hitchhiked into downtown Seattle and swiped a money bag from a Brinks security guard who was making a deposit, taking off with it like a child on fire. Older, wilier street kids quickly snatched his windfall, beating Art so badly that he woke up in a hospital. That was the moment Arthur Longworth, age thirteen, officially became the state's problem. After questioning him at the hospital, police officers sent the boy to his first receiving home, the short-term stopgap Washington then used for kids who couldn't be with their own families and did not yet have a more permanent place to live.

Art detested these way stations, and he made his unhappiness known. Each time he ran away, police picked him up and brought him to juvenile detention, which began to feel familiar, even welcoming. A scrawny child, he'd roll his mattress pad into a fat cylinder and shove it up against the door of his cell, so he could stand on top and peer onto the hall outside.

Longworth's parents left caseworkers utterly perplexed. Both held solid middle-class jobs, neither came across as drug-addicted, and their other children appeared to be fine. Yet they had foresaken Dawn. They "refused to discuss Arthur," and they had been "less than cooperative" with investigators, said one report in officialese that did not attempt to mask its author's bewilderment. Probing for any hint of connection between the couple and their eldest son, a family crisis worker described Longworth's mother as nearly Stepfordian: "She continually remarked that he had everything, nice clothes and home, etc., however, love was never mentioned."

Teenaged Arthur readily confirmed this impression. Asked by a psychologist to complete a series of statements, he was steadfast:

I suffer . . .

"From my mom."

My greatest worry is . . .

"My family."

I wish . . .

"I had another family."

Art could live at the Youth Outreach group home in the wide-open fields of central Washington, authorities told his parents. He was a shy, gangly kid, so awkward and tongue-tied that staff assigned another boy to act as his older "brother." When Christmas approached, Art's new friend invited him to spend the holidays at his parents' home because Art refused to go to his own. But as the boys were preparing to leave, Art began to cry. He felt like a freak. He didn't know how to act around grownups. He wondered if he was crazy or "retarded," and he was terrified of doing something wrong.

"It appears that he does not have the skills necessary to successfully enter into and maintain positive personal relationships," the Youth Outreach staff observed.

There was little time to learn. Within a year of Art's arrival, Youth Outreach closed, and he was sent back to his family. This was a blow. The group home had felt like a reprieve, a paradise compared to where Art had come from. And once returned, he treated his parents' house like another short-term placement. One winter night, he slid open a back window and dropped to the cold ground below. He marched briskly toward the highway, focused only on the sound of crunching snow beneath his feet. As morning thinned the blue-black sky, Art arrived at a truck stop and scrambled beneath a tarp on the bed of a semi about to hit the interstate. He clung to the truck as it tore down the highway. By late afternoon with snow beginning to fall, Art could no longer feel his fingers. He jumped off when the truck pulled over at the foot of a mountain pass, resolving to continue on foot.

But where to go? Maybe he should try to find Dawn, now living with a foster family. Art had met them once, a few days before Christmas 1979, while he was at Youth Outreach. A counselor had loaded him onto a Greyhound bus with instructions to get off in Tacoma. Someone would meet him at the station, the counselor said. Art spent the two-hour ride figuring out how to evade the juvenile detention officer he expected to see on the other side. But when the bus pulled in, there was Dawn, standing with an elderly couple. She still wouldn't speak, but Art's little sister threw her arms around his waist and stayed glued to his side. On Christmas morning, her foster parents even had a gift for Art. He sat cross-legged on the floor by the tree and tore open the wrapping around this unexpected, rectangular package. Two cartons of Marlboro cigarettes slid into his lap. Art, just a few weeks shy of his fourteenth birthday, whooped with joy. By boys' home standards, he was rich.

Stomping over Snoqualmie Pass in the drifting snow, Art grinned at the memory. He'd begged Dawn's foster parents to let him stay after Christmas, wheedling and bargaining as they drove him back to the bus station. But he never held it against them. They had saved Dawn, and that knowledge kept Art warm now, as night fell. A few more miles of walking and he felt nothing at all, no ground beneath his feet, no aching limbs, not even the weight of his body moving through space. It was kind of like floating, Art thought, easing himself into a fluffy snowbank. State Patrol discovered him curled up by the side of the road several hours later, nearly frozen to death.

The officers brought Art to a shelter for runaways, which duly sent him back to his parents. Within days, he'd fled again. He should have been in the eighth grade. But between all the receiving homes, detention stays, and his year at Youth Outreach, Art had been enrolled and withdrawn from so many schools he couldn't stand the thought of memorizing another floor plan of classrooms and hallways, introducing himself to a new crop of teachers, answering questions from more curious strangers. *Where do you live? What do your parents do?*

Instead, he wandered downtown in whatever burg he'd been sent to and panhandled for change.

"Ever had nowhere to go?" he would write of those days, scratching his memories onto a yellow notepad inside a prison cell. "The experience is a discomfiting feeling of being unanchored, of not belonging anywhere."

The staff at Youth Outreach had described Art as "a very likeable boy." But he'd developed a stutter, which came out under stress, and constantly moving from one placement to the next was beginning to erode any sense of identity other than survivor. By the time Art landed at the Kiwanis Vocational Youth Home in Centralia, in 1980, he had no friends and only a few possessions—a radio, some baseball posters—most of them discarded by other kids moving on to their next placements. During his first night at the Kiwanis home, Art listened as the boy on the bunk below him was raped. *Get off me! Get off!* the kid screamed. Lying just a few feet above, Art clenched his hands into fists, his body coiled tight against anyone who might try that with him. The next day he stole a knife from the Kiwanis kitchen and slid it under his pillow.

Dawn had found a family, but the kids Art met in group homes barely remembered what that was. There were dozens of them rotating through the Kiwanis complex. It occupied the campus of a defunct coal-processing plant, with a main house, dining hall, storage shed, and barracks holding beds for thirty boys. Most were within a year of turning eighteen and leaving foster care. Art, at fifteen, was the youngest. During twelve months there, he never went to school. Instead, Art felled trees, chopped wood, and fabricated mailbox posts. There was no formal training. The boys salvaged appliances, cleaned parking lots, painted businesses, and tended the grounds of a nearby cemetery, keeping the vocational home afloat with the money they earned. Their primary form of recreation was fighting. Older boys arranged bouts between the peons to determine their constantly shifting hierarchies of favor.

Art feared he might die in one of these sanctioned brawls, buried in the woods and forgotten. But he managed to forge a bond of shared resistance with two other kids. Huddled in the workout room before dinner one night, they used Art's stolen knife to make a blood pact. *Fuck with one of us and you fuck with us all,* they whispered, slicing their arms and promising to kill anyone they needed to in order to stay safe. A few days later, Art found one of his friends crumpled on the shower room floor, catatonic and bloody. This second rape triggered a new resolve. Instead of murder, the boys decided to flee.

That night after bed-checks, the three slipped out of their barracks and ran across the lawn to the main house. One boy boosted Art through the office window, where he found keys to a pickup truck hanging above the manager's desk. Art could have grabbed the key ring and crept out silently. But he stopped. *Fuck you, motherfucker.* The sound of shattering glass as he flipped the manager's desk thrilled him.

The boys jumped into the Kiwanis' pickup and hit the highway. But now what? They'd made no plan. They had nowhere to go and nothing to eat. At a rest stop, they dumped the truck, stole a car, and took off south, finally pulling over to sleep near the Oregon border. When Art awoke, the boy from the shower room was gone like a figment, or a ghost. Art never heard of him again. He and his one remaining friend kept going, stealing cars and ditching them every hundred miles. They got all the way to Yreka, California, before Art's partner in crime was arrested shoplifting snacks from a gas station. Art made it another three hundred and seventy miles on his own, giddy with freedom. He was finally stopped at gunpoint while trying to break into a vending machine. The police brought Art to a county jail, and the next morning to San Francisco International Airport. Art spent the first plane ride of his life in handcuffs, extradited back to Washington where he was deposited, once again, into a cell at juvenile detention. It felt like a homecoming.

Now sixteen, Art was assigned to live at Kitsap Youth Homes in small-town Silverdale, his thirteenth placement in two years. Rather than a program organized around religious instruction or work crews, this facility took a gentler approach, attempting to mimic the structure of a family. An older girl designated Art her "little brother." The live-in administrator appointed herself house "mother." Art went along with these fake siblings and their pretend mom because it implied a trade. If he acted the good brother to these state girls who'd "adopted" him, whatever force arbitrated the cosmic math of the universe would ensure that someone was doing the same for Dawn, wherever she was.

Family labels did not satisfy the hunger to matter that clawed at group home kids. Sex was constant, almost compulsive, because it provided a brief sense of connection, or at least of value. When Art's housemother began inviting him into town for private trips to the movies, he understood the cues. It was a reward for fitting in so smoothly, she said, pressing against him in the dark. On their way home, she pulled the van over to the side of the road, climbed into the back, and beckoned for Art to follow. This routine continued for weeks, until Art's housemother discovered he'd been practicing his growing carnal knowledge on his foster "sisters." The result was expulsion.

But it brought a rare moment of choice. Art could either return to juvenile detention and await another assignment, or move in with a staffer from the group home who'd agreed to act as his foster dad. The man had already groped Art a couple times. But anything was better than a locked cell at juvie. So Art left Kitsap Youth Homes and moved to his fourteenth placement.

He spent his days hunting for odd jobs and nights at his foster father's place, north of Seattle. The arrangement lasted less than two months. Art did not hate the man for his desires, but he had long ago determined that he would never be a victim, never the boy in the bottom bunk. He had stolen knives and vehicles and had sex with a grown woman in the back of a van to protect himself. When he took off, no one tried to stop him. Art's legal guardian, the state of Washington, severed its responsibility with one terse sentence:

"Arthur Longworth refused further services and informally emancipated himself."

He was sixteen years old.

***

Art was accustomed to life as a runaway. But the experience of truly
belonging to no one was dizzying. In order to eat, he burglarized homes.
He hitchhiked north, planning to find work on an Alaskan fishing boat,
but got only as far as the Canadian border before discovering that he
was job hunting in the off-season. He turned back, stole a series of
cars tearing south down the highway to California, and finally crashed
while speeding across the Mojave Desert with Black Sabbath's "Master
of Reality" blasting from the tape deck. After recuperating from his
injuries in a California youth prison, Art was flown back to Washington
and, incredibly, released to the streets once again, after promising a
judge that he would return for his next court date.

Seattle in the early 1980s was a magnet for homeless kids. They
roved downtown in ragtag packs, living communally. Art, disgusted
by their desperate panhandling, much preferred to camp by himself
in public parks, robbing people for food money, rather than begging.
He was shambling through the quiet Wallingford neighborhood one
evening, debating whether to look for a sleeping spot near the Home
of the Good Shepherd shelter for delinquent girls, when he noticed a
huge cedar growing next to an imposing brick building. The foliage was
thick enough that Art knew he could climb it without being spotted. In
truth, he was a little afraid of the Good Shepherd home, believing it to
be haunted. But this grand old edifice, McDonald Elementary School,
felt different somehow, safe.

Seattle children had attended McDonald Elementary for more than
sixty years. But underenrolled and shuttered in 1981, it now sat abandoned. Art didn't know that. He climbed the tree and saw that its limbs
stretched close enough to McDonald's roof that he could use them to
leap across. He found a hatch, pulled on its handle, and peered into a

dark attic. Lowering himself stealthily, Art dropped down and landed at one end of the dusty room. As his eyes adjusted, he spied a strip of light glowing on the floor. A doorway? For a long time, Art sat in the blackness, listening. No footsteps, no voices. Art crept toward the light. He felt for a doorknob and turned it slowly. A short staircase led down. Art followed it, his heart pounding. Just off the landing, he saw a small room with a twin bed, made up with a blanket and pillow. Shocked by this evidence of human presence, Art scurried back up to the attic. For several nights, he slept there in the dark. But it soon became clear that no one used the tiny bedroom. It appeared to be forgotten.

For the better part of a year, Art made his home at McDonald Elementary, roaming Seattle during the day and wandering the school's silent hallways at night. Sometimes he phoned his former foster dad for money, and often he got it. People were many things, Art decided, more faceted than what could be encompassed in a single word like "pedophile" or "thief."

He picked up odd jobs when he could—dishwasher, delivery driver, room service clerk. The notion of Seattle as a glassy mecca of technology would have been absurd at the time. It was a maritime town with rough edges, built on fishing, shipping, and aerospace. Starbucks was unknown. Nothing about Seattle could be called sleek. Vagrants wandered among the crabbers and Boeing machinists. When necessary, Art robbed them. He felt fine about being a criminal. He aspired to become a better one. Any time he got away with jacking someone, Art considered himself a success.

But he had not completely rejected social norms. Art knew he needed some kind of regular job. Busing tables at the Sherwood Inn, he learned from a hostess about Pell education grants. They could pay his way through community college, she said. Art liked this idea. He was good with cars—stealing them, racing them—maybe he could become an auto mechanic. He applied to North Seattle Community College and pored over the course offerings, fantasizing possible futures. On the first day of fall semester 1984, Art awoke with more energy and hope than he'd known in years, maybe ever.

"Oh, I'm sorry," said the instructor in Beginning Auto Mechanics. "This course is full. Someone must have made a mistake letting you in."

Art, finally, lost control.

Later, he would think back to this moment, wondering where his life might have led had the teacher offered him a seat. Instead, Art barged into the registrar's office. He flung tape dispensers and outreach flyers and staplers to the floor, cursing the women who worked there with the same screaming fury that had left a manager's desktop trinkets shattered on the floor of the Kiwanis group home three years earlier.

What were his options now? Art wondered, standing on a freeway overpass, staring down at the cars speeding below. He swung his legs over the guardrail and felt cold metal pressing against his back. It would be so easy to fall forward, just a surrender to impulse. He pictured himself landing on a car and bouncing off its hood, the others behind rumbling over his body. But again came the memory of the boy in the bottom bunk. Stepping off the ledge would make Art pitiable, a victim. It would mean the state had won. He climbed back over the guardrail and walked away.

Soon afterward, Art met Cindy Nelson. She was twenty-five, with a round face and shiny dark hair, trusting enough to believe the shaggy kid hauling files at her office was truly interested in joining Amway, for whom Cindy sold products on the side. They'd become friends. At least, Art acted that way. He'd long since forgotten what a real friendship was. For him, relationships were alliances that served a purpose. But he liked Cindy okay, and it looked like she had it made, with her cute apartment and a little blue Datsun they drove around. She invited Art to an Amway rally, scribbling her phone number and address on a piece of paper. *Such an easy mark*, he thought.

Sure, said Art, worried about covering rent at the boarding house where he was rooming. They could talk about him joining Cindy's sales team. How about meeting up near the university to talk over details? His older sister, Desiree, might want in too, said Art, figuring Cindy would be reassured by the idea of another woman's presence, though he hadn't spoken to anyone from his family in years. Maybe the IHOP on University Avenue? Great, said Cindy, making a note in her appointment book: "4—Art Langworth and Desry." She left her desk early, had her calls forwarded to an aunt's number, and drove to meet the kid from work.

They sat in her car, parked behind the pancake house where college students gathered at all hours. Anyone who'd glanced at them might have thought Art and Cindy were a couple squabbling, not a would-be thief and his victim. She bolted from the car. He ran after, picked her up, and carried her back, shoving Cindy into the passenger side and wedging himself in behind. As she lunged toward the driver's door, Art knifed her in the back. Then he fled, taking the keys. Alone in her car, Cindy slowly bled to death.

Three hours later, after nightfall, Art returned. He arranged Cindy's body in the passenger's seat and got in on the driver's side. With Cindy slumped beside him, Art drove north through the city. In rural Snohomish County he pulled over on a bridge and heaved her into the water. He'd chosen Cindy because she was kind to him, because she'd made it easy.

"She didn't see who I was," he told me nearly four decades later.

***

Despite the Becca Bill in 1995, which allowed police to bring street kids into detention, and the *Braam* settlement of 2004, which resulted in nine years of dogged work by an oversight panel, despite reams of research and millions of dollars funneled toward reform nationally, little in foster care had changed when I got in touch with Longworth thirty-five years after he was sentenced to spend the rest of his life in prison. But he had undergone a metamorphosis.

For his first decade behind bars, Longworth behaved in a manner that confirmed the words of prosecutors who'd called him irredeemable. He was locked in solitary confinement so frequently he'd spent a combined five years in isolation before turning thirty. Within the inmate hierarchy at Walla Walla prison, this did not go unnoticed. A biker gang was so impressed by Longworth's easy violence that after he emerged from a stint in the hole, trudging wide-eyed and blinking onto the tier, they recruited him as a debt collector for drug sales. Longworth was honored. It was the first time he could recall being viewed as an asset to anyone.

To keep sane in solitary, he read as much as possible. He liked long books, works that provided both inspiration and escape. Locked away a decade before Microsoft became a household name, Longworth had never seen the internet. And he had been denied education because the Department of Corrections felt those classes would be wasted on someone who was never going to leave. Yet Longworth had a better grasp of literature, foreign languages, religion, and the workings of government than many college graduates I knew. This self-instruction had begun during one of his many tours in the hole. Wild with boredom, Longworth had spied a paperback on the floor outside another cell. Here was a task, a mission to focus his mind. He fashioned a tiny grappling hook of staples bound together with thread from his underwear, which he tied to a plastic comb. Wielding the contraption like a fishing line, he slid the comb beneath the bars of his cell, flicking it hard enough to cast its staple-hook beyond the book. Slowly, he dragged it back toward him. The operation took well over an hour. It demanded so much concentration that Longworth hadn't even bothered to read the title. "Fucking shit!" he said when *One Day in the Life of Ivan Denisovich* was finally in his hands. He'd never heard of it. Also, it was short. And its author, Aleksandr Solzhenitsyn, foreign. All negatives in Longworth's view. But it was all he had.

Longworth opened the worn front cover and realized he'd hooked himself the story of a prisoner. Goddamnit, that was no escape. And in the Russian gulag? How was that going to mean anything to him? Longworth sighed. He told himself to read a few pages a day, if only to eat up some time. This plan failed immediately. Longworth devoured the hundred and eighty-page novella in one shot. Upon finishing, he flipped to the beginning and read it again. The writing was plain, but it spoke to him. Particularly the idea of a government locking up its own people. He could not shake the sense of a parallel to something that churned inside him, unarticulated.

Longworth was in his late twenties then, decades from becoming the man I met at fifty-six. But the shift creating that person had taken root. In the visiting room at Walla Walla, as he passed the time chatting with his latest pen pal-turned-girlfriend, Longworth gazed at an older inmate who'd written a novel based on his life as an addict and thief. Jimmy Fogle's manuscript had found its way to director Gus Van Zandt, who was going to turn it into a movie, or so Longworth had heard. And now, sitting across the visiting room was the actor Matt Dillon, talking quietly with Fogle at a small table. A celebrity's presence did not impress Longworth nearly as much as the dawning realization, made real in front of him, that you could tell your story and accomplish something, even inside a maximum-security prison. You could connect with people.

Longworth had always been an avid reader, even during the years he stared at the ceiling from his bunk in juvenile detention, sure that he'd never amount to anything. But he was thirty-nine before he tried to write. The work of turning feelings into words and using them to transmit experience felt nearly mystical. He was puzzled by people who spoke airily of writing as a "gesture of hope." To Longworth, it felt like pure desperation. The day he picked up a pen for the first time, he had no idea what hope was.

But as he wrote, Longworth's free-floating rage began to harden into a recognizable shape. It looked, in his mind's eye, like a creature, some sort of beast. As he saw it, two government systems had intertwined to structure virtually his entire life. Leaving foster care at sixteen had been like jumping out of a plane with no parachute. He'd had no family support, a seventh-grade education, and zero ability to build connections with people who might help. How could anyone expect an outcome other than the cell he lay in now? Longworth saw his story replicated in one inmate after the next. They'd been children twisted into survival machines by Washington's child welfare system, then locked away by the same state government for the very behaviors it had created. Nearly half the kids in Washington's youth prisons had child welfare case files,

Longworth discovered. Yet no one talked about this. As far as he was concerned, foster care was creating a societal emergency. But to the outside world, this conveyor belt he saw channeling thousands of kids into locked cells was invisible.

By then in his fifties, Longworth had earned some gravitas. Younger inmates dubbed him "the professor." He led the reformatory's local chapter of the Concerned Lifers Organization, whose members met on Monday nights to discuss improving themselves, the prison, and if possible, corrections policy. Out of this group, Longworth culled another, comprised solely of men who had grown up in foster care. There were many to choose from. But Longworth was picky. He was after something much bigger than a support group. Longworth wanted men who were literate, people who could see the pattern he'd observed and explain how it had shaped their own lives. He wanted to reach beyond the prison walls with evidence that was unignorable, a report that would quantify and explain this foster-care-to-prison phenomenon. He called his crew the State-Raised Working Group.

Each man he invited had a particular attribute. Longworth, who still stammered in public, found a natural spokesman in Percy Levy, an imposing former addict serving his fifth adult sentence. Everyone saw possibility in Percy. He was obviously bright, undeniably charismatic. But Percy, who'd been put into foster care at age ten after his mother stabbed him, ran from every home, wandering back to downtown Seattle in search of the parent who'd nearly ended his life. A social worker named Chris met Percy at a youth shelter and offered to become his foster dad. He enrolled Percy in a suburban high school and bought him a red sports car. But Percy couldn't stop fighting—in school, on the streets. Repeatedly, he landed in juvenile detention, then did time in three of Washington's youth prisons. By nineteen, Percy had a ferocious crack habit. At thirty-two, he was sentenced to serve a quarter century for armed robbery. The first time he met Longworth, in the prison yard, Percy's radar crackled. It was odd for an older white guy to approach a Black man like him, especially with such a personal overture—"I heard you were in foster care. Would you like to join a group I've started?" He wondered if Longworth was some kind of weirdo, pressing an agenda he could not yet discern.

There was Jeff Foxx, a stoic figure revered by other Black inmates, who'd been placed in foster care at age four, after his mother abandoned him. Jeff was shuffled through five homes in eight years during the 1980s. He was sexually abused, had trouble concentrating in school, and repeated fifth grade. By seventeen, understanding that he was about to age out of foster care with no means of support, Jeff began selling drugs. He was desperate, paranoid, and at eighteen, he rampaged, killing his pregnant girlfriend, her sister, mother, and the mother's boyfriend on a Sunday morning in 1992. Like Longworth, he was sentenced to life without possibility of parole. The two men met at Monroe prison, though not by accident. Longworth was always on the lookout, scouring crime stories for any mention of a defendant's past in foster care. This was a *thing*, Longworth explained to Jeff, a machine they'd been shaped by, with predictable ends.

Also in Longworth's growing circle of activists: Faraji Bhakti, who had been born to crack-addicted parents in 1980 and handed over to the foster care system at eight, with his brother. Faraji moved through ten homes—he'd tick them off: the nice place; the farm with rabbits; the house with an alarm on the refrigerator door—only to discover when he aged out in 1998 that his parents had stolen his identity. They'd used his name and Social Security number to dodge bill collectors, collect payday loans—whatever they needed. Faraji, then eighteen, was homeless, with his credit destroyed before he'd even begun to build a life. He got a job at McDonald's, sold drugs when he could, and cycled through prison three times over the next ten years. During his third stint, naturally outgoing Faraji could not help noticing the dour white guy in his writing class, who seemed to take himself so seriously. The dude was such a curmudgeon. They did not vibe at all. But when he heard Longworth read aloud, Faraji sat up straighter. He began to notice Longworth across the circle at inmate meetings and grew to appreciate the older man's dry humor, his impatience with guys who talked on and on. *Okay, he's just a real linear thinker, super-analytical*, Faraji decided.

"Y'know, Art was in foster care too," a mutual friend told him as they stood on the chow line. And one day, after hearing some of Faraji's poetry, Longworth asked if he might consider writing something about foster care. He liked the way Faraji was able to create a sense of community in an audience.

When he had a half dozen men in the State-Raised Working Group, Longworth began inviting outsiders to listen in. He wrote to philanthropists and nonprofit leaders and government officials—including Ross Hunter, who oversaw foster care as secretary of Washington's Department of Children, Youth and Families.

New to government work, Hunter was one of the first to respond. He had been among the earliest managers at Microsoft in the 1980s—Yale-educated, from a background of East Coast privilege. At thirty-nine, he retired from tech a millionaire. He need never work again. But Hunter, a Quaker, believed in social justice, and in his ability to make a difference. In 2003, he ran for elected office, representing the Seattle suburb where Bill Gates made his home, and over the next thirteen years Hunter became well known at the state capital for a healthy ego and sharp elbows. His eventual appointment to lead the agency overseeing child welfare raised eyebrows across the state. Hunter had no experience of poverty or trauma. His strengths were data analysis, management, and an unshakable belief in his own brainpower.

The visit with Longworth's State-Raised Working Group humbled him immediately. Deep within the bowels of the reformatory, Hunter watched Black inmates sitting in community with white supremacists, Longworth leading all of them through a research-based discussion about foster care. Never in Hunter's high-flying career had he attended such a well-run meeting. The secretary returned for three more sessions, mesmerized by what he was learning about the hand-in-glove relationship between these two systems. How could it be that, after all the lawsuits and expert panels scrutinizing foster care, a prison lifer with a seventh-grade education had been the one to point this out?

***

One afternoon in 2019, while Longworth was organizing an agenda for the next meeting, he stood to receive a letter handed through the bars of his cell. (With its rough brick walls and open tiers, the Washington State Reformatory still looked much as it had on opening day, in 1910.) He peered at the business-sized envelope with an attorney's name printed in the return-address spot. Longworth received lots of correspondence, but it usually came with handwriting on the outside. This letter explained that his name had shown up in old state files listing former residents of the Kiwanis Vocational Home. His experience there had not been an anomaly. Dozens of other men had endured the same brutalities, said the lawyer, asking if Longworth would consider joining a suit against the Kiwanis and Washington state. He signed up that day.

This was around the time Longworth first heard the term "foster-care-to-prison-pipeline." It irked him because he found it imprecise. In Longworth's view, the pipeline was more like a circuit. A snake that fed on its own, an ouroboros of misery, its outputs becoming fuel to keep the beast alive. Foster care was the mouth of this creature, the entryway to a system that had devoured everyone he'd ever known. "I wanted the guys to understand that it wasn't their badness that put them here," he told me, the words coming fast. "It was a systemic thing."

CHAPTER 4

The Legend of Singing Heart Ranch

The cycle Art Longworth recognized was not merely a modern-day failure, some twenty-first century corruption of a once grand solution. To the contrary, from its earliest inception foster care has been used to address the twin American impulses of concern for children and fear of them—particularly children of the poor.

In 1909, one hundred and ten years before Maryanne Atkins stood in court demonstrating one possible outcome of the government-as-parent, a little girl named Vera Kloskie held tight to her father's hand as he marched up the front steps of the Spokane Children's Home, on North Hemlock Street, in Spokane, Washington. Vera was four, and because her mother had died a month earlier, Peter Kloskie believed that turning her over to an orphanage—and the possibility of a new family— would give his eldest daughter the best chance at a better life. But Vera, who lived into her nineties, never forgot the abandonment. Peter ushered her inside the large brick building and visited twice over the next two years. After that, Vera told friends, she never saw him again.

I learned this from talking with her neighbors, long after Vera's death in 2002. She'd had a hard edge all her days, they said. But she loved children, to whom she told her stories of foster care in its early years, when kids in orphanages were eagerly handed over to almost any adult who asked. This was before the government provided support for those who took them in. Initially, the arrangement was more like charity in return for free labor.

The question of what to do with indigent kids has confounded authorities since colonial times, when poor families with new mouths to feed routinely sent older sons and daughters to earn their keep with strangers. Some historians theorize that the mass hysteria behind the Salem witch trials sprang at least partly from suspicion aroused by these outsider waifs. This crossover, where children in trouble become kids to fear, has been part of the American story from its earliest days.

By the nineteenth century, when throngs of immigrant families surged into East Coast cities, the number of unsupervised youths was a five-alarm emergency. Some thirty thousand children were sleeping in vestibules and doorways, banding together in gangs with names like the Dead Rabbits and Plug Uglies, surviving on whatever they could steal. New York City's chief of police George Matsell was so vexed that he railed in his semiannual report of 1849 at the nuisance of these juvenile vagrants. They were "idle and vicious," he wrote, "destined to a life of misery, shame and crime, and ultimately to a felon's doom."

The problem, like the crisis of homelessness today, was pervasive enough to attract the attention of elites, including an ambitious young man from Yale University named Charles Loring Brace. Educated as a minister, Brace opened the country's first youth shelter around the time of Matsell's report, and he agreed with its gist. These urchins were "far more brutal than the peasantry from whom they descend," Brace observed, later chronicling his work with street kids in a book, *The Dangerous Classes of New York*. "The murder of an unoffending old man . . . is nothing to them," he wrote. "They are ready for any offense of crime, however degraded or bloody."

But Brace, a progressive, believed that with a bit of help a young person could escape this fate. His solution, an orphanage known as the Lodging House for Boys, opened in 1854, at 128 Fulton Street in Lower Manhattan. Each of its hundred and thirty young boarders got a bed and a footlocker. Even within their degraded ranks, there were divides. "Regular" boys slept on a floor separate from the "irregulars," who were deemed tainted by "all the ills that dirty flesh is heir to," a reporter for the *New York Times* opined. Savvy beyond their years, these youths knew "at the age of twelve more than the children of ordinary men would have learned at twenty," the reporter continued. They could "cheat you out of your eye teeth, and are as smart as a steel-trap." It took a special person to handle such boys, he concluded, praising Brace for his dedication.

The minister's plan was to educate, house, and feed each one, then find them jobs and permanent homes. His ideals were quickly overwhelmed by the numbers—New York's streets were teeming with vagrant kids. Brace conceived a new plan. Right after college, he had toured Europe and learned about the custom of families "placing out" children whom they were unable to care for. Maybe he could do the same with the lodging house boys and their ilk, sending them to live with families in the fast-growing American West. They would escape the evils of urban life and, in return for shelter and sustenance, provide free labor to farmers.

New York City progressives embraced the idea as a model of pragmatism. Orphaned kids would be scrubbed down, dressed up, and packed onto westward-bound trains with a Bible in hand. The trouble was, not all of them were orphans, and the question of whether they were to be treated as adoptive children or workers was left somewhat murky. Living with a family was surely better than sleeping on the streets or in an orphanage, Brace reasoned.

After a few trial runs to farms in Connecticut, Pennsylvania, and upstate New York, Brace's fledgling organization, the Children's Aid Society, shipped its first clutch of kids to the Midwest in September 1854. When the last of these trains pulled into a Texas depot in 1929, seventy-five years later, more than one hundred and fifty thousand children had been uprooted from East Coast cities and transplanted to live among strangers. The youngest lost all contact with their biological families. Those old enough to remember where they'd come from were strongly encouraged to forget.

***

In many communities, the arrival of one of these trains was a major event. Crowds greeted them, full of families that had placed orders for the type of child they wanted, often specifying gender, hair type, and eye color. A notice in one Nebraska newspaper read:

All children received under the care of this Association are of SPECIAL PROMISE in intelligence and health, and are in age from one month to twelve years, and are sent FREE to those receiving them, on ninety days trial . . .

Other advertisements highlighted the children's physical attributes. (Virtually all of the train children were white.)

Homes are wanted for the following children: 8 BOYS: Ages, 10, 6, and 4 years; English parents, blondes. Very promising, 2 years old, blonde, fine looking, healthy, American; has had his foot straightened. Walks now O.K. Six years old, dark hair and yes, good looking and intelligent, American. 10 BABES: Boys and girls from one month to three months. One boy baby, has fine head and face, black eyes and hair, fat and pretty; three months old.

At each stop the children were divided into groups, those who had been preselected for adoption split off from the rest. Any not spoken for were marched from the train depot to the local playhouse, where they presented themselves by hopping onstage to recite a poem or sing a little ditty. (This practice is believed to be the source of the idiom *putting children up for adoption*.) Prospective parents then got a chance to inspect them up close, prodding the kids, squeezing their arms for proof of sturdiness, peering into their mouths to check for oral health. Those selected went home with their new families immediately. The rest trudged back to the train. At the next stop, the process would repeat.

The practice of sending kids west and placing them with families was widely viewed as a humane gesture. But in hundreds of pages of history about this period, I found no mention of anyone asking the children for their opinion. Years later, elderly survivors of these early experiments in foster care described childhoods of mute confusion and swallowed fear. Well into his seventies, Lee Nailling, one of the very last train children, recalled the journey. He remembered standing with his younger brothers, ages six and three, at a 1920s train station in New York. Their father, believing another family might provide better for the boys after his wife's death, handed Lee a letter in a pink envelope. "Write me when you get settled," he said, tears running down his face. He told the boys to look forward to "wonderful new lives."

A tall woman with bobbed hair escorted the three brothers to their assigned seats. None of them understood what was happening, or where they were going, or why. Other children were quietly weeping as the train pulled away.

"The next thing I knew it was morning," Nailling recalled in a story for *Guideposts* magazine in 1991. The train had come to a stop. "I was handed a brush and damp cloth, and told to tidy myself and my brothers. I washed their grimy hands and faces and brushed their hair, then reached for my coat." He checked the pockets, expecting to feel the crinkle of his father's pink envelope, but it was gone. Lee grew frantic, searching everywhere, even crawling beneath his seat to check the floor.

"What are you doing?" the tall woman chaperone demanded, standing above Lee. He tried to explain about the letter, but she shushed him.

"Straighten up and sit down," he remembered her saying. "You're starting a new life now. A clean break is best."

Lee understood then that she had taken the envelope. More than seventy years later, he was still bitter. He remembered the way his heart twisted as he turned toward the train windows, watching the blur of trees and towns speeding past. "Her matter-of-fact words weren't unkind. But all I could do was hate her."

The boys were ushered from one train onto the next. "The big problem was that you never knew what the future held for you," Nailling said. When their train finally arrived in Texas, young Lee and his brothers walked across the town square to a church. An adult pinned squares of white cloth to their coats, printed with the numbers 24, 25, and 26. They stood before a crowd of would-be parents who looked them over, opened their mouths, poked at their ribs.

"It was all I could do to resist the urge to bite," said Nailling, recalling the way one man shoved a hand into his mouth to check his teeth.

***

Vera Kloskie was born in the midst of this period, in 1905. She would later recall being so poor in the years before the orphanage that her family lived on toast spread with lard. In search of work, Vera's father had moved them from Iowa to South Dakota, where Vera's mother died giving birth. Now an unemployed single dad, Peter Kloskie gave Vera's little sister to a couple, who adopted her, and took off for Washington with four-year-old Vera in tow. Two years later, in 1911, the federal government would begin providing aid to widowed single mothers. But single dads like Peter Kloskie routinely turned their kids over to orphanages. A family chose Vera from among the hundred kids living at the Spokane Children's Home when she was six.

"Back then, if you wanted a child for whatever reason, you could just go and pick one out," her former neighbor said. He'd been a boy listening to Vera's tales and hadn't asked many questions. But his memories had an ominous quality. The family's teenage son had treated Vera as a plaything. She'd barely learned to read when her foster brother shot out her eye with a BB gun. "He was a mean little bugger," she told the neighbor boy half a century later, her eye permanently mangled.

In addition to household chores, Vera earned her keep by working in a garment factory. Child labor was not yet against the law, and when a needle from her sewing machine stitched through Vera's forefinger, she had to use her own meager earnings to pay for its extraction. "Vera was always pretty sour about that," said the neighbor who grew up on her stories. By that point, she'd become a legend in Idaho's Priest River valley, a tough, frugal woman with a mysterious past that spanned the history of American foster care. She knew its infancy in orphanages, its early years as an unregulated source of free labor, and the way it sometimes lost track of children.

In 1999, Vera told a newspaper reporter that she'd fled her foster home in 1912, at age seven, and spent the next few years wandering the West, one among untold numbers of unaccompanied children roving the country at the turn of the twentieth century.

**

Brace's child-removal project went by several names: The Emigration Plan, the Home-Finding Department, and finally, the Department of Foster Care. (The term "orphan train" came from Hollywood, via a 1979 television movie.) In general, the program was hailed as an enormous success. Eighty-seven percent of its 105,000 transplants had become "creditable members of society," the Children's Aid Society announced in 1910, a half century after re-homing its first shipment of kids. Two of the boys grew up to become governors (John Brady, of Alaska, and Andrew Burke, of North Dakota). Several more became mayors, congressmen, and local representatives.

But not all of Brace's adoptees were the grateful, docile children their new parents anticipated. Having previously survived by their wits in orphanages or on city streets, more than eight thousand were uninterested in complying with family rules and found themselves returned to New York. Another five thousand died, disappeared, or were arrested, Children's Aid reported. One of these kids, a foster child named Charley Miller, became the first person executed by the state of Wyoming. He was seventeen years old.

Blond and blue-eyed, Charley had been born to German immigrants in New York City. When he was six, in 1880, his mother died of septicemia due to miscarriage. Several months later, Charley's father committed suicide. The couple's four children ended up at the New York Orphan Asylum on West 73rd Street, where Charley's sister and two brothers were quickly adopted. But Charley was turned down by families again and again. The problem was his chronic bed-wetting.

Believed to be the result of uncontrolled masturbation, bed-wetting was understood by Victorian-era authorities to be a red flag for latent delinquency, a sign of inborn criminality, and possibly, insanity. To cure Charley, orphanage workers whipped him. When that brought no change, they had him circumcised—at age twelve. But the bed-wetting continued. "I had a disease. I couldn't stop it," Charley later testified. At thirteen, he was packed onto a train and briefly housed by a couple in Virginia, who soon sent him back. Several months later, the orphanage shipped him to Minnesota. The farming couple who'd signed for Charley needed a hired hand more than a son, and their discovery of his morning shame only further hardened them against him. But no report of problems with the adoption reached Children's Aid in New York. When an agent with the organization visited to check on Charley Miller, he reported that the boy was "doing well in an excellent home."

Charley's story is chronicled by Cornell University professor emerita Joan Jacobs Brumberg, in her 2003 book *Kansas Charley: The Boy Murderer*. Brumberg became interested in the case as an early example of juvenile execution. But to me, it was all about foster care. The parallels between Charley's life "on the tramp" in the 1880s and Art Longworth's on the roadways and riverbanks of Washington state a century later were stunning.

Deeming Charley defective, the Minnesota farmers finally dumped him at a train station without food, money, or even a ticket out of town. For two years he rode the rails as a hobo, hopping off to find work where he could, stealing food when he could not. His favorite escape was dime-store novels. In their pages Charley lost himself, fantasizing that he was a cowboy, roving across the West. But Charley's life was no grand adventure. He was jailed briefly in Pennsylvania and gang-raped by other drifters in a boxcar. Not long afterward, Charley Miller, age fifteen, bought the pistol that would seal his fate.

In Colorado, Charley befriended two young men, middle-class gents from good homes. With their newly purchased Western garb and pockets full of cash, Waldo Emerson, nineteen, and Ross Fishbaugh, nearly twenty, considered hobo life a lark, an escapade. They met Charley while roughing it at a campsite one night and allowed him to tag along. But Charley was a real hobo—smelly, ragged, unsophisticated—and to his new companions he quickly became a nuisance. They tried to shake him in Nebraska, promising to meet up at a certain street corner in Sidney but never showing. Instead, Emerson and Fishbaugh went to a restaurant and enjoyed a hearty meal while Charley, barely a hundred pounds, remained famished wandering the street outside. He found them later at a saloon. The young men bought Charley a beer and, for themselves, several pints of whiskey. Now drunk, all three crawled into a Union Pacific boxcar on a train heading west and passed out.

A few hours later, as they crossed into Wyoming, Emerson and Fishbaugh awoke, made their way to the dining car, and had breakfast. Bellies full, they returned to the boxcar and settled into a satisfied snooze. Charley, lying awake, guzzled the last of the booze, shot each man in the head, rifled their pockets, and scurried off the train. He bought food, clothes, and a haircut with the money he'd stolen. But Charley took little pleasure in his crime. He tracked down his older brother in Kansas and confessed three weeks later.

The idea of childhood as a period of unique vulnerability was a relatively new concept in 1890, when Charley was tried for murder, and his case became a flashpoint, crystalizing two opposing stances toward young people that persist to this day. Charley had killed not in self-defense or the heat of an argument, but with an approach that looked to many like cold opportunism. In their view, murder was murder and should be punished as such, no matter who had committed it. However, new progressives countered that there was such a thing as child trauma, and it shaped behavior. Justice demanded acknowledging these facts, they said.

Child abuse itself had been officially recognized for less than two decades, ushered to public awareness by the case of a nine-year-old named Mary Ellen Wilson. She'd been found tied to a bedpost in a New York City tenement the year Charley Miller was born. Held captive by her stepmother, Mary Ellen did not know how to walk on grass. She did not even know her own age. "Woods, fields, green things growing, were all strange to her," testified social worker Etta Wheeler, pleading with a judge for permission to save the girl. "She was wholly untaught, knew nothing of right and wrong except as related to punishments."

Mary Ellen's case became notorious, and legally, the first acknowledgement that children require protection. But consensus on what that should look like proved elusive. The same year Mary Ellen was discovered, the National Prison Reform Congress complained that Charles Brace's trains full of children were merely dumping East Coast problems onto the social welfare rolls of the West. Charley Miller's case exemplified these competing views around the question of America's response to harm caused by traumatized kids.

His story, covered in newspapers from New York to San Francisco, convulsed the country. Charley never offered a clear explanation for his murders—as maddeningly opaque as every young killer. On the stand, he referred matter-of-factly to the "two young fellows" as "the ones that I killed," a plainspoken description heard by jurors (and journalists) as chillingly casual. "His calmness in admitting the killing was something simply amazing," said the Cheyenne *Sun*. To the writer, it sounded like Charley was recalling an act as unremarkable as "carrying a package to the depot." At a distance, Miller's face didn't look bad, he added, "but a close study reveals an expression of fiendishness." Charley's apparent nonchalance was particularly striking compared to the demeanor of his victims' parents. They wept. They described their boys as "saintly." Charley was no desperate child, they said. He was "a drunken demon."

The teenage defendant did little to dispel this interpretation. In jail, Charley smoked cigars and played harmonica. He chatted with anyone who came to visit, including a newspaperman to whom he confessed his crime. Like Maryanne awaiting trial in juvenile detention more than a century later, Charley's two years in jail were virtually the first he'd known regular meals, reliable shelter, and a clean bed. After his interview with reporter Albert Stewart was written up for all to see in the *Daily Republic*, Charley's lawyer decided the only hope for acquittal lay in convincing jurors that his client was insane. To build this argument, he coaxed Charley to talk about masturbating up to four times a day.

That admission, along with testimony about his continued bed-wetting, only made him look more depraved. Thus, irredeemable. The jury took fifteen minutes to return a guilty verdict. A month later, Judge Richard Scott sentenced Charley Miller to death.

The trial set off a national debate about the true character of America, a young nation built on Christian ideals of charity and forgiveness but given to behavior that belied both. Petitions piled up on the desk of Wyoming governor Amos Barber, beseeching him to save Charley's life. "Oh, don't you think he is too young to have such a dreadful fate?" wrote a woman from Missouri. "This poor boy was wholly blind to the crime and his own poor soul's condition."

Many others, however, saw Charley's candid acknowledgment of murder as evidence of a terrifying internal void. "He is utterly lacking in moral responsibility," wrote one reader to the editor of a Cheyenne paper. "They had money and he wanted it. He therefore killed them in cold blood and with as little compunction as a man would crush a fly which pestered him."

In her book Brumberg, the professor and social historian, attributes Charley's behavior to severe childhood trauma, total lack of emotional support, desperate hunger, and intoxication. But his fate hinged on politics. Governor Barber, negotiating a spate of violent skirmishes between Wyoming's cattle barons and small ranchers, had an interest in quashing his state's growing reputation for lawlessness. Charley's case provided the vehicle.

On the last night of his life, Charley recited some of his poetry to the jailers who'd become his companions and bequeathed them his few possessions. He munched several doughnuts, smoked a couple of cigarettes, and went to bed. The next day, April 22, 1892, the state of Wyoming hanged him on gallows built specially for the occasion. Sixty invited dignitaries gathered in a walled-off clearing outside the Laramie County Courthouse to watch while a crowd of onlookers collected outside, some shimmying up lampposts to get a better view. Charley himself had sent out gilt-edged invitations to his own execution.

"Please be quick. You are choking me a little," he said, complaining of discomfort as the noose was placed around his neck.

Reading about Charley Miller, I thought about Art Longworth scraping by on thievery and odd jobs before he stabbed Cindy Nelson on the streets of Seattle. I remembered the way Maryanne Atkins had been described as cold and manipulative after she shot Emmanuel Gondo in his car. Were there truly demonic teenagers, young people permanently devoid of empathy? The question has bedeviled American criminal courts for more than a century.

"People are afraid of kids—not unrealistically," forensic psychologist Kenneth Muscatel told me as he considered Maryanne's case. He was the person who'd once opined that she was "probably an emerging sociopath." Muscatel had built his career on the fact that children could do horrible things. "But they are also victims," he observed, "so what is justice?"

***

After Charley Miller's execution in 1892, public sentiment over delinquent kids and how to handle them split into two camps: those who maintained a belief in hard punishment, versus those who advocated something that looked more like love. The following decade, a two-volume tome titled *Adolescence* was published by psychologist G. Stanley Hall, the first major work of scholarship to frame the period between childhood and adult life as a distinct developmental stage, in fact a critical time, during which a person's brain and character were forged. "No age is so responsive to all the best and the wisest adult endeavor," Hall wrote. "In no psychic soil, too, does seed, bad as well as good, strike such deep root, grow so rankly, or bear fruit so quickly or so surely."

While Hall considered adolescence a fascinating phase in human development, he noted that it was also the least understood—"in most crying need of service we do not yet understand how to render," he wrote. Brumberg's research backs this up. Other than Charley Miller, she found nearly sixty examples of juvenile execution between the end of the Civil War and 1900.

But policies toward youth were slowly shifting. In 1912, eight years after the publication of *Adolescence*, President William Taft established the federal Children's Bureau, officially recognizing the government's obligation to protect young people. His decree came too late for Vera Kloskie. By then, she was wandering the West on her own, a runaway from foster care.

Vera would soon find her way back to Spokane, working as a chambermaid at the city's glamorous Davenport Hotel, the first in America to offer in-room commodes. Vera, age fourteen, might have been cleaning toilets when President Woodrow Wilson declared in 1919 that there should be codified standards governing children's health, labor, and general welfare. It was time for a "Children's Year," he announced.

Vera's childhood was long gone. She left the Davenport in 1921 and, at sixteen, married a mechanic who was nearly fifty. Though she loved children, Vera never had any of her own. She told friends that she'd been sterilized by doctors at the orphanage, a common practice rooted in the belief that the poor had deficits of intellect and morality that could be culled by limiting their ability to reproduce. Vera and her aging husband instead became homesteaders on a vast tract of ranch-land near the Idaho border. There, Vera cultivated an abundant garden, cooked enormous feasts, and became an ersatz godmother to the kids next door, telling stories of her bitter youth in the early years of American foster care.

Though electrical power came to the Priest River valley by mid-century, Vera continued to cook on her woodstove. She refused to install a telephone, and she saved everything, down to cellophane bread bags. "Tough as nails and sharp as flint," said the man who eventually bought her hundred-and-sixty-acre property. "I have no doubt she was abused in foster care—there was an edge about her. But she could be very kind, especially to children."

After her first husband died, Vera remarried in middle age. The tale of her romance with cowboy Jeff Gevrez is, like the rest of Vera's story, wrapped in mystery. But a few details have been repeated enough to become legend. Vera and Jeff had been pen pals when he showed up at her ranch one day, everything he owned piled in the back of his truck. Gevrez had apparently misinterpreted Vera's polite invitation to visit as an overture. Offended by his assumptions, she made him sleep in the barn. But she offered breakfast in the morning, invited him to dinner that night, and three days later the two were wed, so the story goes. Gevrez was a romantic in every sense of the word. His favorite saddle bore a silver medallion in the shape of a heart, and Vera, who softened under his attention, named her home after it. Singing Heart Ranch was a respite, she told friends, the first place she had ever felt truly safe and free.

She lived there into her late seventies, finally selling the land and moving to a small apartment in town in the 1980s, around the time Arthur Longworth was dumped from foster care onto the streets of Seattle. Decades later, after his attorneys settled their lawsuit against Washington state and the Kiwanis group home, Longworth, from prison, used the money to buy Singing Heart Ranch.

***

Whatever histories brought them into the child welfare system, one fact unites Vera Kloskie with Charley Miller, Arthur Longworth, and Mary-anne Atkins: All grew up low-income or poor. A survey of Washington parents with kids in foster care during the early 2000s found that all were living on less than $40,000 a year. Most were scraping by on less than $20,000. Nearly a third had been homeless, the present-day incarnation of the same destitute families that had so offended philanthropists like Charles Loring Brace in old New York. Class-based from the start, foster care was never conceived solely to protect kids. It has always been a tool for controlling populations seen as crime-adjacent, an instrument of government motivated, in turns, by concern, judgment, and fear.

The irony is that foster care was seeded from the start with a fatal flaw essentially guaranteeing the delinquency and homelessness it sought to prevent. In 2018, pediatricians named it: Removing children from their parents could cause "irreparable harm" to the "architecture" of developing brains, with "potentially lifelong" effects, the doctors said. Their warnings were directed not toward foster care, but the practice of separating immigrant families at America's southern border. Severing children from their mothers and fathers was "wreaking dramatic and long-term damage psychologically and to the physical structure of the brain," a Harvard University pediatrics professor told *The Washington Post*. The consequences, he added, would reverberate far beyond politics.

Foster care has been doing the same thing to kids for a hundred and fifty years.

***

By the 1920s, Brace's orphan train movement was no longer necessary. Newly professionalized social workers were taking an organized approach to the question of children in need. And in 1935, the federal government authorized the first welfare payments to poor families through the Aid to Dependent Children Act. Congress permitted local officials to set their own eligibility criteria for these stipends, however, and many southern states passed "suitability laws," explicitly barring women with children born out of wedlock. Caseworkers had the authority to investigate clients at will and could cut benefits to any they deemed unsuitable. In Alabama, sixteen thousand kids, most of them Black, were immediately dumped from welfare rolls because their mothers had live-in boyfriends. In Florida and Tennessee, mothers labeled "unfit" were told to turn their children over to relatives or risk referral to the courts for "child neglect."

By 1961, Congress sought to create national standards. States could no longer withhold welfare benefits from families unless they had first tried to help them. And if a family remained unwilling to bend to the authorities' determination of wholesomeness, the government would pay for foster care. It made no sense "to declare a home unsuitable for a child to receive assistance, and at the same time permit him to remain in that same home, exposed to the same environment," reasoned Arthur Flemming, secretary of the Department of Health, Education and Welfare.

The policy sounds well-intended. But many social historians see this moment as a dire turning point. With Flemming's decree, the child welfare system shifted "from providing services to intact white families, to taking Black children from theirs," writes Dorothy Roberts in her 2022 work, *Torn Apart*. (Roberts is the same sociologist who tried to help Washington state reform its foster care system as a member of the Braam panel in the early 2000s, and she came away from it convinced that the nation's entire approach to child welfare was corrupt.) In one fell swoop, she observes, Flemming enshrined the practice of hobbling Black families by evaluating them for benefits while removing the children of those judged unworthy.

Afterward, foster care was transformed. In a single year, between 1961 and 1962, the system grew from 163,000 children to 272,000. Those numbers look quaint today. Child welfare agencies now touch the lives of more than a third of U.S. kids by the time they turn eighteen, including 53 percent of all Black youth.

CHAPTER 5

How to Build an Activist

In 2006, while six-year-old Maryanne was navigating life with a drug-addicted dad, and Art Longworth sat in prison, trying to figure out how to make his days mean something, a lanky teenager across the country in Bridgeport, Connecticut, lay on the floor of a sparsely furnished living room, watching *Law & Order* reruns. The popular crime drama had been around for more than a decade, its original stars now celebrities and its tightly scripted plots becoming formulaic. But not to the fourteen-year-old boy staring at the screen. The storyline told of a murder victim killed during a car jacking. The television detectives had been unable to solve key questions about her death until they discovered an overlooked bit of evidence, a recording she'd made secretly, while pleading with her assailant. She'd talked about her family, her children, letting the recorder run all the way up to the blow that killed her. Watching this episode, the boy had been rapt. But at the revelation that a victim had recorded her attacker, he sat bolt upright, vibrating with an idea.

The boy's name was Sixto Cancel, and for years he had been trying to convince an investigator with Child Protective Services to take him away from the woman who'd adopted him out of foster care. Sixto's new mom, whom he called Gladys, had taken in three other children as well, but Sixto was the only one who was Black. He hadn't given much thought to this at age nine, when Gladys became his guardian. But as he grew to a gangly six feet, Sixto could not ignore the way she treated him differently from her other kids. They had new clothes; his were used. They attended private schools; his was public. Gladys had adopted Sixto, yet she seemed to hate him. And he noticed that she crossed the street whenever she saw people walking toward them who were Black, like him. Soon, she began to speak her feelings out loud: *You make me sick, you faggot nigger! Take this money and go!* he recalled her shrieking, as she peeled off a few hundred-dollar bills from the monthly adoption support sent by the state. Sixto ran into the night. He slept wherever he could find a safe place, usually the couch of a friend. Sometimes, Gladys locked him out for days.

Sixto tried to explain this to his CPS worker, Yvette, begging to be returned to foster care. He had always been a talker, piping up about perceived injustices even as a little kid. And though the possibility of angering Gladys terrified him, Sixto kept trying to make the state understand: He had been adopted by a racist who seemed to value him only for the paychecks. It was hard to tell if Yvette believed Sixto, or if she considered his claims merely exaggerated. Either way, she did not remove him. The federal government provides all states with financial incentives to encourage "a forever family" for kids in foster care, and the last thing Connecticut's Department of Children and Families wanted to do was admit failure by dissolving Sixto's adoption and taking him back.

But now, watching *Law & Order,* Sixto suddenly saw a way to prove what was happening. He would tape Gladys screaming at him. He wanted people to understand how it felt to be constantly berated; what it meant to realize you were living somewhere only because of the $875 in government money you brought in each month. Yvette would hear the disgusting things Gladys spat at him, and she would take Sixto away. Then he could go back into foster care. Anything to escape the house on Beechwood Avenue.

Sixto taped a digital recorder to his chest, pulled a t-shirt over it, and stood as close as he dared while Gladys let loose. He was thrilled. There was no way Yvette could doubt him now.

At their monthly check-in, Sixto pushed "play" and watched his social worker's face. Yvette looked concerned, but she said the recording would make no difference. As evidence, it was useless because Sixto had made it without Gladys's knowledge, a violation of state law. This news landed like a kick to Sixto's gut. Standing at the bus stop afterward, he could not control his tears. He kept replaying the conversation with

Yvette in his mind, unable to believe his misery mattered so little to people with the power to do something about it. Headphones clapped over his ears, Sixto blasted gospel music and prayed. *Please let all this pain mean something. Please let it lead somewhere.*

Yvette had, in fact, been moved by what she heard. A few days later, she agreed to accompany Sixto to Gladys's house and open an investigation. Sixto understood how it looked on paper. He'd long ago stopped spending time at his adoptive home, moving from the couch of one friend to the spare room of another. In the language of a case file, he appeared defiant, uncontrollable. But he was sure if Yvette actually got a glimpse of Gladys, she would see. She would recognize the cold, angry woman that Connecticut had assigned Sixto to live with, and she would save him.

***

They pulled up to the two-story, clapboard home and all was peaceful. Sixto sat in Yvette's car, noticing that the vehicle usually parked in Gladys's driveway was gone. Nor could he hear the Spanish-language news she watched religiously. Yvette knocked at the front door. No one answered. She knocked again, looking back at her teenage client with a puzzled frown. He got out of the car and led Yvette around to the side of the house, where they could peek into the living room through Gladys's sheer white curtains. But there were no curtains. And the living room was empty, the old TV gone, the floors barren, the vinyl-covered sofa vanished. Sixto and Yvette circled the building. They knocked on windows and called out uselessly until the meaning of the silence was clear. Gladys had packed up and left without a word to the state, abandoning her adopted son like an impulse buy she regretted.

At the time, in 2007, many Americans had read headlines about international adoptions that turned into domestic disasters. They knew about orphaned infants in Romania, who flinched at human touch after months spent alone in their cribs. They'd heard about refugee children from Africa, who struggled to adjust to life in white suburban homes. But few news stories pointed out that thousands of American children adopted from foster care each year are eventually returned to the system. Not until 2010 did the government even track those numbers. Maryanne had confessed to me sheepishly, in prison, that before it happened to her, she didn't realize it was possible to be "un-adopted."

Yet broken adoptions have long been one of foster care's saddest secrets. Between 2008 and 2020, more than 66,000 children were given back to child welfare after being taken in by families who later changed their minds. The reasons for these turnarounds are as heartbreaking as they are unsurprising: a little kid in need looks very different from a teenager reeling with fury from a torn-apart heart. Would-be parents who want to be rescuers, or believe gratitude creates fertile ground for love, find themselves painfully disabused of those notions. In Brooklyn family court, up to 25 percent of prospective adoptions fall apart before the arrangement even becomes official. Another 10 percent, like Sixto's and Maryanne's, are reversed afterward, an emotional wound so severe that a psychologist who evaluated Maryanne before her murder trial cited "abandonment by her adoptive family" as a direct contributor to the explosive rage that left Emmanuel Gondo dead in his car.

For most kids, the next stop is a group home, where bedrooms look more like detention cells, food is served on a cafeteria tray, and any relationship with an adult is defined by their job title. Kids understand implicitly what this means: They are unwanted. Sixto had been so horrified by the sight of his brother in one of these facilities that after the discovery at Gladys's, he begged Yvette to find him a new foster family instead. His sibling, once an ebullient chatterbox, now spoke in a medicated monotone, like a person without a soul.

Yvette made the required notes in her file: Sixto was refusing adoption, and there were no relatives to step in. Options for a foster family would be few, she warned. No one wanted to take a teenager like him—opinionated, stubborn, and ready to argue. But, unexpectedly, an usher from Sixto's church did. Their arrangement was awkward from the start.

Sixto's new foster mom wanted a boy who would act like a son. Sixto saw himself as more of a boarder. After eleven foster placements, his disastrous adoption, and two years shuttling between the sofas of friends, he was numb. He refused to say "I love you." He did not hug back. The last straw, ironically, was a fight over *Law & Order*. Sixto wanted to stay up late and finish watching his favorite program; his foster mom insisted he go to bed. The argument that ensued was blistering. The following day, during a class trip to New York City, Sixto got a phone call from Yvette. She would be taking him to an overnight emergency placement after school. His belongings had been tossed in a garbage bag and dumped at the Connecticut Department of Children and Families.

Sixto realized young that college would be his only chance to create a different kind of life, his best shot at escaping the bruised streets of Bridgeport. But he hadn't fully grasped what it would take to get there. Researching the necessary steps, he grew increasingly anxious. Fewer than 5 percent of kids who age out of foster care at eighteen earn bachelor's degrees, and Sixto understood that any hope of vaulting himself into that exalted group would require a scholarship. Which meant taking the SAT. Despite his many moves, Sixto had managed to remain at one high school, a fact that separated him from most foster kids, almost half of whom drop out before earning a diploma. But his grades were spotty.

Sixto's networking abilities, however, were Olympian. He'd joined the NAACP youth board at thirteen, while still living at Gladys's home. Two years later, Sixto joined the youth board of Connecticut's Department of Children and Families. The position was merely advisory, but it had given Sixto his first chance to speak publicly about foster care to people who wanted to listen. It also connected him with other foster kids, which was how Sixto woke up to the fact that when he left the system, his support network of social workers and stipends would vanish. The full import landed with a thud when he visited Connecticut's former youth board president for lunch. She was twenty, living in a tiny studio with no table to sit at, no plates to eat from, no utensils to hold. Once, she had dined with philanthropists and legislators. Now Vanessa sat on the floor with her baby, watching TV in an empty room.

By this point, Sixto had added yet another entry to his resume. The Jim Casey Opportunity Fellows were foster youth specially selected for training in advocacy by the Annie E. Casey Foundation, America's preeminent philanthropy dedicated to the welfare of young people. Through the fellowship Sixto learned about the system's many levers and how to pull them. He was schooled on the policies that had governed his life, and coached on using personal stories to explain them to others. It was like lifting the hood of a car; suddenly, he could see the gears of the bureaucracy that had raised him. He met with lawmakers who used terms like "systems change." He befriended mentors who explained how to sock away money in interest-bearing CDs and build up enough to buy a car, which would save time wasted waiting for public transit. He began to grasp the way one step forward led to the next. Like Art Longworth, who spoke of being raised by a faceless entity he called The State, Sixto referred to himself as the product of a strangely disembodied parentage. He called himself "an Annie E. Casey baby," the progeny of a government system and the private nonprofit trying to smooth its jagged edges.

Despite his insecurity about college entrance exams, Sixto's extracurricular zeal won him an interview with the admissions team at Harvard University. Squeak by with an SAT score of 500 on the verbal and 500 on the math, they said, and we might let you into our summer school remedial program. Pass the summer course, and we might let you enroll in September.

On it! said Sixto.

Even reaching that low bar would require tutoring, he knew. A test-prep class seemed like a natural for his charter school. But Sixto's idea of what was right, and just, and obvious ran once again into stonewalling that left him bewildered. *Oh, there's no money for that*, people said, echoing the refrain Sixto had heard all his life: *No, it's not possible. No, the system doesn't allow that. You think you know better, but you don't.*

He couldn't see why money should be an obstacle. All he needed were a few teachers willing to donate their time and someone who could drive students to meet with them on Saturdays. Sixto asked around. Everyone he approached said yes.

He called the program Stellar Work, and for two years it ran on nothing but goodwill. Students kept coming. People began to ask what would happen to the tutoring club when Sixto left for college. After his training as a Casey fellow, he knew exactly whom to approach about permanent funding. Send us a proposal, said his contacts at the Department of Children and Families. Sixto turned in two. The first would support one year of Stellar Work at $4,000; the second offered a two-year plan at $8,000. Instead, the state of Connecticut opted to fund Sixto's program at $22,000 during its third year. The foster child who'd been unable to make himself heard had turned his needs into an idea, and the idea into a plan, and the plan into an effort that would ripple beyond the parameters of his own life.

Sixto's test scores never got high enough for the Ivy League. He opened the thin envelope containing Harvard's rejection letter the same month the university's John F. Kennedy School of Government sent him a commendation for working on the Connecticut youth board. But Morehouse College in Atlanta accepted him, despite—or perhaps because of—his application essay. It was titled "America's Angriest Colored Child."

***

Now nineteen, Sixto was older than the average college freshman when he arrived for orientation at Morehouse in the summer of 2011. He also had experience—in advocacy, system navigating, and sheer survival—far beyond most of his peers. Yet he landed awkwardly. On a campus tour, Sixto chafed at a feeling he could not name, a sense of being out of place. He found himself arguing over minutia. Confronted with paperwork for financial aid, he balked at the numbers and refused to sign. By day's end, sitting in a large room with thirty other students, Sixto was ready for war. A professor stood at the front of the hall, encouraging incoming freshmen to ask questions about campus life, academic expectations, the food. A young man at the all-male school raised his hand to inquire about the dress code—was there one? Yes, said the professor. All students were expected, in fact required, to wear "men's clothing" at all times. No handbags, or scarves, or anything of the sort. Sixto, who is gay, out, and proud of it, let fly. What was the thinking behind this rule? he asked. It sounded like a swipe at homosexuals, or cross-dressers, or anyone who didn't conform. When the professor's answer failed to mollify him, America's Angriest Colored Child stalked out to the parking lot. Driving back to Connecticut, he pulled off the highway in Virginia, rolled onto the campus of Virginia Commonwealth University, which had already offered him financial aid, and enrolled then and there as a political science major.

Sixto had vaulted himself to a place most foster kids never see. He had set himself up with tutoring, built a network of supporters, and successfully advocated within a state bureaucracy that felt aligned against him. Nevertheless, the advent of college created mounting apprehension. Vanessa's empty apartment loomed in his mind. He thought of the former youth board president sitting on her floor, eating meals with a plastic fork, and he began to appreciate the enormous gulf separating him from freshmen whose parents would buy them dishware without thinking twice.

At a dinner with Connecticut's leader of Teach for America, Sixto mentioned his upcoming move.

"You all set for that?" asked the director, Nate Snow. "Do you have enough clothes? What about furniture—do you have a desk? A lamp? An alarm clock?"

Sixto began to feel queasy. He owned none of these things, and he was due at VCU in a week.

"Meet me at Target tomorrow," said Snow.

Sixteen hours later, the two wheeled eleven shopping carts out of the store, piled high with the basics of young-adult life.

What would he have done without Snow's generosity? Sixto wondered as he unpacked in his small apartment a few blocks from campus.

Where would he be, if not for the Casey Opportunity Fellows and all he had learned through them—everything from navigating statehouse politics to buying a car? What about the thousands of foster kids never selected for that program?

In every life, Sixto believed, the two most important days were a person's birth and the moment they understood their purpose. He pegged his to the afternoon he'd stood at the bus stop in Bridgeport, trying to hold back tears and praying that his suffering would mean something, someday. He longed to make his experiences matter. When he allowed his mind to wander, it told him a story of childhood misery transformed into fuel that powered an engine that changed foster care.

Born in 1992, Sixto had grown up with the internet. By the time he stepped onto the campus at Virginia Commonwealth nineteen years later, in 2011, technology had transformed American life. But not foster care. The U.S. child welfare system—a web of thousands of separate state and county agencies—still operated via lumbering communications networks from the 1980s. Paperwork was processed so slowly that Sixto missed the funeral of his older brother, shot to death in Puerto Rico, because he knew he'd never get permission to fly there in time. But what if technology could be used to improve foster care? It would be like electricity, he thought, a force people had lived without for millennia that, once discovered, changed human history.

Sixto's first idea for marrying foster care with tech was a website. He wanted to design something foster kids could consult as they approached their deadline to age out. For Sixto, that moment had felt like running toward a cliff with no parachute—utterly terrifying. The website could address this experience. It would serve as an electronic mentor for kids who had none, offering a menu of videos to guide eighteen-year-olds, step-by-step, through the process of realizing their goals. It would start with the basics: how to buy a car, secure a college scholarship, apply for government benefits. That alone would be more ambitious than the state's Preparation for Adult Life classes, which focused on modest goals like how to do laundry and buy groceries. Sixto even had a slogan for it:

When the shit hits the fan, think of us. But for the moment, the website existed only in his mind.

The summer after freshman year, Sixto landed an internship with the California nonprofit Together We Rise. It had been founded by a law student as exasperated with foster care as he was. At nineteen, Danny Mendoza had been deemed too young to serve as a legal guardian for his nine-year-old cousin, who was living in a car with his mom. Frustrated by the bureaucracy, Mendoza soon discovered there were hundreds of people like him, who wanted to support foster kids but felt thwarted—entire corporations, in fact. No single entity coordinated their efforts, which resulted in a scattershot of redundancy and unmet needs. Mendoza decided his organization (later renamed Foster Love) would act as a clearinghouse, connecting kids and their requests for aid with outlets that could help.

When Sixto arrived at Mendoza's office in Chino, he found a funky loft buzzing with twentysomethings. Music blasted, the walls were scrawled with graffiti, and college students sprawled across the space, working on laptops. This was nothing like the drab conference rooms of Connecticut, and Mendoza—young, charismatic, driven—resembled no philanthropist Sixto knew. Maybe you didn't need advanced degrees or decades in government to make a difference.

Back in Virginia for sophomore year, Sixto leapt into action. He befriended a videographer and explained his website idea. He built an office in the storage room of a Chinese takeout restaurant, gathered a dozen friends, and collected a few donated computers. He buttonholed anyone who would listen, explaining his concept to funders, telling journalists how he'd been inspired by the *Choose Your Own Adventure* children's books, where readers made key decisions for each character, shaping the plotline themselves. Sixto wanted his website to function that way. Foster kids would log on, type in their goals—going to college, or buying a car, or getting a job—and click through a series of questions, choices, and tasks. The most striking thing about it, he thought, was that nothing similar already existed.

Sixto kept telling his story about the departure from Gladys's and the way no one seemed to care about the needs of older foster youth. Speaking requests began to trickle in. Among the most painful wounds of his childhood had been the gut-kick recognition of how little his wishes mattered to a system purportedly set up for his well-being. But where government had turned away, now Sixto could barely keep up with all the nonprofits that wanted to hear from the foster kid who'd made it to college. By 2012, he was staring at an invitation to speak at the Clinton Foundation's Global Initiative University conference, a three-day gathering of student leaders specially selected for their activism. It was networking on steroids. Sixto would be thrust into a room with hundreds of other young organizers. He would connect with entrepreneurs in technology, funders from philanthropy, and consultants who could help him turn his ideas about improving foster care into an actual vehicle for change.

Organization name and speaker's title, said the registration form.

Sixto paused for a moment. *Think of Us, CEO*, he wrote. He was twenty years old.

***

After such a long time of begging to be heard, telling his story felt like therapy. Sixto described the day as a tiny child that he'd crawled into a neighbor's kitchen cabinet, trying to hide from police who'd come to take him from his mother, and listeners were rapt. He narrated the moment at the bus stop in Bridgeport when he'd first grasped that his desperation to leave Gladys's did not matter, and he could feel the rough edges of that psychic gash healing. To the researchers and academics who sat before him, these convenings were routine, with their ubiquitous coffee urns and thumbnail bios. But to Sixto, they were rocket fuel. He leaped on stage to talk to college kids in Vermont and tech workers in California and politicians in Washington, DC. Even when he wasn't talking, Sixto vibrated with urgency. At formal luncheons he listened to funders and policy experts, his head cocked to the side, his leg jiggling beneath the table, feverishly marking time.

He was not naïve. Sixto noticed the way listeners nodded appreciatively as he and a parade of former foster youths narrated their journey to the dais. But every one of them was under thirty, still kids. What would happen to his audience when he crossed that bright line? Telling his story had helped Sixto feel seen, finally, but he understood that every young person on a conference hall stage was furthering someone's agenda. When they grew too old to be useful, the speaking invitations would dwindle, their voices heard no more.

For the moment, he kept quiet about this concern. The Clinton convening turned out to be a bonanza. Sixto met activists working on the problem of "opportunity youth"—euphemistic nonprofit-ese for the country's four million unemployed, undereducated sixteen-to-twenty-four-year-olds, who frequently wind up in homeless shelters and jails. Huge numbers of them were former foster kids. He connected with a consultant who explained how to translate his website idea into a pitch that could attract funding. And, crucially, he grasped the power of data to move lawmakers. Human experience could be quantified, Sixto saw, and those numbers, when presented to the right people, became evidence to drive change.

After the Clinton conference, Sixto was on fire. He convinced the stock market guru Charles Biderman to grant him $6,000 for a Think of Us website leading foster kids through the realities of life after state care. He leveraged Biderman's support into funding from a half-dozen philanthropies. The more he connected with people, the more Sixto's hazy ideas about a marriage between child welfare and technology began to take shape. No longer did his horizon end with a website. Now, he was asking bigger questions: How could the experiences of foster youth be captured as data? The system made millions of decisions about thousands of kids each year, but the kids themselves rarely got a chance to speak. Everyone recognized the system's miserable outcomes. Why couldn't youth voices be used to reshape it?

Sixto had always been bold, but through public speaking he'd plugged into a network of advocates who pointed him toward the federal Children's Bureau. The year was 2016, and President Obama had declared the White House "the people's house." Sixto would hold the administration to its word. What about hosting a tech-style hackathon, but for foster care? he asked. Few kids who'd grown up in the system held master's degrees in social work or psychology, but they possessed valuable expertise. The idea proved intriguing enough to White House staff that they invited two hundred leaders in child welfare, technology, and law to a spring summit. For forty-eight hours the experts huddled with youth from foster care, hammering out ideas for overhauling the system.

Though Sixto's profile and influence were growing, Think of Us remained headquartered next door to the Chinese restaurant in Richmond and staffed by his friends. None of them were professional fundraisers. Few had the energy of their founder. Some eventually lost interest, and others realized that full-time activism was impossible as a full-time student. Sixto himself had pushed aside coursework in favor of public speaking. By 2018, he was the only employee left. He closed up his storefront and moved to New York City with a single suitcase and a near-religious fervor to keep going. He'd been invited to the White House a half-dozen times. But he still hadn't graduated from college.

Though on his own with Think of Us, Sixto was not entirely alone. He'd maintained his relationships with technology officers from the Obama administration, two of whom reached out on his behalf to a young woman named Sarah Sullivan. She knew nothing about foster care, but Sullivan understood how to manage a team of coders who could build an app to accompany Sixto's website. At their first meeting, in a friend's backyard garden, Sixto and Sullivan spoke barely at all about child welfare or government systems. They talked instead about fated connections. Sullivan was mulling several job offers at the time, and Sixto's was unquestionably the riskiest. To this day, she isn't sure why she said yes.

Immediately after Sullivan signed up as the only full-time employee at Think of Us, $2 million in anticipated funding fell through. There they were, the visionary founder with no money but a wealth of life experience, and the manager with tech expertise but no knowledge of child welfare. Road trip? suggested Sullivan. To help her get up to speed on the problems Sixto's app would tackle, they could meet with kids on the cusp of aging out. Sullivan would hear directly about their needs, and Sixto could continue strengthening his network of connections. Sullivan wanted to understand exactly why so many foster youth ended up homeless or incarcerated. Precisely where had child welfare fallen short? And for those who'd avoided the pitfalls, what possibilities did they see? What did they need to make their goals real? Sixto believed he already knew the answers, but he agreed to set up a series of meetings for Sullivan.

In October 2019, the two began their cross-country tour, interviewing more than two hundred former foster kids, foster parents, and social workers in New York, Minnesota, and California. Sixto certainly didn't anticipate learning more about foster care. He accompanied Sullivan mainly to oversee the education of his new director of products. Yet he emerged from their six-month research project staggering under the weight of those voices. "Lots of us are living workshop to workshop," a nineteen-year-old in San Francisco told him, ticking off her tricks for surviving on the $25 gift cards handed out at Preparation for Adult Life classes.

Despite the galvanizing nature of that moment at the bus stop when Sixto prayed through his tears, he'd devoted little sustained attention to his own sadness. His three-year frenzy of public speaking and fundraising had been helpful for keeping those thoughts at bay. But now, as he listened to young adults across the country, he heard his own life story echoing. He thought back to kids he'd known at college, how the most basic aspect of their lives—the ability to call home—had been foreign to him, like a different language. He saw with new clarity the ways children from intact families gradually learned to take on responsibility, building toward independence, while his youth had been about learning to pack fast and quash emotion. Survival in foster care required a certain passivity, an emotional circuit-breaker that shut off caring about anything. But it left young people stunted. Most never learned how to envision a goal and make it real. The very idea of goals was dangerous. The San Francisco teenager surviving on gift cards was savvy. She knew where to find discarded food before it went bad and how to make those money cards stretch. But she had no idea how to build a life.

***

In March 2020, Sixto and Sullivan wrapped up their research trip and returned to Washington, DC, with hundreds of hours of interviews. It was a Friday afternoon, and they were flush with the energy of their new venture. They planned to start building the Think of Us app the following Monday. Instead, the world went into lockdown.

Sixto and Sullivan looked at each other. They had just spent six months talking with some of the twenty thousand kids about to be cut from foster care during a global catastrophe. The magnitude was paralyzing. But only momentarily. Sixto shifted into crisis mode. He reached out to his old mentors at the Casey Foundation, who gave him $50,000 to dole out to youth leaving the system—as many as he could find.

Still riveted by the idea of turning their experiences into data, Sixto hatched a plan. What if each person who got one of these mini-grants had to answer a few questions about their circumstances? The responses might be enough to form the beginnings of a lived-experience database. Sixto put the word out on Facebook: He had small cash awards available for anyone leaving foster care who was willing to complete a short poll.

That very evening, Sixto dashed off a questionnaire. It covered the basics, like whether the grant-seeker had a job or was in financial crisis. Had they ever been adopted? Were they LGBTQ? Did they live with a guardian, or alone? Were they on the street? Sixto hoped for perhaps a thousand replies.

Within a week, more than twenty-seven thousand young people had responded. They lived in small towns, big cities, rural areas, and suburbs in all fifty states and the District of Columbia. Nearly 30 percent said they went hungry several times a month. More than two thousand struggled daily to find food. Four thousand said they were homeless, living in shelters or sleeping on friends' couches. Thirty-three percent—nearly nine thousand young people—said they'd had brushes with the criminal legal system. The same number said no one had ever talked to them about housing before they left foster care. Sixto's questionnaire had generated 146 pieces of information per grant applicant, for a total of 3.9 million data points codifying the recent life experiences of American foster kids. Nothing like it existed. No dataset so broad, deep, and detailed about the intimate realities of being a foster child. As far as Sixto was concerned, Think of Us had hit the mother lode.

No matter what age they'd entered the system, or where, several patterns in the data were consistent: Every person who'd spent time homeless or incarcerated had either run from a placement and ended up on the street, like Maryanne; or they had been adopted as children, rejected by their new families, and returned to foster care, like Sixto (and Maryanne); or they'd landed in group homes, where every relationship was transactional, like Arthur Longworth. And many of those who'd managed to stay with a single foster family were virtually shoved into homelessness when they turned eighteen and the monthly stipends stopped coming. At that point, their foster parents bid them goodbye with a wave at the door and a hearty "Good luck!"

The alumni from group homes upset Sixto like no others. He had never shaken the memory of his younger brother, slumped and dead-eyed during their visit in Connecticut. The moment came rushing back as he listened to interviews from the foster-care tour. One youth after another described being watched so closely that going to the bathroom was the only chance for privacy, and those moments were strictly monitored. (To their embarrassment, many group home alumni were unable to shake the habit of requesting permission to use a restroom, even years later.) Those who attended school off-site were ashamed to tell other kids where they lived, which left them isolated, unable to build friendships and utterly adrift once on their own.

At best, the aged-out foster kids said, they had a high school diploma and an hourly-wage job. But not one of them could rely on the kind of safety net Sixto's college friends took for granted, the ability to call a mom or dad for help with money, or a job application, or just basic life advice. Many had no reliable connection to another soul.

***

"Network! Network! Network!" Sixto urged a crowd of advocates, congressional staffers, former foster kids, and child welfare officials from the Obama, Trump, and Biden administrations. It was May 2022, two years after he'd put his questionnaire on Facebook, and hundreds of well-wishers were gathered for the unveiling of his dream, a research and policy-development lab for analyzing youth data to change foster care. Sixto called it the Center for Lived Experience.

He was standing onstage at a Washington, DC, event hall in an iridescent-blue suit. Catering staff wove through the crowd, offering hors d'oeuvres. Around the dance floor, mounted wall screens flashed quotes from his own case file: *Sixto refused adoption and there is no viable family option,* said one, recalling the single sentence jotted down by an exhausted caseworker so many years before. It turned out, she had been wrong.

At a family reunion shortly before the launch in DC, Sixto learned that he'd had an aunt who was a licensed foster parent and lived less than sixty miles from Gladys's house. He'd never needed to feel so lost and alone. He'd never needed to wander through the homes of a dozen strangers. But he didn't know that as a bewildered child, nor as a nine-year-old adoptee, or a thirteen-year-old running the streets of Bridgeport. He had no idea this relative existed, and apparently no one in Connecticut's vast child welfare bureaucracy had bothered to check.

Known as kinship care, the practice of placing foster children with relatives instead of strangers was rare in the 1990s. Families riven with addiction or mental illness should be removed from a child's life, the thinking went, as if inborn bonds could be overridden with paperwork.

It is one of the most exasperating examples of illogic in a bureaucracy rife with them. Despite decades of research on attachment problems in foster youth and their disastrous life outcomes, the government steadfastly refused to consider that children might connect better to people they already knew. And in rare cases where neglected kids were handed over to aunts, uncles, or grandparents, the state never provided financial support. It was either pay strangers to take in children, or have kin handle the expense on their own.

"We have a wrong design!" Sixto bellowed into a wireless mic as the DC crowd applauded.

Increasingly, an emphasis on kinship care is becoming standard when caseworkers take children from their parents. But this is new. On the night Sixto paced the stage in DC, child welfare had staggered along virtually unchanged for a century. Many of the bureaucrats who'd perpetuated its harms were standing in front of him. But now, rather than being punished for defiance, Sixto was hailed. Celebrities jostled to be photographed by his side. Paris Hilton arrived in a black sheath dress and sunglasses, posing for paparazzi with her arm slung around Sixto's waist. She'd just come from an afternoon on Capitol Hill, visiting legislators to press his most recent campaign: abolishing group homes.

It had been a decade since he spoke at the Clinton Foundation event in 2012, and four years since the Think of Us board disbanded. Now Sixto had a multimillion-dollar budget and a staff of forty.

Shortly before the evening in DC, I'd asked him if any bonds remained from his childhood in Bridgeport. Normally, words and ideas tumbled from Sixto's mouth, one on top of the other. But this time he tilted his head to the side, running through a mental Rolodex. "No," he said curtly, his sunny expression gone hard.

I turned toward motivation. What exactly was driving him?

"For a very long time, anger was my driving force," he said. But that had changed. "At a certain point it becomes more about what good you can do. When that switch happens it's no longer about your unique experience, but the collective."

Though in his element—smiling for cameras, pressing flesh—Sixto's keyed-up nerves remained evident. During an onstage discussion, his foot jiggled compulsively, creating the impression that he was ready to spring off the dais and dash to the next moment, the next conversation, the next campaign. He quipped about an unnamed funder who'd dismissed the notion of placing more foster kids with their own kin. "The apple doesn't fall far from the tree," Sixto recalled them grumbling. His audience booed. He had them all now—former foster kids and bureaucrats, activists and philanthropists. He'd taken the wounds of his childhood and turned them into sculpting knives, carving out a sense of purpose and then identity, shaping himself into someone who could no longer be denied.

But Sixto still acted like someone running for his life. He was in a race to transform foster care, and the race had transformed him.

CHAPTER 6
Boat Against the Current

Among the thousands of former foster kids who answered Sixto's original questionnaire and reported moving from state care into homelessness, nearly all had spent at least part of their adolescence in group homes. The experience had so torqued Art Longworth's youth that he remained outraged about it forty years later. If I was going to connect the dots from foster care to living on the street, the realities of life after a group home were essential to understand.

Monique Thompson had stumbled across Sixto's social media callout while online, searching for a job. She'd answered mainly because of the $130 stipend Sixto was offering. To Monique, this felt like a life-changing sum. She owed two hundred dollars on her cell phone, and the service was about to be shut off. The first time we spoke, she was living in a state-subsidized apartment, still looking for work. To save her cell minutes, we talked over Zoom. Behind her, on an otherwise bare wall in Monique's dim bedroom, she'd hung a white board covered with a biblical verse in neat bubble letters, Psalm 140:4, the Prayer for Protection: *Protect me, Lord, from the power of the wicked; keep me safe from violent men who plot my downfall.*

Monique had been removed from her family at age five. But unlike Sixto, and despite her prayers, she had never been adopted. After stumbling through ten foster homes, multiple crisis centers, and seven hospitalizations for suicidal behavior, Monique, at fourteen, was sent to the Bayes Achievement Center, a group home about an hour north of Houston.

Some group homes effect a family-style atmosphere, like Tasha's place outside Seattle, where Maryanne had been one among six girls. Others, like the Kiwanis facility where Art Longworth learned to fight, are structured like work camps. Many feel more like prisons or hospitals.

Bayes, in rural Huntsville, Texas, presented itself as a therapeutic boarding school for children with severe behavior problems, many of them developmentally disabled. Monique did not strike me as disabled so much as dissociated from her life.

She knew she had "mental problems," as she put it. She'd been dosed with psychotropic drugs virtually from the moment she entered foster care in kindergarten—clonidine to calm her; Zoloft for depression; Risperdal, an antipsychotic, to improve her mood and behavior. Also, at various times over the years, Trileptal, a mood stabilizer; trazodone for insomnia; Concerta for ADHD; Ativan for anxiety; Seroquel for depression; Lexapro to sleep; and Lithium for "suppression of anger," in the words of her case file.

The anger was understandable. Monique, at five, had accused her stepfather of sexual abuse in response to questions from a teacher about why she kept scratching her crotch. The allegation blew her family apart. None of them backed her. Monique's mother, who'd spent time in foster care herself, refused to believe her daughter. Monique's grandmother, who presided over the family home, told investigators that she "did not want to get involved in this situation." Doctors deemed their investigation "inconclusive." But for Monique's safety, and that of her baby sister, the state removed both girls. A psychologist who examined Monique at the time said that her "long-term prognosis hinges upon whether she is able to grow up in a stable, secure, loving, and otherwise appropriate home environment." His notes proved prescient.

Monique was among twenty-eight thousand children removed from their families in 2001 because of suspected sexual abuse. That particular horror is actually one of the least common reasons children are taken into state care. Among the three million calls to Child Protective Services each year, reports of neglect are far more typical. Nearly 60 percent of the 296,000 kids who entered state care the year Monique did were deemed victims of neglect. And while many children suffer multiple forms of maltreatment simultaneously, neglect underlies fully 74 percent of foster care cases.

But evaluation of mistreatment is not a science. As interpreted through the eyes of some twenty-nine thousand screeners and investigators working in Child Protective Services, any number of problems may qualify as child neglect, including empty refrigerators, shut-off power, children arriving at school unbathed and hungry, and children left at school or daycare after dismissal time. All of these things signal a family struggling, and most suggest poverty. None is evidence that a child is unwanted or unloved. Yet the government spends ten times more on foster care payments to strangers than on services aimed at keeping families together. When Monique was taken away, her family was living on about $20,000 a year, most of it from her mother's job as a waitress at Golden Corral.

Much of the time, neglectful parents are drug-addicted or mentally ill. But as advocates frequently point out, a drug test is not a parenting test. A Black mom who smokes a little weed can reasonably worry about having her fitness questioned—especially if she is poor—where white middle-class families almost never face that threat.

And the undeniable truth—long ignored by the system but foundational to its young charges—is that whether their parents starved, stabbed, beat, or abandoned them, many children spend their time in foster care pining for reconciliation. Kids are, it seems, neurologically programmed to forgive.

Considering the allegations, Monique's home may have been too dysfunctional to fix with any kind of government support. Medical evidence confirming her claims was indeterminate, but Monique's behavior spoke volumes. Foster parents who knew nothing of her history reported sexual acting-out well beyond the imagination of a typical first-grader. Monique also threw chairs, kicked out stairway banisters, cut herself, and wept if other children moved in to a foster home where she was staying, afraid they'd soak up all the attention. At seven or eight years old she had no way to explain these feelings, but state-contracted therapists kept telling her to write them down in her journal.

"What do you wish for?" a psychologist asked when Monique was in the third grade.

"I want my life to change," she said.

With each new placement, her behavior worsened until, at thirteen, Monique kicked a staffer at the crisis shelter where she'd been sent after her latest foster parent had had enough. This resulted in a call to the police. When the officer arrived, Monique bit him. She spent the next two weeks at the Montgomery County Jail.

"Due to lack of immediate maternal attachment, there is a concern," a therapist wrote at the time. "Prognosis is poor."

***

In April 2010, a month before her fourteenth birthday, Monique landed at Bayes. She was terrified. Despite her propensity to fight—"intermittent explosive disorder," in the words of the state—Monique considered herself a shy person, prone to drawing away. Throughout the hour-long drive from juvenile detention, she talked about dying. Her case worker stared straight ahead, hands clenched on the steering wheel. At Bayes, the staff rummaged through her meager possessions as Monique stood by, watching helplessly. They confiscated her beloved Bluford High books and the metal rap she liked to blast in her headphones, though they allowed her to keep a small stuffed bear. Monique slept in a room where all decorations had to be approved by the staff and meals arrived on a tray. But Bayes did provide a certain stability. Monique wore the same outfit every day—a blue polo shirt and khakis—which was okay, since she didn't have many clothes. The uniform made her an oddball at Huntsville High School, where she was dropped off each morning in a van.

Shortly after she arrived at Bayes, the staff listed Monique's career goals in her file: "Lawyer, beautician, physical therapist, or a writer." Counselors at Huntsville High guided her toward cosmetology. Monique liked fixing people's hair, doing their nails, and a program manager at Bayes promised to refer her to a friend who worked in the salon at JCPenney as soon as she passed the state licensing exam. Each week, Monique got a half hour of therapy, along with her meds, and though she'd been below grade level in elementary and middle school, at Bayes, Monique began to get straight As. She "has a clear plan for her future," a caseworker wrote, declaring herself "excited and proud" that Monique was "on the right track."

Paging through her file, I could not help wondering about these sunny assessments. Since early childhood, psychiatrists had noted that Monique would need long-term therapy and "ongoing support." Yet caseworkers kept writing that she was headed toward "independent living." Three months before her eighteenth birthday, Monique's latest social worker wrote that she would "age out of care with all of the resources needed to be a productive adult." When I met her seven years later, Monique was holed up in a dark apartment, too wracked with anxiety to venture outside. Were her caseworkers merely acting with fake-it-till-you-make-it optimism? Or were their goals more self-serving? If, for example, a worker's notes indicated that all appeared well while Monique was at Bayes, how could the state be blamed for whatever came later?

During senior year, when she wasn't learning how to mix hair dye and manicure nails, Monique focused on her senior prom. Its theme was "The Great Gatsby," America's parable of aspiration and decline. To get a dress, Monique's caseworker drove her into Houston for a charity event known as Giving Gowns, where a bevy of women outfitted girls in donated formalwear. One of them introduced herself as Monique's "fairy godmother" for the day and led her through racks hung with satin and organza, pulling out one dress after another and holding them against Monique's petite frame. Midway through the fittings, they all sat down to a luncheon with pink place settings and linen tablecloths, while a seamstress tailored Monique's final choice with a few deft stiches. Never in her life had Monique's looks and desires attracted so many hours of continuous attention. It was like a dream. She was so giddy afterward that on the way home Monique suggested she and her caseworker get their nails done, like real girlfriends. But Monique's worker had other obligations, she informed her client, who sank into glowering silence for the rest of the ride back to Bayes.

Foster care employs about ten thousand similar staff, most of them social workers, who keep track of children after they are removed from their families. They are supposed to visit with their young charges monthly, ensuring that kids are healthy and clothed wherever they are living—be it in a foster family, group home, or juvenile detention cell. But many caseworkers are so overloaded they can't meet those deadlines. The majority quit within two years. During her time at Bayes, Monique was handed off to at least three different workers, who affected varying degrees of friendliness but moved on to new assignments, or jobs, with barely a goodbye.

By prom night, Monique had rebounded from her disappointment after Giving Gowns. She'd arranged her hair in flapper-style finger waves and emerged from her bedroom, beaming. People gaped. It was Monique's Cinderella moment. For four years, no one had seen her in anything but khakis. But a few weeks later, on her eighteenth birthday, Monique would turn back into a teenager with no one and face the question of what came after foster care. She had failed the cosmetology exam by a single point.

***

While Black children like Monique make up about 13 percent of America's youth population, they comprise nearly a third of the young people raised in group homes. Whether those residences are homey or institutional, their outcomes are almost universally awful. A *Lancet* review found that 80 percent of kids living in group facilities were below average in cognitive development and had problems forging healthy bonds. The researchers examined group home studies from a hundred and thirty-seven countries. Patterns were the same everywhere. The more time spent in so-called congregate placements, the less likely a young person would emerge ready for life as a functional adult.

With salon work at JCPenney off the table, Bayes scrambled to come up with a new plan for Monique. Texas, like most states, connects all foster kids likely to age out on their own with a Preparation for Adult Life counselor, whose job is to guide them to independence. Monique's counselor met with her at Bayes and helped her apply to Texas Southern University, where she planned to major in physical therapy. The state would cover her tuition as long as she maintained decent grades.

Monique couldn't wait to get there. The rules at Bayes were stifling. She'd needed them once, but she was grown now, ready to fly. Despite all the ways she'd felt "outcasted" during high school—as the only Black girl in cosmetology, the only one who couldn't invite a friend over, or hold a job after school, or go to the movies at night—not until Monique landed at college in the fall of 2014 did she fully appreciate the differences between herself and other students. Four years of asking permission to use the bathroom left her wide-eyed at life on an open campus. She taped a class schedule above her bed and tried to keep focused, but the lack of structure made her sweat. Trying to describe the experience of freedom, she choked out a single word: "Overwhelming."

One morning in January 2015, after she'd stumbled through her first semester at TSU, Monique awoke to her phone ringing. A man was on the line saying her mother had died. Monique thought it was a prank. When she finally understood the news was true, she took it as a sign to drop out. She was on academic probation anyway.

Here, Monique faced a fork in the road. After thirteen years in foster care, she thirsted for autonomy. But she was unable to handle the anxiety that came with it. Getting monthly checks through Extended Foster Care required that Monique be employed or in school, so she found a job at McDonald's and lived for two years in a new home with a new foster mom. But Monique was no longer a little kid. She wanted to run around at night. She wanted boys to come over. Her foster mom kicked Monique out at twenty. Suddenly, she was homeless.

Monique found an apartment near Lone Star Community College, where she could enroll and keep her state benefits coming. But to move in, she needed a security deposit. For a summer, Monique lived in limbo, sleeping at a shelter and attending school until Texas's

Department of Family and Protective Services could catch up with her dreams and provide a housing stipend. Because the shelter was far from her job at McDonald's, Monique quit and began selling blood plasma for food money. Her first draw brought $25. The next, $40. She worked her way up to $60 before the blood center said she had to stop. After a few days off, she began the cycle again. Between that and occasional stripping, Monique was able to keep her cell service on.

Most kids who age out of foster care want nothing more to do with the child welfare system. Not Monique. She clung like a puppy to her Preparation for Adult Life counselor, Brianna Jones. It was Jones's job to make sure every kid on her caseload knew how to sign up for the government services to which they were entitled. Monique had been her best pupil, successfully registering for college and negotiating housing subsidies. While living at the shelter and waiting for her benefits to kick in, Monique connected with an advocacy group that posted her portrait online as a "Foster Care All-Star." In the photograph, Monique's skin glowed. Her lips were parted, and she faced the camera with a sunny smile. The text noted that she'd been a student at TSU and met Olympic gymnast Simone Biles. It talked about her plans to complete a degree in physical therapy and open her own business. Nowhere did the website point out that Monique was homeless.

Jones could have predicted all of it. Year after year, she watched her clients age out of foster care and tumble straight into shelters or prisons. Kids would sit in front of her at fourteen for an initial conversation about their life goals. At sixteen, Jones began teaching them how to apply for food stamps and do laundry. She explained the virtue of buying groceries in bulk, lectured about shopping lists and keeping to a budget. But she knew the kids weren't listening. Every one of them was daydreaming about the mothers and fathers they'd lost. Were their parents better now? Would they want them back?

Officially, Jones's jurisdiction lasted only until each client's twenty-first birthday. But often they'd call her later with updates: "I graduated!" or "I had a baby!" Monique was different. Twenty-five years old and still checking in every week to chat about nothing. Most of the kids on

Jones's caseload were street-hard by the time they walked into her office. Everything they did was aimed at conveying self-sufficiency. Monique showed only her need.

For Jones, the main source of tension between them was her former client's inability to hold a job. Monique had no trouble getting hired—at Panera Bread or Starbucks, or a hospital gift shop—but she walked away from every gig after a few months, sometimes a few weeks. Jones kept telling her to accept where she was and work her way up, step by step. But how was that any way to build a life? Monique wondered. How was she supposed to self-advocate like all the counselors and social workers had taught her to, while working a late shift for minimum wage? Monique hated riding the bus for an hour just to get to some crap job where it felt like half her salary went to taxes, only to spend another two hours going home. (Public transit ran less frequently after 9 P.M., and Monique often walked long stretches of highway in the dark. "That's how girls get trafficked," she kept saying.) It felt like running on a treadmill, going nowhere.

The first time we met, Monique wore a hoodie pulled so low over her forehead that her eyes, nose, and mouth were scrunched into the space of a drawstring hole. It was the summer of 2021, and she had just turned twenty-five. On her next birthday, the Extended Foster Care benefits would end. Which was why Monique spent most of her time scrolling job sites, trying to get a foothold on her future.

While we were getting to know one another, Monique and I spoke every week. She had managed to secure the apartment in North Houston, leave the homeless shelter, and enroll at Lone Star college. But the question of employment had become a bugaboo. Monique's most promising lead was a position as "foster care ambassador" for the Texas Network of Youth Services, a nonprofit that would pay her $150 a week to attend conferences and talk about her experiences as a ward of the state. "I'm thinking about a career in public speaking," she told me.

There is a growing army of foster youth who appear at these events, deployed to give texture and legitimacy to the agenda. Monique was thrilled by the opportunities to "network," despite her crippling social anxiety. At a conference in San Marcos, she sat on a dais with a half-dozen other former foster kids, telling her story. But she bleached out the details. She alluded to having been homeless but did not describe marching up and down the highway to sell her blood plasma. She read from a script, robotic and monotone, barely raising her head to make eye contact.

The panel was full of foster kids who'd run from their placements. They explained to the audience of teachers and social workers how that usually landed them in a cell at juvenile detention. Here, again, Monique was out of place. She had never been a runner, not really. She tried it once in sixth grade, when her foster mom threatened to send her to a youth shelter. *That ain't happening*, Monique said to herself. So she left. But when the sky grew dark and the streetlights came on, Monique returned, head hanging low. She didn't know what she was doing out there. Where was she going to go?

Monique's downward spiral from foster homes to crisis shelters and finally the Montgomery County Jail had been spurred by the last in a series of hoped-for adoptions that disintegrated. When a new girl visited the home where Monique was living—just to get a look at the place—Monique was sure she understood what was happening: There would be no adoption. The other girl was prettier. Their foster mom would like her better. Any mother-daughter relationship she'd believed in was a mistake, an invention. Brought up sharp by this new certainty, Monique threatened suicide. The woman who'd seemed like an answer to her bottomless craving for love took Monique to a hospital and left her there.

Adults often marvel at the "resilience" of children. But based on what I'd seen, a more apt description would paint them as survivalists, hanging on. That was Monique, clinging to foster parents and case-workers like a human vine. Yet one family after the next requested her removal. Wherever she went, Monique fantasized about the apology her mother would someday offer for failing to protect her, and then she'd have a family again.

Nothing close to that ever happened. At Bayes, Monique learned that the system had deemed her "unadoptable."

"It's such a crap realization when you think you're going to be loved and then you realize that it's not gonna happen," she'd told Sixto Cancel's researchers. She'd hoped she might still find a family, even as a teenager living in a group home. "It hit pretty quick that was a fantasy."

Monique wanted to be so many things—a public speaker, a model, an entrepreneur. When reality intruded on her dreams, she shrugged it off with a vow to keep scouring job sites. Every time we spoke, she had a new idea. "A ballerina," she said, as if this was a reasonable plan for a woman in her mid-twenties who'd never taken a dance class. But what Monique wished for more than anything was something she found difficult to articulate. It was her Achilles heel, the unprotected underbelly that defeated her again and again. How did you tell a social service agency that what you really needed—aside from food and housing and a job—was someone to belong to?

***

One day in the fall of 2021, a man emailed Monique. He called himself a producer and said he'd seen pictures she posted online, posed provocatively in neon-green stretch pants and three-inch nails, her hair long and wild. The man said he'd pay her $100 to model. "It's something out of nowhere!" she rejoiced to me over the phone. "It's a miracle!"

Monique had been watching *A Star Is Born* on television the night before, the Judy Garland version from 1954, and to hear from a self-described producer the following morning felt like a sign. She spent hours imagining where this unexpected contact might lead, how it could change her life. So thrilling was the vision that she'd forgotten to ask the producer for details. She didn't know who he worked for or what he intended to do with her pictures. After he failed to write back, Monique spent a week curled up in bed with her teddy bear.

She sent me a page from her journal to explain what she wanted people to know about life after foster care:

When walking on the street they are vernable to anybody to help thats why youth turn to drugs suicide stripping and end up in trafficking. Maybe even self-harm because what more can I do inflict More harm on myself. the resources and jobs keep us in a cycle what About next month are we going to sweep the problem under the rug? Now I'm stress angry, sad and hungry. The only communication I had because im alone trying to get out of debt from being homeless and still made no progress. I'm serious giving up crying now I vented on In a journal like therapist and professionals recommend but still doesn't fix the problem

The girl had a big heart and even bigger dreams, and Jones, her onetime caseworker, wanted to see them come true. But year after year, Monique's singsong voice glossed over an inability to manifest her ideas, as if the psychological foundation that allowed others to envision a self and persevere until it became reality was missing. Despite all the positive evaluations during her time at Bayes, on her own Monique fumbled every test of independence. On an application for Social Security benefits through Extended Foster Care, Monique checked boxes affirming she had problems "managing money," "remembering," "concentrating," "getting along with people," and "understanding or following directions."

Jones believed all of these deficits were rooted in Monique's lack of family. How could you build a sense of self when the artifacts of your identity—school photos and treasured books or favorite clothes—were dumped in a series of garbage bins behind a string of foster homes? Monique still had the old stuffed bear that had been with her since middle school, but other than that there was no anchor to her past. As far as Jones could tell, this hunger for family was more problematic than Monique's impractical dreams. It got her into trouble constantly. On rare occasions when she tried to visit her grandmother and cousins back home, Monique's relatives demanded whatever cash she had. She handed it over dutifully, her government aid intended for school, stipends meant for food.

Jones could barely contain her disgust.

"Monique, let me explain," she'd say. "I know you want that family feeling, but this is not the family you want."

Monique would smile and nod in agreement. "I'm just waiting on something to happen."

***

In April of 2022, Monique heard about a job that she considered perfect, night shift guard at the Harris County Jail. The position had a solid salary and health insurance. She filled out the paperwork, thrilled to receive an auto-reply confirming receipt. "They said they gonna be in touch soon!" she crowed. Monique had left a few things off her application, like information about the time she bit a cop and wound up in juvenile detention. But she didn't see how that could matter—she'd been a kid. Anyway, Monique told herself, foster care records were sealed.

As Monique tried to finish up her community college coursework and prepare for another youth conference, we spoke less frequently, keeping in touch via text. I sent a note on her birthday.

"How are you doing?" I typed.

Moments later my phone buzzed with two pictures of Monique, her right cheek scored by three jagged cuts in bloody, diagonal lines. A medic was in the lower corner of one photo, examining the back of her legs. "I haven't left my house in a week," she texted. "I'm really struggling."

The next day, we spoke for an hour. Monique and a friend had gone dancing at a South Houston club called Cloud 21. I Googled it and found a dismal looking low-rise in a strip mall. Inside, black leather couches were arrayed around shiny chrome poles. Monique said she'd been dancing there until a bouncer told her to leave the floor—the professionals were trying to work.

"I'm like, 'okay, that's fine,'" she said.

Monique had left the dance area, but she had no intention of leaving the club. And suddenly, everything went sideways.

"The night went off—I mean, I didn't do anything! I walked off the stage, but I told them I wasn't leaving because I didn't do anything wrong!"

Cause-and-effect storylines often seemed to be beyond Monique. Everything came out in a jumble of words tangled with emotion, but out of sequence. The description of her night at Cloud 21 had this quality. Somehow, drinks "were thrown" and a gun "was pulled." Monique said the security guard lunged at her, and then the dancers were clawing her face, pulling out her hair, grabbing for her phone when she tried to record what was happening. In the melee, Monique lost her glasses. "I couldn't really protect myself because I couldn't see, and I was crying. There was blood on the floor, and my hair was everywhere!"

Afterward, Monique was convinced people from the club were looking to hurt her, so she refused to leave her apartment. She spent weeks at her computer, trying to identify the women who'd attacked her by their Instagram handles so she could call them out on TikTok.

"I need to speak my truth," she kept saying.

"Okay, but you also need to eat," I said. "How are you getting food?"

"Smoothies," she answered.

I'd sent her a juicer for Christmas, and it appeared this was now Monique's main source of sustenance.

"But how are you paying for your phone and rent?"

"I have been up all night, looking at different ways I can do quick cash. At this point, I don't know."

"What about the jail job, the county government position?"

The process had gone smoothly, Monique said. She'd filed the paperwork three months prior and received regular updates as her application worked through the system. She'd taken a drug test—negative. She'd taken a TB test—clear.

"And then I went to the psychological."

"Was that a written test or face to face?"

It had been a series of fill-in-the-blanks, Monique said, with many questions about her background, including criminal history. Again,

Monique omitted any mention of biting a police officer in middle school. Just as she finished up, the evaluator summoned her for an interview. Facing him across the desk, it became immediately clear that the department knew all about Monique's history—even more than Monique herself, since she hadn't yet seen her complete foster care file.

"They were able to get into everything, even when I was in school and I was fighting with the police and my foster mom had to come get me!"

Monique was shocked that this information had been accessible. But she was not surprised at the verdict from Harris County about her fitness for the jail job. The psychological exam sealed her fate.

"They said it's a stressful place, and they didn't want to put me in that situation because I've already been through a lot. I mean, I was answering their questions, and they were like, maybe this job is a little bit too . . . Just basically, no."

Though disappointed, Monique largely agreed with the decision. Night-shift staff often had to deal with suicides, she'd heard, and she knew she couldn't handle that.

I wondered about the details Monique chose to reveal and the words she often let drop: "Suicide." "Trafficked." "Vulnerable."

For all her goals and dreams, Monique understood that she'd grown up with serious emotional problems and that living in a group home had done nothing to address them. Being taught how to keep her room clean was not enough to navigate adulthood. She was grateful that Bayes had helped her graduate high school and kept her off the streets. But she'd landed there anyway.

CHAPTER 7
Invisible Science

The most painful part of Monique's story was her desperation to bond with the foster families who took her in and her compulsive sabotaging of those connections, each and every one. Even at Bayes, she imagined her caseworkers as older sisters or friends, until they brought her up short and reminded Monique that they had hours to log and paperwork to file, that their relationship was a job. While her hunger for family remained, the years at Bayes had at least pointed Monique toward the notion of the future. For that reason, she found it difficult to talk about living in an institution, reluctant to criticize the people who'd provided her with food, shelter, and consistency.

Jay Perez-Torres had no such qualms. When we met, Jay was twenty-seven—nine years out of New York City's foster care system and struggling to keep his fury at it from drowning his efforts to build a new self, far from the frightened, humiliated child he'd been. The search for a reliable place to call home had dogged Jay most of his life. New York's Administration for Children's Services allowed him to live with his ex-stepmother when Jay was in middle school and his dad went to prison. But Jay's father, an explosively violent man, made that arrangement unsafe once he'd been released. So, at fifteen, Jay was sent to a group home in Harlem.

On move-in day during the winter of 2010, Jay heaved the garbage bag he used as a suitcase onto an X-ray scanner and walked through a metal detector. On the other side, a guard patted him down—arms, legs, and crotch—searching for weapons. Jay had already spent time in juvenile detention for gang activity, and he'd visited his father in prison upstate. As far as he could tell, the biggest difference between those places and where he stood now was an orange jumpsuit. Jay was a hulking five-foot-ten and two hundred pounds. His arms were sheathed in tattoos, and he'd long ago given up dreams of having anything like the kind of childhood he saw other kids living. But as he stood in the main hall, looking around at the place he'd secretly imagined as a home, Jay felt his chest tighten.

For the prior two years he had wandered the city. Sometimes he stayed a few days at his ex-stepmom's place; other times on the couches of friends. Once, when he was thirteen, he lived alone for six months in a vacant apartment where his dad had been doing construction work. His dad disappeared, but the landlord allowed Jay to stay. When his father resurfaced, they sometimes stayed together at a homeless shelter or with one of his dad's girlfriends. Jay's life as a kid was endlessly itinerant, scattered in fragments across four of New York's five boroughs. Because there was no place he could reliably store his belongings, Jay kept everything he owned in a Hefty bag that he lugged around the city—clothes, food, schoolbooks, Social Security card, even his birth certificate.

He'd never envisioned the Catholic Guardian group home as a permanent base, but he had allowed himself to fantasize that it might be an island of calm in this odyssey. Peering around the day room, he ripped himself for those hopes, for imagining he'd get his own bedroom with a door that closed. About fifty teenage boys sat in the wide-open hall, hunched over cafeteria trays or talking with visitors. No one looked up to meet his gaze. Surveillance cameras blinked from every corner. A guard pointed him toward the place where he would sleep, a cubicle separated from the main room by a thin partition with an enormous window. Jay got the message. There would be no privacy. People could watch him every minute, as he slept, or read, or changed his clothes.

The front door pat-down was not merely a move-in formality. It was Jay's daily after-school ritual. Catholic Guardian was one of about sixty nonprofits paid by New York City to manage its foster population— sixteen thousand kids in the 2010s, when Jay was part of the system. And despite rhetoric about creating dignity, preserving hope, and providing "nurturing and therapeutic environments," the message conveyed through security cameras and scanners was unmistakable: the kids living there were guilty. Of what, Jay was unsure. Years later, he would look back at the group home in Harlem and think of it as the place that finally crushed his soul.

Though naturally sociable, it was easier for Jay to avoid making friends at a place where people came and went without warning or farewell. Instead, he walked the city. He'd wander Times Square, soothed by the sight of anonymous tourists, none of whom would look twice as he slipped into a side entrance of an AMC movie theater and sat for hours in the dark. Or he'd go to the park and watch other kids throwing footballs, so free of the cares that hounded him. Jay worried about his father, whom he found terrifying. And about his stepmother, who was too afraid to let Jay stay with her. He scanned the streets constantly for gang bosses to appease and rivals to avoid. By the time he returned to his bed at the group home at the end of each day, Jay was exhausted.

The longer he stayed in foster care, the angrier Jay became. His 6 P.M. curfew made it impossible to join the football team at school because practices kept him too late. The same went for field trips with his AP History class. Jay had no money for extras anyway, and requesting a voucher or reimbursement through one of his ever-revolving caseworkers meant alerting them with enough lead time to fill out the necessary forms. Even when he was organized enough to do that, the money always came too late. Everywhere he turned, Jay saw himself confined, barred from the freedom to be silly, even to laugh. He seethed with jealousy at other kids who didn't have to lug their lives around in a garbage bag. In his schoolbooks, Jay drew pictures of men punching and kicking each other. Within two years of leaving the Catholic Guardian group home, he was booked for assault.

***

Anna Bennett, the student advocate on staff at Manhattan Comprehensive Night and Day High School, was in the second month of her first full-time job after college. Her assignment was getting sixty seniors at this last-chance school across the finish line to a diploma.

"Hi, are you Jay?" she asked the husky kid slouching through Manhattan Night and Day's halls. It was the spring of 2012, and Bennett had whittled her caseload down to a handful of still-unknown students, which included Jay. She needed to get him to answer her list of questions codifying the "barriers" keeping Jay from graduation. For a kid at Manhattan Night and Day, those might be anything—a job, or childcare obligations, or missing credits, or simply the lack of an alarm clock to wake up in the morning. Bennett's mission was to zero in on the problem and devise a fix—practical, efficient, and without judgment. Often, this meant working with teachers to rearrange a student's class schedule. Sometimes it involved phoning a kid to rouse them from sleep. Generally, it was not complex.

But Jay had never shown up in her office, which prevented Bennett from doing her job. In the room she shared with three other advocates, Bennett stared at his photograph and reviewed his transcript. Jay had withdrawn from three previous high schools, and his grades were mostly Ds and Fs, though Bennett noticed his test scores were quite good, considering. She roamed the halls, surprised she hadn't noticed him yet—an eighteen-year-old whose arms were covered in ink. When she finally spotted Jay skulking toward class, Bennett was struck by the way this enormous kid seemed to be trying to disappear—head down, avoiding eye contact, walking close to the wall.

At the sound of his name, Jay looked up and nodded quickly, as if trying to quiet any further conversation in public.

"C'mon in," said Bennett, waving him toward her tiny desk in room 212.

Bennett had grown up comfortably in Seattle, and she was often shocked by the gulf between her childhood and the one inhabited by the kids she was supposed to help. She ticked through her list of eight questions to get the basics on Jay: full name, family members, medications or other special needs, home address, and transportation route to school—hardly entry points for a deep interrogation. That was not Bennett's aim. She was going for pragmatism, trying to find the shortest path between a spotty transcript and the graduation stage.

Jay tried to answer. But he was thrown by this white woman with big, searching eyes, who knew so much about his crap grades and lousy attendance. Every question she asked bumped up against topics he didn't want to discuss. Such as where he lived (nowhere specific, a friend's house, a homeless shelter); who his friends were (gang members he could not name); what his parents did for work (his father was presently unemployed and navigating a new legal case; his mother was dead).

Bennett kept probing.

"How do you get to school?"

"I take different routes."

Bennett gave him a quizzical look.

"So, it's not safe for me on certain streets," Jay whispered. "There are people who would like to harm me."

Bennett nodded slowly, reminding herself to keep her expression neutral. She noticed that her officemates never paused in their work. If they were eavesdropping, they were practiced at doing it imperceptibly.

"Actually, there's not really any place that's safe."

"And when your father is around, where does he stay?"

"With friends, or in a shelter. I wanted to live with my stepmom, but he wouldn't let her take me. They're not together anymore, so I guess she's not really my family."

"And when did all this moving around start?"

"When I was thirteen. CPS came—I guess a teacher told them I was wearing the same clothes every day."

Jay rubbed his hand over his face, and it took Bennett a moment to realize he was crying. This muscly kid, hunched over and shaking.

But he kept talking. Jay told Bennett about his father's rages, about gangsters who'd put a gun to his head, about being beaten so badly he'd wound up in the hospital thinking he was going to die. And he told her, haltingly, about beating other kids too.

Bennett was not an experienced interviewer. She was floored by the information pouring out of Jay. After two hours, she looked up from her notes and took a breath.

"Okay, that's probably enough for today. You should be getting to class now anyway."

"Yeah," Jay replied, "I'll see you around."

Bennett watched him trudge down the hall. She closed the office door and stared at her colleagues.

"What just happened?" she said. "What do I do with all this?"

Bennett's workmates urged her to keep her hopes realistic. A kid with a history like Jay's—four high schools, intermittent homelessness, gang violence, and multiple brushes with the law—might never graduate. And college? Get ready for a long road, they said. But Bennett kept thinking about Jay's test scores and the way he'd seemed so relieved to talk, so willing to be helped. His biggest problem, as far as she could tell, was getting safely to class.

After that first meeting, Jay stopped by room 212 almost daily to say hello—unless he'd heard that a rival set was looking to jump him on the way to school. Then he stayed away. But he explained this problem to Bennett, who sat him down in her office with Google Maps, and together they devised a new route.

***

Jay would indeed graduate from high school, but not on any grand stage. It was in the summer, months after the rest of his class. Bennett had helped him enroll at a community college with the idea that he could transfer from there to the state university in Buffalo and leave his shattered childhood behind. Jay didn't entirely believe in this plan, but he could sense his world shifting. He knew he wouldn't attend graduation—no one in his family would have shown up, and he was still apprehensive about appearing in public, let alone on a stage. But he wanted Bennett to know what she'd meant to him. On his last day of high school, Jay gave her a framed drawing. It was Anna's name, done graffiti-style.

Bennett kept the picture, but Jay slipped from her mind. At twenty-three years old, she was still trying to figure out the shape of her own life, practically a kid herself. But Manhattan Night and Day had changed the way Bennett saw kids on the street and her understanding of poverty as part of a larger system. She puzzled over the answer so many students had given when asked about role models, the people they looked up to. "Me, I am my own role model," they'd tell her. In their lives, no one else had shown up.

Bennett would leave the student advocate job after two years and land in philanthropy focused on strengthening community within schools. A decade later, her life felt worlds away from the small office at Manhattan Night and Day, so it was a shock to open her email one morning and see Jay's name.

"I just wanted to let you know what happened to me, Anna. I'm in a PhD program now, in criminal justice," he wrote. "You changed my life and I think you should know."

Bennett burst into tears. She'd felt so young and awkward, so unequipped to solve the questions posed by Jay's life. The time between their first meeting in her office and the summer day Jay presented his framed drawing had been less than a year. She'd never imagined it had any real impact. She dug out the picture and reread the note Jay had included on the back:

> Dear Anna, I know that I can't put in words how much I appreci-
> ate the help you have given me . . . Me being the big tough guy
> I cried realizing that I made it . . . I graduated, I survived! You
> are one of the people I have to thank for this. I will never forget
> you . . . You saved me, and now I will save the world!!!!!

***

As Jay told me his story over many Zoom calls, I wondered about its Cinderella quality, the way he credited one inexperienced young woman with such a life-changing effect. He had transformed from a kid try-ing to become invisible, into a scholar who sat in the front row of his graduate courses, and he said the metamorphosis had started with her. By the time we met, Jay was in his final year of doctoral studies on extremism. Once, he'd been afraid even to think about his gangland past. Now he was writing about violent radicalization. His dissertation was titled "Words Matter."

But even as an adult, Jay remained haunted by his years in foster care. With friends he was secretive, even toward those he considered his substitute family. He wouldn't speak Spanish in front of them. He refused to connect on social media, and he took pains to ensure they would never meet anyone from his childhood. A decade after his wandering youth, Jay remained acutely aware of the differences between the world he'd come from and that of most graduate students. They were not covered in tattoos. And those who owned pets were unlikely to be caring for a pit bull like Jay's dog, Chance, who he doted on like a child. He knew he'd come from the gutter, but he did not want to be treated as a curiosity. Nor did he want to explain his decisions as a teenage gangster, especially the ones he still felt bad about. Was it hiding to cover old tattoos, or was it a sign of growth?

In college, Jay had stared down at his right forearm with its insignia of his former gang set and decided to color over it with new ink in the shape of a golden koi. Japanese mythology tells the story of the koi fish swimming upstream, vaulting over life's hurdles. Those that reach the pinnacle, a waterfall, are transformed into dragons. Jay got two large koi tattooed onto his forearm. One pointed down toward his wrist, covering the old gang marker. The other was headed upward, toward his shoulder. Someday, he told himself, he would complete the sleeve with a golden dragon across his back.

***

Hearing how angry Jay had been as a kid reminded me of Art Longworth, who talked about a gap in his psyche that he attributed to growing up in state care. Where he'd been an awkward runaway at first, reduced to tears of panic at the idea of meeting a normal family, Longworth, by sixteen, had hardened into something wilier. He forged associations, rather than friendships, brief alliances geared toward a common purpose, like breaking out of the Kiwanis group home, or robbing people. Aside from his ability to create these fleeting connections, Longworth considered himself completely unsocialized when the system spat him out, unfit to function in mainstream society. From prison, he'd written to me about his sense of aloneness in those days, even around other kids. This void felt not like sadness, but a continuously roiling rage.

In Maryanne Atkins's case files, the same overflowing fury showed up a hundred different ways, all framed under a single repeated phrase, *reactive attachment disorder*. This was the root of her behavior problems, said the trio of psychologists who'd interviewed Maryanne in jail while she awaited trial for murder. The same diagnosis appeared on page after page of Monique's file too.

The field of attachment theory is somewhat controversial. Its basic tenets hold that evolution has hardwired humans to turn toward others for survival, at least in infancy. For creatures unable to move or even eat on their own, these early, preverbal attachments are a matter of life or death, and their quality shapes a child's brain, creating a blueprint for later interactions with the world. Ruptures in this developmental process cause problems with "emotional regulation, relationships, and communication," wrote psychologist Marty Beyer, who testified at Maryanne's sentencing. Beyer had evaluated hundreds of foster kids and she'd seen the same patterns, again and again.

In Maryanne's case, a negligent mother and abusive father had created a fever of need that made family life with her all but impossible for well-meaning foster parents. The same was true of Monique, whose foster families repeatedly called the state to have her removed. By the time the girls landed with families who wanted to adopt them, they were constitutionally unable to trust, clinicians said. Their neurobiology would not allow it.

Maryanne's adoptive parents may have been unprepared for the behavior displayed by their new daughter, but they caught on fast. "She did/does not know how to have a family," the Atkinses wrote to Maryanne's middle school, trying to prepare her teachers shortly after she'd moved in. "She is able to make friends easily, but getting close and maintaining a relationship seems impossible for her." Because she'd never learned to connect, Maryanne had "a lack of understanding of others," the Atkinses said. She appeared devoid of "empathy, remorse, regret or compassion." Less than two years after they wrote those words, Maryanne had killed a man.

Jessica Berliner, the prosecutor who'd pushed to have Maryanne locked away for a quarter century, told me she'd agonized over the question of fairness. At her son's high school football games, Berliner sat in the bleachers watching other sixteen-year-old girls, noting their coltish flirting and childish dramas. Any of them could be a potential Maryanne, she thought. But she found arguments about the science of still-developing juvenile brains too simplistic to satisfy the demands of justice, and perhaps naïve. In her view, being a minor should not necessarily shield one from the consequences of taking a life.

"She's just this little girl that I had to let go," Berliner said as we sat in a clattery Seattle coffee shop, discussing the national sea change in youth crime laws. "I don't think the brain science told us anything we didn't already know, that teenagers are impetuous and self-centered. If reform is just to pat yourself on the back so you can feel good, it's not going to work."

Despite those views, shared by many in law enforcement, Washington legislators had begun to inch toward a more youth-friendly interpretation of justice. Just as Maryanne was sentenced to nineteen years, the state passed its "Juvenile Rehabilitation to 25" law, allowing minors charged as adults to serve their time in a juvenile facility until their mid-twenties. Apart from infancy, adolescence is the most plastic phase of human development—for good or ill. The rationale behind "JR to 25" held that imprisoning a teenager like Maryanne with career felons would only lock in the behaviors of those surrounding her, but in a youth facility focused on rehabilitation, a young person convicted of murder could change.

I was skeptical. Not because I believed Maryanne was inherently lethal or irretrievably broken, but because it seemed unlikely that an understaffed program run by workers earning little more than the minimum wage would be able to deliver the kind of transformation promised by JR to 25.

At Washington's women's prison, counselors had doubts of their own. On top of Maryanne's constant rule-breaking and multiple stints in solitary confinement, she had managed to get her picture posted on a website for incarcerated women seeking pen pals. "I'm looking for a long-term friendship. I need somebody to lean on and someone to be there for me," she wrote next to the same photograph that had once appeared on escort websites.

Washington has only one long-term lockup for girls, the Echo Glen Children's Center, and through all the years Maryanne sat in juvenile detention awaiting trial, she had listened to other kids talking about it. Echo Glen was a place of wide-open fields surrounded by forest and staffed by caseworkers who actually liked kids. It was coeducational, with no barbed wire fence, and it hovered in her mind like some sort of Valhalla. But at the time, only minors could go to Echo Glen. The day Maryanne turned eighteen, she gave up hope of ever seeing it.

The JR to 25 law presented an unexpected reprieve. In November 2019, after Maryanne had been in prison for eight months, a panel of evaluators visited her to discuss the possibility of a transfer to Echo Glen. Though she had dreamed of this moment, once it was in front of her Maryanne dithered, running back and forth between her cell in the isolation unit and the conference room where her interviewers waited. Echo Glen was the respite she'd pined for. But prison had a structure she was beginning to understand. And what about her new girlfriend, the woman whose name was now tattooed on her face? Overwhelmed by these choices, Maryanne gave up and told Echo Glen's evaluators to go home. She would stay in prison.

Within hours of that decision she called her lawyer, sobbing. She begged for another chance. It took months of work from Colleen O'Connor, but the state finally agreed to a second interview. This time only two women showed up.

"Sorry I was such an asshole before," said Maryanne.

They spoke to her for an hour and promised to mail their verdict in a few weeks. If she incurred even one infraction during that time, Maryanne would make the decision for them. They knew all about her history of running away in foster care. Attempt anything like that at Echo Glen and she would be returned to prison immediately. No warnings, no second chances. Maryanne tried to keep a leash on her hopes, but she couldn't help envisioning the possibility of grace. Echo Glen floated before her like some sort of gauzy dream.

"I have a good feeling," she told me during a prison visit, looking into the distance, imagining the fresh air.

***

The more I pored over Maryanne's story, and then those of Art, Monique, and Jay, the more it began to look like the very structure of foster care systematically undercut children's ability to form the kinds of emotional bonds that are essential for resilience, the ability to bounce back from life's disappointments and frustrations. I was mulling this idea, interviewing forensic psychologists about the role of attachment in delinquent behavior, when I saw a panel discussion about foster youth in the legal system. A professor from Loyola Law School in Los Angeles described the child welfare system as a pipeline funneling kids directly into juvenile detention halls, typically when they ran from their placements. In juvie, they bonded with other kids like them, just as Art Longworth had decades earlier. It created a sense of belonging, however fleeting, and with no connection to adults who might model another way, it was no surprise that huge numbers of foster youth eventually landed in prison, the lawyers said. In Los Angeles County alone, a hundred and twenty were arrested each month—nearly fifteen hundred a year.

One after another, the lawyers rattled off miserable statistics about foster children destined for locked cells. Then I heard a word that surprised me. "There is only one intervention that has been shown, conclusively, to make a change in kids' brains that translates into lasting behavior improvement," said an attorney named Jennifer Rodriguez. "That intervention is *relationships*."

Rodriguez ran a California nonprofit called the Youth Law Center, and she was the only person on the panel who had been in foster care. She did not talk about the system's structure or its choke points, the places where children were handed from one bureaucracy to another. Rodriguez focused instead on a more human problem: attachment. "For a very long time now, we've known that little ones, infants and toddlers, are wired to connect for survival," she told me later. "When we disrupt that, even if it's for what seems like a positive reason like ensuring the child's safety, we know there are consequences when they grow into adulthood."

Then forty-three, Rodriguez had been raised in San Francisco in the 1980s by a mom who was schizophrenic. While still in middle school, she ran away and found shelter with a man who took in packs of street kids like her. "They either sold drugs for him or sold themselves. That's what I did," Rodriguez said.

California's child welfare system knew about Rodriguez. Though she had a social worker who urged her to turn herself in and enter foster care, Rodriguez kept skittering away. Living on the streets was scary, but also thrilling. To a thirteen-year-old girl, the independence was intoxicating. All the street kids felt that way. They believed they were taking care of themselves, making their own money, their own choices, even when those choices resulted in criminal charges for shoplifting or prostitution. Not until she was robbed at gunpoint did Rodriguez finally give up and enter state care.

Kids who have criminal records are rarely placed with a family. Like Art Longworth before her and Jay Perez-Torres after, Jennifer Rodriguez spent her adolescence in a series of group homes. When she aged out of the system in 1994, Rodriguez was a high school dropout. Back to the streets. She talked her way into a Job Corps program—the administrators were reluctant because of her history—where she earned a GED and found her way into a medical assistant's program because it sounded like the shortest route to a regular paycheck.

The problem was, nothing in Rodriguez's past had set her up for that kind of stability. "Normal," to her, meant staying up all night and sleeping through the day. She had no grasp of science or math, and no idea how to support herself as an adult on her own. For a year she lived with a man in his truck. Nevertheless, she managed to stay in school. To address her deficits in science, Rodriguez signed up for a community college biology class, which meant explaining to the teacher why she could barely do middle school math.

The teacher pointed her toward law studies, which led her to the University of California, Davis. There, the former foster kid discovered legal advocacy around children's rights. At last, Rodriguez thought, she'd found her path. But not until she had a child of her own in 2004 did it all come together—her past, and her budding law career, and what she saw now in the eyes of her infant son as he gazed up at her: the critical missing link in foster care, a parent-child connection.

Rodriguez had applied for a Youth Law Center fellowship focused on connecting pregnant foster youth with doulas, since these young moms-to-be, having no models, needed to be taught how to bond with their children. She did not get the job. But the agency's director, intrigued by Rodriguez's unusual path, hired her anyway. The mission: Scour research on child development and bring it to foster care agencies nationwide, showing them how their practices lined up with brain science—or not.

Among the first researchers Rodriguez met in this quest was Mary Dozier, a developmental psychologist at the University of Delaware, who'd overturned her own career to focus on the chemistry that underpins attachment in infants. Dozier's work initially focused on schizophrenic adults, some of whom had grown up in foster care. She was trying to determine whether any thread connected their present mental illness with their pasts. But one night, while watching television news,

Dozier made a sharp turn. The footage on her screen showed a baby girl being taken from her foster mother, shrieking as if in physical pain, as if she was dying. What were the psychological effects of trauma like that, Dozier wondered. Would they fade? Or did they create permanent neurological gouges? *I need to understand this*, Dozier thought. Within weeks, she had convinced her graduate researchers to shift their focus away from adults and toward the other end of the life cycle, infancy.

The first thing they discovered was how rapidly babies in foster care form attachments. Among infants, it could happen in less than two weeks. Toddlers, however, were slower to bond. Instead of reaching out when frightened or in need of comfort, a healthy sign, these foster children turned away. They appeared to reject their caregivers, and their foster parents tended to respond in kind, becoming distant, often brusque. This created a vicious cycle, with worsening behavior from the child that frequently ended with a call to the state, requesting removal.

But Dozier discovered that these patterns could be altered. A technique she developed called Attachment and Behavioral Catch-up, or ABC, was designed to help caregivers better interpret children's signals, and it brought rapid changes to their behavior. A few months later, while listening to an endocrinologist speak about his work, Dozier had an epiphany.

The lecturing scientist was describing his experiments with infant squirrel monkeys, explaining how stressors altered their internal chemistry. When the infants were separated from their mothers but remained within earshot, their cries were intense, piercing. Those placed in cages far away, unable to smell or sense their mothers, stopped crying. Anyone judging by behavior alone might assume that these babies were less distressed than the others. Their biology told a different story: All of the baby monkeys secreted the stress hormone cortisol when separated from their mothers. In those who were isolated, this stress indicator soared, and it remained elevated for days.

Sitting in the lecture hall, Dozier suddenly wondered about the children she'd been studying. Might their behavior around attachment have a similar corollary in their biology? Her first experiments had shown that ABC could change a baby's behavior. The task now was to determine whether their cortisol levels registered a parallel shift.

To begin, Dozier created a benchmark by measuring stress hormones in the saliva of two-dozen babies placed in foster care. It was easy to do with a cotton swab soaked in saliva. As expected, she found their cortisol levels were elevated and remained so throughout the day, rather than rising in the morning and dropping around bedtime, which is a more typical pattern. "Adversity affected a very basic biological function," Dozier wrote. Disturbance to a child's cortisol system interfered with their sleep cycles, alertness, and ability to focus—for instance, at school. Children with flat cortisol patterns also seemed to have trouble handling basic emotions like disappointment and anger. Since every child in foster care had endured some version of trauma, and likely had flattened cortisol as a result, Dozier next asked, could those levels be changed?

She sent parent coaches into foster homes for ten weekly sessions to teach foster parents the ABC techniques—more closely following children's cues and responding immediately when they showed distress. After three months, Dozier measured the children's cortisol levels again and found that they now showed steeper up-and-down slopes across a day. Parenting could literally affect a child's biology—even if the child wasn't your own.

To Jennifer Rodriguez, puzzling over a tool to improve foster care outcomes, this finding was a revelation. She remembered the 1990s news stories about abandoned infants in Romanian orphanages and how, despite being fed and sheltered, they withered in their cribs, unhugged, untouched. Without human contact, Rodriguez marveled, the babies failed to thrive. As she listened to Dozier talking, Rodriguez thought back to her own teen years and all the ways she'd sent exactly the wrong signals to her caregivers. "That's what we do—miscue completely—and it's not cute like with a baby that just turns around and withdraws. Teenagers are more likely to tell you to go fuck yourself."

Or worse. Precisely the kind of behavior that prompts foster parents to request a placement change, if not call the police.

Group homes compounded the problem, as Rodriguez recalled all too well. She'd known she was only a job to the staff who supervised her, nothing more. There was no connection, no attachment. I thought of Jay, whose group home in Harlem felt more like a prison. And of Monique, medicated and monitored at Bayes, who now seemed wholly unable to build a life on her own.

Was it any wonder thousands of kids stumbled out of the system unable to get a foothold on adulthood? Transitory living is standard in foster care, and a study in 2020 found that suicidal ideation increases by 68 percent with each new placement. A child in Florida moved more than fifty times in 2016 alone. Another in the same Florida county trudged through forty-three placements. The phenomenon is not specific to one state or region. A lawsuit against Kansas's Department of Children and Families claimed that a fifteen-year-old boy under the state's care had been shunted through one hundred and thirty placements over eight years, many of them in group homes.

"It really should be no surprise," Rodriguez told me. "When you look at the data, even when you control for every other variable, the youth in those kinds of facilities are almost three times more likely to end up getting pushed into juvenile justice. It's about the structure of the institution—they're not parented. Nobody loves them. They're an object."

***

Soon after she met with Dozier, Rodriguez began wondering about possibilities for teenagers. Their cortisol levels were already set. But brain scans indicated that neural pathways shaped by trauma could be reshaped. As G. Stanley Hall recognized a century ago, the period of greatest plasticity in human development, after infancy, is between the ages of fifteen and twenty-four. And the tool that most powerfully effects change is neither drug therapy nor counseling. It's a nurturing relationship with a trusted adult—any adult, whether biologically related or not.

"All of this research kind of came together to show us, it's families," Rodriguez said. "Families are the most powerful force we know for disruption and dysregulation in children. The absence of love and nurturing can quite literally destroy a child. But family is also the most powerful force we have for repair."

Rodriguez's boss at the Youth Law Center was simultaneously mulling a related problem: Why were there so few excellent foster parents? Why was it so difficult to find and recruit these people? The usual answer—not enough money in the work to balance its demands and disruption—frustrated Director Carole Shauffer. No one said that about joining the Marines or the Peace Corps. Those jobs were also demanding and low-paid, but they never seemed to lack for recruits. It had to be something else.

Shauffer began interviewing foster parents to see if they had ideas. She spoke to hundreds, in cities from Miami to San Diego, and came away with a discouraging summation: fostering was seen as bottom-of-the-barrel, something few people were proud to be. "If you say you're going into the Peace Corps, people go, 'Oh, that's so cool,'" Shauffer mused. "If you become a foster parent, people say, 'Why would you want to do that? Aren't all of them just in it for the money?'"

As a brand, fostering was corrupted, Shauffer began to believe, because the practice itself was rotten. Foster parents were not treated as important players in a child's development. Quite the contrary. They were warned never to get too close to their wards because the kids, if not adopted, would eventually move on. And once gone, foster parents were barred from having any further contact.

The system held foster parents accountable for no outcome beyond keeping a child alive. It treated them as glorified babysitters, interchangeable way stations. And it wanted to move children among them easily, often with less than an hour's notice—the very opposite of what kids need to build the pathways for attachment. No wonder Tasha Smith told Maryanne to call her Auntie. "Mom" took too much of a toll.

Together, Shauffer and Rodriguez conceived an entirely different approach to foster care. Their Quality Parenting Initiative positioned foster parents as professionals, integral to a child's case and part of their future. In this vision, foster parents would speak to a child's birth family—conversations that are typically forbidden—the night they arrived. They would ask about a kid's favorite foods and TV shows and hobbies, then put the child on the phone to speak with their mom or dad.

This was a radical change. When Rodriguez began pitching it to child welfare departments across the country, in 2008, officials looked at her like she was speaking Martian. Those who accepted the logic could not see how a mammoth bureaucracy comprised of a million children, foster parents, biological families, and caseworkers could possibly adapt to embrace it.

"What is the primary goal for your system?" Rodriguez asked the head of each state agency.

Invariably, the answer was: Avoid children dying. Avoid liability. It was not about healing kids. Foster care was seen a stopover, not a therapeutic intervention, even though thousands of children languished in it for years. And the changes that Rodriguez was pushing seemed only to open the door to more risk.

CHAPTER 8
The Butterfly Effect

The D train from Coney Island had a comforting rumble. That was part of the problem; it always lulled Tina to sleep. She'd lean her head against the smudgy window, listen to the ka-chung ka-chung of metal wheels on the track, and it was hard to keep her eyes open, hard to stay alert. Outside, New York City was cool and rainy. But the subway was warm and, at night, usually empty, since everyone was holed up at home because of the pandemic. She could hop on at Stillwell Avenue, ride all the way up to the Bronx and back down through Brooklyn again without talking to another person. Even then, Tina couldn't really sleep, not deeply enough to forget. You had to guard against the creeps. And in the morning, little shards of commuter conversations cut into your dreams. Tina could feel people staring even when her eyes were closed. Like now. She shook herself awake. The smell of perfume and coffee announced a new day, and she knew she looked horrible, like a homeless person, since that's what she was. But fuck these people in their business suits staring down at her.

How did it come to this, Tina wondered. Three months earlier she'd been on her way, sixteen years old and taking care of herself just fine. Found a room to rent in Philly and paid for it with money she'd earned. Now she was living on the subway. It was better, sort of, when she could kick it with the girls from the Children's Center. They'd laugh and smoke on the platform, stay out of the rain, and maybe swipe some candy from a newsstand. But Tina knew this was no solution to her problems. How long could you live on a train?

After the financial district, when the subway car emptied out, she let her mind wander back to Pennsylvania and the year with her mom, then back before that, to Philly and all the foster homes, then all the way back to Florida and the years with her grandma. Could anything have changed her path? It had been such a relief when the state first figured out about her mother. It meant she got to move into Grandma Momo's development in Florida, which was like a vacation when you were eleven and coming from winters in the Northeast. Except that she'd fucked it up by fighting with everyone. Sometimes multiple fights a day. She couldn't even explain why, exactly. The only thing she knew for sure was that blabbing about what her mom's boyfriend's dad had done to her did not make the anger go away. If anything, it got worse, like volcanic lava moving too fast for words. So Tina kept her mouth shut and let her fists do the talking. She was good like that. Good at taking care of herself.

Her grandmother saw things differently. Providing a home for Tina made her blood pressure spike. It strained her back. Then she had a stroke. When Tina was twelve, it was back to Pennsylvania and her mother's apartment in Pottstown. Sometimes they even slept in the same bed, like a parent and child who loved each other. Unless her mom had a guy over. Then Tina was on the air mattress in the living room, which is where she was sleeping when a rough hand shook her awake. She smelled the sweet-sour alcohol breath before full consciousness, and she could sense what was about to happen. When she opened her eyes there was her mom, with that hard, pinched look on her face that said things were about to get real. She was screaming something about a phone charger. Tina had grabbed it from the bedroom to make sure she got up on time, to avoid more screaming about oversleeping. But you couldn't explain that when your mom was lunging at you with a knife. The blade punctured Tina's air mattress and her mother's hands landed around her throat, and as usual, the police showed up. This time, they sent her mom to jail. Tina went into foster care the next day.

It was hard to keep track of all the schools and therapists and medications and caseworkers she spun through over the next three years. But Tina couldn't blame Grandma Momo for refusing to take her back. She knew she was a lot to handle. And foster care seemed okay, at least for the first week. After that, in the chaos of bumping along from one placement to the next, school remained her safe zone. She did okay when she wasn't fighting. It felt good when people saw she was smart.

Mature for your age, they said. But then they'd bring her to court, where some judge she'd never met, in front of a room full of strangers, would ask her mom about taking Tina back.

"I'm not ready," her mother always said. And within days Tina was again fighting anyone she could. Social workers kept using the same word—*regression*—to describe this behavior. But as far as Tina was concerned, the problem was nothing so clinical-sounding. The problem was wanting something impossible.

She would never describe herself as an innocent. But foster care had been a shock. You had to be on your guard with *everyone*—with your caseworker and your foster mom and the other kids sleeping next to you in whatever house they sent you to. Always so much drama. Fights about everything. Escalations over nothing. She'd kept her side of the bargain, showing up to class, making decent grades. Barely fighting at all. But then came the Montgomery County van pulling up to school at dismissal with a woman driver in uniform, who waved Tina over to the window.

"I'm here to pick you up," she said.

Tina opened the door and got in. She was used to strangers telling her to do things.

"What's all that stuff in the back?" she asked, noting the pile of garbage bags heaped in the seat behind her, clothes spilling out.

"That's yours," the driver said.

"Why's all my shit in this van if you're taking me home?"

"I didn't say I was taking you home. You're going to detention. You'll get your next placement there."

Whatthefuck? Didn't she and her caseworker, Taneesha, have a deal? Do well in school and you can stay where you are, Taneesha had promised. Tina hated detention. The girls there had serious charges and many pounds on her. All Tina had was a foster mom who complained when she smoked weed. Why should she have to put on an orange jumpsuit and sit in a locked cell when she hadn't done anything wrong? Okay, yes, she'd punched a boy who was messing with her—what did they expect? She was never going to back down if she felt threatened, and now it was going to land her in lockup. *This is not happening*, Tina decided, staring at the snowy streets outside.

Tina had never been afraid to brawl, but she knew how to be quiet, how to think. She plugged her phone into the door charger, happy to watch it sucking up the state's electricity. As the van maneuvered through Northeast Philadelphia, she turned in her seat, dumped the gym clothes and notebooks from her book bag onto the floor, and refilled it with shirts and underwear from the sacks of clothing piled behind her.

At the last traffic signal before the streets became highway, the van slowed. From here out, there would be no more red lights, just a straight shot to the locked doors of juvenile detention. Tina began counting to herself.

One . . . *Wait till the light turns green, gotta be green when you jump out.*

Two . . . *She's gonna have to go forward—there's cars behind us—and I'll be gone down one of these little streets.*

Three . . . *Check the phone charge, almost three-quarters full, should be good.*

Tina had never run from a county car before. But she wasn't scared. She liked being on her own, and this was her moment.

Four . . . *Go!*

With military precision, Tina snatched her phone, flung the van door open, and hopped down to the slushy street. She zigged to the right, circled around the block, and zagged left. No way that driver would be able to follow, not even with her eyes. It was weird being on the run. You felt free, but jumpy. Excited, but lonely. As soon as she could find a good spot to hide, she'd text her old foster sister Keisha. Keisha knew this town. She'd find some place for Tina to crash. Tina marched through the cold and tried to look like she knew where she was going.

Keisha texted back the address of a friend in West Philly who would let her stay a few days. It was a trek to get there, involving a bus ride, train ride, and miles on foot. Tina arrived soaked and numb. For three days she camped on the guy's couch. When he started to paw at her, she split and slept in a laundromat. *It's all good, I got this,* Tina kept telling herself.

But during that week on the run, she learned through friends that her cousin had been killed. The news shattered Tina's resolve. With no more fight left, she called her mom. *She won't turn me in,* Tina thought with a smile. *She hates the cops too.*

Their reunion after two years apart was nothing like the long tight hugs Tina saw on TV, where moms and daughters held each other, rocking back and forth like they were on a boat. Not that she'd expected this. But Tina could never kick away the secret hope that someday her mother would surprise her by being different. No such luck. Her mom opened the door with a shrug. At least she let Tina fall asleep in her bed instead of on the living room floor.

***

"Tina, c'mon out of there! There's someone to see you," her mother yelled, just as Tina had finally dozed off.

Weird. She hadn't been home more than an hour. Not even Keisha knew where she was.

"Who is it?" Tina yelled.

"The police! They're here to talk to you."

The officers did not take Tina away. They merely wanted her to confirm that she was the girl who'd run from the van, so they could close out the missing person report Taneesha had filed.

Sure, said Tina, signing her name with a flourish before heading back to bed. One thing about life on the run, it was exhausting.

Two hours later, Tina's mother was shaking her again. The officers were back.

"You gotta get dressed," she said.

"Why, Mom?"

"So the police can take you to detention. Taneesha said to wait for your new placement there."

***

Such a long road she'd traveled just to end up in the same place. After detention and two group homes, Tina, at fifteen, was sent back to her mother. Everyone kept saying the point of foster care was to find kids a stable place to live. But as far as Tina could tell, the state seemed focused only on getting her back to her mom's house. How could anyone claim that was stable or safe? All the money Pennsylvania spent on family therapy was wasted because any idiot could see counseling wouldn't work unless a person believed they needed to change. Tina and her mom would sit in a room, Tina crying, and her mother yessing the therapists, and her grandmother, recently moved up from Florida, staying quiet to avoid saying anything that would set off Tina's mom. It was ridiculous, Tina thought, like a play everyone agreed to perform. What she wanted seemed so simple: Just be a different kind of mom. Just stop hitting me. But Tina's mother didn't stop. She called the police on her daughter so many times that the cops in Pottstown got used to calming both of them down. If Tina's cuts and bruises were bad enough, they'd bring her to the hospital for a night to clear the air. Then Tina met a guy.

"You're too cute to be spelling things wrong," she typed under his Facebook post.

He was a few years older, the friend of a friend, and their relationship grew from e-flirting, to phone calls, to real life. In January 2020, when Tina's mother, predictably, threw her out, she knew exactly what to do. Get a bus to Philly. Find a room to rent. Buy a bus ticket for Dante from Facebook to come down from Brooklyn and stay with her. She'd never had a real boyfriend before.

Each of these things Tina envisioned, then enacted. She'd always been that way. When Tina had a goal, she could make it happen. But within a few weeks, the friend who'd provided a room realized that renting to a stranger could bring in lots more money. *She picked that girl over me*, Tina kept telling herself as she loaded up her backpack and boarded a bus for New York City.

She knew the city, had been there plenty of times to visit family. But now there was no auntie to meet Tina as she marched through the Port Authority terminal, gripping the shoulder strap of her backpack like a ripcord. A few scraggly-looking men followed her with their eyes. Tina, built like a hydrant with curly hair dyed fire-engine red, cut them with a look. There were still days when she wished her mom was the kind you could call for advice. This time, the thought brought only the roar of rage and behind it, the ache of betrayal. She wouldn't give two seconds to that shit. Betrayal meant that you'd believed in someone, which required admitting that you got played. And Tina was never gonna cop to that. She was free now. On her own. In a city she loved. Everything would be fine.

Tina found Dante in Brooklyn. He said he would take her out to eat. They went to a diner in Coney Island and the food was horrible. "I ain't payin' for this shit," Dante said. "Let's ditch."

They were standing outside the restaurant when the manager called the cops, who found them almost immediately. That was how Tina learned her mother had filed a missing person report.

"But you kicked me out!" she shouted into the phone, making sure its speaker was on so the officer could hear her mother's reply.

"I only filed that report to cover my ass," said the voice on the other end of the line.

Tina had proven her point to the police, but it made little difference. Instead of sending her back to Pennsylvania, the officer decided that Tina, still a minor at sixteen, should be handled as a runaway. Which was how she landed at the Administration for Children's Services youth shelter in Manhattan, cold, wet, and hungry. The six-story stone building had been erected in 1912 as the city morgue. A century later, the Children's Center housed perhaps a hundred kids awaiting foster placements, many of them teenagers. Despite this clientele, the lobby was decorated with six-foot posters of Elmo and Cookie Monster. *What am I, a fucking baby?* thought Tina.

Upstairs, a huge dormitory was filled with bunk beds laid out in rows, just like the orphanages she'd read about in novels. Older girls slept in separate rooms of six or eight. Some of them had been there for months. Tina was livid. After three years in foster homes and group homes and detention cells and treatment centers, she'd intended her arrival in New York to be a debut, a coming out, her chance to show everyone she could make it on her own. Now she was sleeping in a place where kids smeared shit on the walls and stored knives in their lockers. Tina could hardly blame them.

"Time to go!" staff yelled in the morning, banging on the girls' door. They had to be out by noon, when the shelter was locked, not to return until early evening. Officially, the kids were expected to go to school. But Tina arrived at the Children's Center in the spring of 2020, just as the country was going into lockdown. New York City's board of education had shuttered its schools, and by the time the board determined that the remainder of the academic year would be online-only, it was April, with so little time left on the calendar that no one bothered to enroll Tina. She was living in limbo—under her mother's guardianship, but kicked out of the house; too young to find a well-paying job, but locked out of school during a global disaster. When the doors to the Children's Center closed behind her, Tina once again had nowhere to go.

***

"C'mon, Tina!" hissed Dante, looking over his shoulder to make sure she was following. It was late on a Sunday afternoon in April, six weeks after Tina had landed in New York. She knew what was about to happen, but when Dante's eye landed on a slight Asian woman, Tina held back. Dante had tailed the woman from the subway, down the sidewalk, and toward an apartment building, the kind with no doorman. When she pulled open the front door, he slipped in behind. Tina was ten paces back, her heart racing.

It had been a rough couple of weeks. She'd found a few girls at the Children's Center to run with, but they were harder than the kids she'd known before. They robbed people just to fill time, sometimes right in front of the Children's Center. They never talked about the victims—most of the time, Tina couldn't even remember their faces. You didn't think about details like that. It was all action, just a blur. None of them gave a shit about being arrested. Being underage was pretty much a get-out-of-jail-free card, Tina knew. But there was something stressful about it anyway, an anxiety that thrummed in her whenever she wanted something and knew she'd have to steal to get it. She was ashamed of this feeling— she sure didn't want anyone feeling sorry for her—yet she could not shake the sense of being swept up in something she wished wasn't happening. You needed friends in a place like the Children's Center, a crew to have your back. These girls liked her okay, but not if they thought she was a snitch. So, Tina stood by when they grabbed women's cell phones and purses. She wasn't going to hurt anyone. She'd seen enough violence.

Walking behind Dante, she could see that the woman had no idea she was being followed. Even in the lobby, pulling letters from her mailbox, the woman didn't look up. Dante clocked her on the side of the head. But instead of dropping her bag and holding her face like he'd said she would, the woman held on to her purse. Dante tried to yank it away, but she wouldn't let go, so he dragged her across the tile floor. Tina gave the woman a few kicks to show Dante she was with him.

"I have a knife—gimme your purse!" she yelled.

Why did this woman keep fighting? All they wanted was her wallet. Why not just give it up? She didn't want Dante to hurt this woman. And she didn't want the woman to act in a way that would make him have to. Sometimes she pictured herself as a crime-scene negotiator—pretty fucking ironic, she thought—trying to beam into her boyfriend's brain and tell him, *you don't need to keep beating this person up. And person,* she'd tell the victim in her mind, *you don't need to keep getting beat up.*

But she said none of these things. People made their choices, and Tina wouldn't blame hers on anyone else. Still, she had the slightly nauseated feeling of being on a theme park ride she was afraid to jump off.

The woman finally let go of her bag and Dante tore out of the vestibule, the purse under his arm. Tina followed him to the park, her heart pounding so loud in her ears that she could barely hear what he was saying. They hid in some bushes until all was quiet. Then Tina and her boyfriend hustled down to the subway, where Dante punched her in the head as they waited for the train.

That's when Tina began sleeping in the subway. If you went AWOL for seventy-two hours, your placement would be cancelled, the Children's Center girls said. Still, she could not believe how low she'd fallen, scrunched into a corner where her bench met the wall, pulling her hoodie down over her face. What was that thing she'd read about the butterfly effect? How something as quiet as a butterfly beating its wings could cause a hurricane half a world away. The idea obsessed her. What if her mother had never filed that bullshit missing person report? Then she never would have been listed as a runaway. And if she hadn't been a runaway, the cops wouldn't have taken her to the Children's Center. And if she'd never landed at the Children's Center, Tina was pretty sure she wouldn't have got caught up in all the shit she was hiding from now on the train. But you couldn't change the past. The worst thing Tina could imagine was sitting in a locked cell, wishing she could go back in time.

***

The police caught up to Tina a few days later. As expected, she was released after arraignment to await trial at the Crossroads Juvenile Center in Brooklyn. A few years earlier, Tina might have faced prison for the multiple charges she'd racked up. But in 2017, New York passed its "Raise the Age" law, which channels almost all minors accused of crimes into youth court and diversion programs. Prosecutors described Tina as "antisocial" because of the half-dozen robberies she'd been accused of committing in a mere three weeks—now including the assault on the woman in the vestibule, which was the most serious of all.

Her lawyer presented a different interpretation. Yes, Tina was full of attitude, but all of it was posturing. In reality, she had been a sixteen-year-old child adrift, alone, and struggling to survive in New York City. Multiple arrests did not make Tina "some kind of super-predator," he said, wielding the term that had become a source of shame for the entire youth justice system. To the contrary, Tina's rapid plummet showed how badly she was flailing, her lawyer suggested. She'd never wielded a knife, despite her threats. Nor had she been accused of coercing anyone into committing these crimes. It appeared, in fact, that she was the one being coerced. She was not an adult. Not a career criminal. Just a kid in trouble, way over her head.

New York, reluctant to stop putting teenagers in prison, was the forty-ninth state in the nation to repudiate the "super-predator" era and begin bending juvenile crime laws toward rehabilitation over punishment. Considering her foster care history, Tina's lawyer argued, her case was better suited to Family Court with its emphasis on therapy, rather than criminal court and incarceration. The judge agreed, with a ruling that was comprehensive, if somewhat unrealistic. Tina would be sent home to her mother, now living in Ohio, and enrolled in the Center for Alternative Sentencing and Employment Services (CASES). Instead of prison, she would get education and job training. If she completed the program successfully, Tina's record would be cleared and sealed.

For seven months, Tina complied. She phoned her supervisor every day. She applied for twenty-seven fast-food jobs and dutifully followed the prompts in her online journal on Handling Difficult Feelings. "Difficult feelings and irresponsible behavior are connected," the website informed her, directing Tina to make better choices through a computer screen. The lack of face-to-face counseling was a result of the pandemic, which also prevented Tina from meeting her defense attorney in person. But she developed enormous affection for him anyway, such that she began to imagine pursuing a degree in law herself.

For now, though, Tina was back home with her mother, the woman who had choked, stabbed, and terrorized her since childhood. She had not mellowed. Tina's new caseworkers requested an emergency clothing voucher from the state of Ohio to buy pants and shoes that fit her because Tina's mother refused to provide them.

After two months at home Tina was arrested again, just like in the old days when her mother would drink, and they'd argue, and the fights would escalate to her mom calling the police. Except this time, Tina and her mother were unknowns, living in a small town in a new state where the cops were unfamiliar with their history. The police booked Tina into the Jefferson County Jail for investigation of a domestic disturbance, though she was charged with no crime.

CHAPTER 9

A Room of Her Own

Tina's swagger had helped her navigate multiple government systems. It had propelled her onto a Greyhound bus to arrive alone in New York City at sixteen and kept her company through long bouts of aloneness. But a stream of anger coursed beneath her every move toward self-sufficiency, and it tripped her up constantly. In that sense, she was like any teenager—hungry for independence, unequipped to handle it. In her case, of course, there was no parent to turn to when she stumbled. Tina knew this, which was why the approach of her eighteenth birthday, in May 2021, provoked something close to panic.

As early as 1986, the federal government recognized that cutting kids off from support at eighteen virtually guaranteed thousands of homeless teenagers landing on America's streets every year. All of those kids had been taken from parents deemed unable to care for them, and few of those families had changed enough to welcome their children back. The majority of young people leaving foster care at eighteen had no place to call home. Congress earmarked $70 million in housing vouchers for these eighteen- and nineteen-year-olds in the mid-1980s, and doubled that amount by 1999. But it barely made a dent—mostly because few states were connecting the kids to the money.

In 2008, shamed by the miserable outcomes for foster youth detailed in the Midwest Evaluations, Congress passed the Fostering Connections Act to get serious about improving the hand-off to independence. As long as they were living with some kind of supervision—even just a monthly phone call from a caseworker—former wards of the state could get about $1,000 per month to cover rent, food, and clothing until they were twenty-one. But there were conditions. The District of Columbia required that aged-out foster kids have a checking account with at least $100 in it and no unresolved criminal charges. Hardly realistic for vast numbers of young people—arguably the ones who needed help most. Generally, they had to be either employed or in school. That had kept Monique afloat in Texas, which was among twenty-six states participating in the federal program. Another was Ohio, where Tina, in the spring of 2021, was weeks away from turning eighteen.

In the back seat of a state car, she tapped at her phone, her lifeline. Tina didn't know what she would do when she got back to New York City, but the staff at Youth Intensive Services in Youngstown, Ohio, hadn't asked for much evidence of a plan. They took Tina from the Jefferson County Jail into their residential treatment program after her lawyer got involved, and they were almost as eager for Tina's birthday as she was, since it would mean the end of their obligation. Turning eighteen also marked Tina's official emancipation from foster care and her transfer to state-supported "aftercare." This chain of bureaucracy boiled down to a check in the mail. Tina needed it to arrive by her birthday, before the group home turned her out.

She had lots of ideas about ways to meet the state's requirements for aftercare—ideas for her someday-education in law, and for where she wanted to live, and for jobs that would help her reach these goals. But without a check, she had no way to start making them happen. All she had was her phone. It was the first thing she'd bought with the money earned by working at McDonald's in the court-ordered CASES program, and the first account she'd ever opened in her own name. Next, Tina signed herself up for an online bank account, the second piece of proof that she was on her way to adulthood. But she still needed her check.

"I'm gonna be homeless!" Tina kept telling the staff at Youth Intensive Services, as her birthday drew close and her mailbox remained empty.

Don't worry about it, they assured her, everything will probably work out fine. In the parlance of child welfare, as Tina knew all too well, *probably* meant you'd better have a contingency plan.

As expected, her birthday came and went with no communication from Ohio's Office of Families and Children. Instead, the group home bought Tina a one-way ticket to New York City and dropped her at the bus station. There was no other choice. Legally, they could not hold her. Nor would they be reimbursed for the cost of keeping her. Nor did they want to release her to the streets. "I got this! I know people in the city," Tina reassured them, watching as they drove away. It stung a little, realizing no one wanted to wait and see her safely aboard, though she would never ask for that. She turned toward the bus station doors and tugged. Nothing budged. She pulled harder. A small piece of paper was taped to the inside with a hand-scrawled note: *Locked due to pandemic.*

"Whatthefuck!" Tina fumed. Now she would be waiting outside, alone, on this empty strip of nowhere.

When the bus arrived two hours later, Tina marched straight to the back, sank into the last seat, and pulled out her phone. "We good? I'm heading in," she texted her friend Yvonne, who'd said Tina might be able to crash at her grandmother's place in Brooklyn. Tina was about to start plotting her subway route from Port Authority.

"Nah, she rented that shit," Yvonne texted back.

Tina saw no point in yelling at the latest person to let her down. Instead, she began scrolling her contacts, texting friends, relatives, friends of relatives, and relatives of friends—anyone who might have a couch where she could park until she figured out the next move. By the time her bus pulled into the station seven hours later, she'd reached an aunt who let her stay for a month. But within a few weeks of turning eighteen, aging out of foster care, and landing back in New York City, Tina was, once again, homeless.

The aftercare money finally showed up in Tina's bank account a few weeks later. But it wasn't nearly enough to support someone trying to live on her own in one of the world's most expensive cities. For the next five months, Tina was a nomad. She stayed briefly at the Covenant House shelter on West 41st Street. When a man there grabbed her breast and another man threatened to punch her for making a stink about it, the staff moved Tina to a shelter for victims of sexual assault and trafficking. She despised the place. The women were dead-eyed. Everyone stayed in their rooms. No one spoke. She insisted that they move her again—Tina had no problem speaking up when unhappy—which was how she landed at a transitional-living program for homeless youth in the Bronx called Rising Ground.

I met her a few weeks later, introduced by the social worker who'd helped get Tina's robbery cases moved to Family Court. The social worker thought Tina could be "a star." I understood why in our first conversation. She carried herself differently from most teenagers, grasped information more efficiently, could see the chess board three moves ahead. She was living at Rising Ground, finishing her high school credits through the School of Cooperative Technical Education on East 96th Street, and commuting an hour on the subway to make sandwiches at a deli in Tribeca from 5 P.M. to 1 A.M. Then it was back to the subway for another long ride up to the Bronx.

***

In her travels, Tina had met a man on the train who said he'd help her out if she needed it. For the move to Rising Ground, she did. Tina had a backpack, tote, and several shopping bags full of clothes she didn't want to lug from the women's shelter in Brooklyn to her transitional living program in the Bronx, so she called the guy. He rolled up in a nice car. She got in. On the drive north he pulled over and raped her. "You're my prostitute now," he said.

The rape was horrible but not life-changing, Tina insisted. She refused to give it that much power.

Her days were tightly structured, designed to keep Tina too busy for old patterns. But a schedule did not address the realities inside a teenager reeling with hurt and anger. She saw herself as constantly under attack. It overwhelmed her smarts and undermined her drive again and again. At the deli job her manager had an attitude, Tina decided, because she'd requested a shift change to accommodate school, and the woman gave her exactly the times that would be most difficult.

The possibility of a miscommunication was not something Tina considered. She tried to swallow her irritation, keep things cordial. But

the work was exhausting, the location inconvenient, and by the end of
the shift Tina and her coworker were at war. Which was when the other
girl blurted out that Tina was about to be fired anyway.

"Now I find out you all been talking shit about me?" Tina yelled.
She walked out without her final paycheck.

Rising Ground presented its own problems. Tina wasn't allowed to
cook in her room. Nor could she leave without telling staff when she'd
be back. Throughout her years in foster care, Tina had butted heads
with the rules of a bureaucracy that to her felt ridiculous, arbitrary,
designed to control more than help. Nothing had changed. When she
took off for a week in Atlanta with her grandma, workers at Rising
Ground searched her room for contraband and found paraphernalia for
smoking weed, though no drugs. This was partly her fault, Tina knew,
because she hadn't notified them of her plans. Did they need to be in
every corner of her life? Everyone talked about independence, but they
kept treating her like a baby.

When Tina returned from her vacation in Georgia, the manager
said she had to go. Fine, said Tina. She hated staying any place for long,
and she'd been there eight months already. Anyway, she'd expected
them to find some reason to put her out. Transitional housing handled
kids in batches, shuffling one group into its barren rooms and counting
the days until they left to make room for the next.

Tina was among 147,143 young people between fourteen and
twenty-one who were connected to some version of foster care in
2021, most of them living in group placements aimed at promoting
self-sufficiency. But as Art Longworth had told me so many times, no
government system can substitute for a real mom or dad. Though well-
intended, none of these programs replaced the traditional milestones of
adolescence—dating, gradual independence, learning to drive a car—
nor could they provide the essential bonds of a family. Texas had tried to
train Monique in budgeting. California caseworkers quizzed kids about
the risks of using credit cards and whether they knew how to do their
laundry. But these tutorials carried all the weight of a passing breeze.
Most kids were either too bewildered by the reality coming at them to

absorb the information, or they were fixated on fantasies of returning to their families. Even Tina, who understood the gravity of her situation, had problems managing her anger long enough to swallow the indignities that challenge anyone trying to build a life. Child welfare systems were trying to get more young people connected to kin. But Tina, like thousands of others, had no relatives willing to take her in. Fewer than half of kids over sixteen leave the system to live with families. Instead, they are on their own.

***

Two years after Tina and her boyfriend ran from the Coney Island diner without paying for breakfast, she suggested we meet for brunch at an Upper East Side bistro. I spotted her outside, sucking on a vape pen before deftly tucking it into her bag as I walked up. She was dressed in a paisley-swirl bikini top, her feet slid into dainty pink mules, and she had straightened her hair. She could have been thirty. Only when we ordered and she made a gag-face at the suggestion of coffee did I remember she was just a kid, not even nineteen.

Tina's latest job was soliciting donations for breast cancer research by approaching passers-by on the street outside Grand Central Station. She could do that kind of work, paint on a bold smile and talk to strangers, brassy and confident. At first, she'd been thrilled by the commissions, which felt more rewarding than working for minimum wage at McDonald's. And she liked the mission, the feeling that she was doing something helpful. Between the breast cancer pay and her aftercare stipends, Tina considered herself flush, doing well enough to ride an Uber home, or take her grandma on vacation to Virginia Beach. Managing her life like a real adult, she told me.

"Someday, I'll have an apartment here," Tina said, gazing up at the skyscrapers surrounding us. When I asked about Dante, who, as an adult, had incurred a more serious sentence for their robbery and still phoned regularly from Rikers Island, she waved off his name with a pffft.

"I don't need love right now. What I need is my own apartment."

The idea of a safe, private place where she could close her door, free from oversight, tantalized Tina. But this experience is so foreign to kids who grow up in foster care that those fortunate enough to land such housing often have problems handling it. In 2021, the U.S. Department of Health and Human Services commissioned a study to determine which kinds of supportive housing worked best for former foster youth. The researchers surveyed nineteen permutations of independent living—apartment-style, dorm-like, some with intensive case management and school or employment requirements; others less structured. They interviewed staff and youth residents at each. But they found it impossible to track long-term outcomes because few clients stayed in touch over time, especially those who left dissatisfied. And while these subsidized apartments provided stability, their tenants' fractured pasts showed up every day. "Some of the folks we serve, they are not used to having a place to keep their things that is secure," one case manager reported. "They are not used to sleeping on furniture. We go and see that they are sleeping on the floor." Though intended to stem the tide of former foster youth living on the streets, these programs were often unsuccessful. "Some of our tenants were so disrupted from physical violence, we had to move them along, and those young folks moved back into homelessness," another staffer said.

Jay Perez-Torres, the gangbanger-turned-graduate-student who'd undergone such a turnaround under attention from his high school advocate, was thinking about this very problem when we met. For Jay, college dorms had provided an answer to the question that dogged his itinerant youth: how to find a home. The apartment where he now lived, surviving on food stamps, protein shakes, and adjunct work, had come by virtue of the lawyer who represented Jay in his assault charge during tenth grade. The day she learned he was in foster care, she'd entered his name on the New York City Housing Authority waiting list. He was sixteen at the time. Six years later, as he was about to graduate from the state university in Buffalo, the Housing Authority got in touch. Jay's name had come up.

He found it bitterly ironic that this saving grace had come by way of the criminal legal system, through his defense attorney. No one from foster care had ever tried to set him up like that. For kids who'd never had their names added to a years-long waiting list, or were too young to sign a lease, Jay endorsed programs like Chelsea Foyer, which operated on the premise that almost no one is ready to be on their own at eighteen, or nineteen, or even twenty-one—certainly not kids without family. The Foyer provided apartments and case management in a desirable Manhattan neighborhood. But its cornerstone was a forced-savings plan. Through it, alums left the program after two years with enough money to set themselves up in their own apartments. At least that was the plan. By coincidence, Chelsea Foyer also happened to be Tina's next home.

When the staff at Rising Ground informed her that taking off for an unapproved trip to Atlanta was grounds for dismissal, they referred Tina to the Foyer. She wrote the required letter, sat for an interview, and within a week threw her bags into an Uber to Manhattan.

She'd been lucky to win a spot. Chelsea Foyer offered studios with kitchenettes and private baths to a mix of young people in need of housing. Fourteen beds went to foster kids aging out of the system; sixteen were reserved for runaways and homeless youth (Tina's designation); and another ten went to adults under twenty-five who had been homeless but without any foster care history.

Instead of charging rent, the Foyer required its forty tenants to kick in a portion of whatever income they were earning, or at least $200 a month, which went into a savings account. "An escrow account," Tina said with pride.

She knew a deal when she saw one. Market-rate rents in Chelsea were easily ten times what she paid at the Foyer, a grand old building erected in 1904, and she loved the idea of leaving with a few thousand dollars saved up for her own place. Now she was really, truly on her way. Over FaceTime, she toured me around her bright new studio, showing off its shiny red cabinets, hardwood floors, and her window overlooking West 24th Street. She'd made it to Manhattan after all.

But I noticed that she'd chosen to sleep on the floor in a nest of blankets. And though she'd set up her bathroom with fresh towels and a new bar of soap, Tina, like most kids leaving foster care, owned no plates or cutlery. She spent most of her earnings on takeout.

Her first meeting with a case manager provided a hard dose of reality. Had she signed up for health insurance yet? If not, she would be unable to keep current on her psychiatric meds. This had never occurred to Tina. In foster care, she'd been enrolled automatically. Now she was facing a mountain of paperwork and deadlines. "No one tells you all the stuff you need to know about what happens when you turn eighteen," she said. "No one told me I need to renew my insurance every year—how you gonna know if no one tells you? So, I didn't know, and now I'm out of my medication until I renew again."

What about a job? her caseworker asked. Employment was a condition of residency at the Foyer, but Tina had soured on soliciting street donations for cancer research. "Man, I quit that job!" she said breathlessly. It was just another form of service work, hardly different from being a waitress, she'd decided. Trying to charm would-be donors reminded her of being a little girl, watching her mother serve diners in an Italian restaurant. The hostess would set her up at a little table off the kitchen, where the cook brought her plates of ravioli while her mom worked. Some nights Tina's mother might make $500, but you had to bring your A-game every day. You had to smile and act nice to get those tips. It was the same working for commissions, and some days Tina didn't feel like chatting up strangers. Fissures of frustration were beginning to crack through her sunny bluster.

"See, my depression comes from anxiety. It starts with mad anxiety, and my anxiety got real bad for, like, a week because all my money comes from commissions. So, on Monday, I just didn't come in. I don't know how I be blowing money like I am. It seems like I decide I'm gonna spare my ankles after ten hours standing, asking people for donations, so I get an Uber to work and it's $20 each way. So that's $40. And $40 don't sound like much, but it's almost $50. And $50 is half of $100, and there you go. It just goes—I don't know how!"

The Foyer aimed to mimic dorm life, unstructured but communal, a place where the young tenants could test boundaries while learning to live on their own. Researchers had found that kids who made it through six months were usually able to complete the program's full two years. The most successful were in their twenties. They came and went to school or jobs, bought and prepared their own food. They had identified career goals, met twice monthly with case managers, and joined the Foyer's many workshops on time management. Tina resisted immediately, preferring to keep to herself.

For teenagers, conceded Director Pascale Larosiliere, it was "extremely ambitious" to expect they'd be prepared to live on their own in New York City after two years at the Foyer. Most had never held a steady job before.

After Tina walked away from fundraising, her caseworker offered new leads for employment. She also pointed Tina toward a community college program that could funnel her straight into graduate courses at the John Jay College of Criminal Justice.

"They just accept you automatically!" Tina exclaimed, more jazzed by this guarantee than she was curious about the program itself.

Before that could happen, however, Tina was expected to attend the Foyer's classes on everything from basic hygiene to understanding an apartment lease. The checklist of responsibilities overwhelmed her. The petty rules of minimum-wage work grated. And every hurdle was beginning to feel like a message. The community college people wanted her old transcripts—could she send the document as a pdf? Could she upload her immunization records? When it became clear that Tina was not going to complete these tasks in time for the first day of fall semester, she chucked the whole thing. "They're asking for too fucking much!" she screamed over the phone.

She was sitting on the floor of her apartment, a black hoodie pulled over her dyed-orange hair, rolling a blunt. "I hate being an adult," she said.

All the years of fighting and running, moving from foster homes to detention cots to residential care, made more sense than trying to manage life on her own in New York City. "I know how to deal with that kid shit, that kid's life, better than all this," she said, talking at warp speed.

Tina was hardly the only youth to chafe under the rules of supportive housing. Five years after opening, the Foyer reported attrition rates of around 20 percent. Staff expected it. There would always be young people who found the Foyer's demands too rigorous or "did not wish to be part of a . . . community," as one report put it.

The Foyer model was inspired by a similar program designed for young people in Belfast, Northern Ireland. It had been imported to New York in the early 2000s after the city's deputy mayor for Housing Preservation and Development visited the UK and returned brimming with enthusiasm. A stringent application would screen in only those youth with the necessary self-discipline. A consortium of government and nonprofit groups surged forward with support, raising $29 million to buy and retrofit an old apartment building on Manhattan's West Side with common rooms, offices, studio apartments, and four-bedroom suites arrayed around a shared kitchen and living room. An additional $1.6 million paid for case management, building maintenance, and life-skills workshops.

The human engine generating all this goodwill was Sister Paulette LoMonaco, executive director of Good Shepherd Services, who'd been alarmed by the same numbers that shocked me. In the early 2000s, twenty-three thousand young adults were leaving U.S. foster care every year, most with neither the skills to live on their own nor family to help them. Thirty percent of the residents in city shelters had spent time in foster care. This was true in New York of the late 1990s, when Sister LoMonaco first took note, and in Seattle around 2005, when I did. It remains true today. About 30 percent of young people leaving foster care will spend time homeless by the time they are twenty-six.

Chelsea Foyer sounded like a brilliant way to bridge this gap. Advocates called it state of the art. By 2009, five years after opening, the Foyer had housed two hundred young people and "graduated" one hundred and sixty-five. At an annual cost of $41,000 for each tenant, Chelsea Foyer wasn't cheap. But it looked like a bargain compared with the alternatives. Jail was $86,870 per inmate. Homeless shelters were cheaper, but they provided no coaching and minimal case management.

In 2016, Good Shepherd Services attempted to quantify its results. It compared the status of residents after two years at the Foyer against a control group of youth who had aged out of foster care without support. The differences were striking. Twenty-nine percent of kids who'd been unable to find their way into a housing program spent time in a shelter. Among the hundred and thirty-eight Foyer graduates polled, the rate was about 17 percent.

The pattern repeated with education and employment. Chelsea Foyer graduates were more likely to have jobs or to be enrolled in school, according to Good Shepherd's data. But it wasn't a terribly rigorous accounting. The study surveyed Foyer alumni two years after their move-in date, meaning most had only recently left. And since the Foyer required its residents to be employed, it wasn't surprising to see these recent graduates doing better on that score than their peers. But what about a year, or two years, or five years later?

"We don't track alumni in that sense," said Larosiliere.

Chelsea Foyer knew how its former residents were faring only if they called with an update or reached out for help. Based on communications from a few dozen alumni, the Foyer had made a difference. Eighty-four percent reported that they were housed a year after discharge, and 91 percent said they were employed. But those results were based on a handful of clients.

Larosiliere declined to reveal the number who left in anger or frustration with no place to go, though she insisted they were "very few and far between." And she seemed unconcerned about the number of young people who moved out of the Foyer before the two years were up. The majority chose to leave after ten months. Were all these young adults ready to function on their own? Or had they bolted, desperate to throw off the kind of institutional oversight that had girded their lives since childhood? Larosiliere could not say.

Staff running Foyers across Britain had cautioned the New Yorkers against gearing their program primarily toward youth aging out of foster care. The UK model worked because it mixed young people at various stages of maturity; the more stable served as quiet motivators for the other kids, who modeled their example. A population full of high-needs residents might present problems, the UK experts warned.

Other cracks appeared. The cost of living in Belfast was nowhere near as high as New York City, for example. (Tina groused constantly about how little she could buy for $15 in Manhattan.) But the biggest difference between the British version of Chelsea Foyer and New York City's showed up around education. The academic deficits among former foster youth in New York were severe—far worse than their social skills—such that the requirement to be in school became a barrier. Former foster kids needed help with everything from learning how to apply to college, to knowing when to withdraw from a course before it became a failing grade, to understanding that remedial classes would not count for credit. The issue of "using financial aid wisely" was a problem unto itself. Within a few years of opening, New York jettisoned the three-pronged European model of housing, education, and career, retooling to emphasize housing and employment only.

Beyond that adjustment, Foyer managers in New York realized they'd been overly optimistic about the mental stability of their young residents. Staff estimated that nearly 70 percent had emotional problems that made them "not well suited to independent living," the Foyer reported in 2009, five years after opening.

The kids who had grown up in foster care had the highest needs of all. "They are overwhelmingly under-prepared for independent living and, in most cases, must be taught basic self-care and life-management skills," a study funded by the Annie E. Casey Foundation stated bluntly. Coming out of the child welfare system, they had been habituated to expect services would always be provided. The Casey writers described this as a "presumption of continued entitlement." Sixto Cancel called it "learned passivity." The government-commissioned report on supportive housing said simply, "The foster care system does not prepare young people to succeed in [these] programs."

All of these observations matched what I saw in Tina. Five months after moving in, she was desperate to get out, boiling with frustration over her flooded bathroom, a freezer caked in ice, a friendship gone awry, dead-end jobs she hated, and case managers who were either too much in her business or not helping enough.

Problems with authority were to be expected, the Casey Foundation pointed out, particularly for kids who had grown up in conflict with adults. Typically, these rifts showed up in relationships with employers. "When difficulties arise, young people often view quitting their jobs as the only recourse," the researchers observed. They might have been talking about Tina at her deli job, or the breast cancer fundraising gig, or any of her innumerable tours through McDonald's.

Despite the facade of independence, kids like Tina were covering deep caverns of worry about being on their own, the evaluators found. This fear showed up as anxiety, which morphed immediately into an impulse to fight, run, or hide.

CHAPTER 10
Closing the Front Door

One of Sixto Cancel's earliest observations about foster care was how poorly it used data. He was perplexed by the system's failure, if not refusal, to analyze the enormous amount of information it had collected about the children it was supervising and make changes in response. As a college student he'd recognized that sifting and interpreting this data could revolutionize the child welfare system. Its sluggishness around analytics had astounded Sixto in 2010, as America rocketed into the information age. A decade later, many states continued to lumber along. Caseworkers had moved from handwritten paperwork to typing their notes into computers, but scrutinizing the patterns within happened only sporadically. In the South, it hardly happened at all.

So, when researcher Christopher Church led several parishes in Louisiana through a study of their own numbers, it represented a first for many. Louisiana has sixty-four of these parishes—analogous to counties—and twenty agreed to share details behind the data they were already required to report to the federal government, basic stuff like how many children were in foster care, and how long they stayed there; how many were eventually reunited with their families, and how many adopted. The city of New Orleans was among those willing to let Church dig through its records to see how they compared.

A native of South Carolina, Church first visited Orleans Parish Juvenile Court at the end of 2017. He met the five judges assigned to child-dependency cases, shook hands with a bunch of attorneys, and hustled back home to work with a statistician. Over the following year he did much the same in nineteen other parishes. This was standard practice for his work with Casey Family Programs, entirely routine.

But back in his home office, Church did a double take, then a triple take. Examining the federal trends and where New Orleans landed within them, Church saw that the city barely registered. In every category, its numbers were too small to show up.

This discovery did not sit well. To data analysts, extreme outliers are nerve-wracking. They throw methodology into question. They raise the possibility of blind spots that might corrupt every other finding. Were there simply no children left in New Orleans? Had Hurricane Katrina wiped them all out? How else could Church explain what he was seeing: lower rates of foster care than any other region in the state, or any region Church had heard of, in any state, anywhere. He scrutinized every possible explanation and came back to one answer: Something was going on in Orleans Parish Juvenile Court that was radically altering the child welfare system in Louisiana's major metropolis.

"I don't think anyone gets what it means for a city this size to have only twenty kids in foster care," Church said to his research partner Vivek Sankaran as they hiked Zion National Park after a conference. "I mean, New Orleans has four hundred thousand people!"

Church and Sankaran marched on, along Zion's prehistoric pathways, past rock formations and down red-dirt lanes that others had walked for eons, puzzling over the Crescent City's historic deviation. As far as they could tell, New Orleans had all but eliminated the churn of children who cycle in and out of the system, spending a few months or a year with strangers before being adopted or returned to their families—only to be taken into foster care again. In New Orleans, far fewer kids were showing up in the system, and most of them left it in a matter of days.

Sankaran, a legal professor at the University of Michigan, had spent a decade observing family courts around the country. Generally, they operated as an assembly line. Judges grew impatient with attorneys who gummed up the works by pointing out matters of law that might slow the conveyor belt into care.

Against that backdrop, New Orleans stood out like the towering rock formations Sankaran and Church were hiking past in Zion, and the person running Orleans Parish Juvenile Court was Judge Ernestine Gray. Precisely how had she achieved these stunning numbers—foster care in the double digits? Had her results affected the rest of Louisiana's child welfare system? Did they change the way caseworkers did their jobs even before requesting a child's removal? And what about the kids who'd been allowed to remain with their families—how were they faring?

"You know, we could go deep on this," Church said to Sankaran, suggesting a full-scale study. They could watch Judge Gray on the bench and pinpoint exactly what was going on in her courtroom. It might have national implications, lessons for dependency courts across the country, Church thought. His partner agreed to make a pitch.

"We need to identify the practices she has implemented," Sankaran wrote to the head of Casey Family Programs, proposing a year-long research project. Before spreading the word about what looked like a remarkable achievement in New Orleans, they first needed to make sure Judge Gray's approach wasn't leading to more hurt children.

In 2020, Church and Sankaran got the green light.

***

"Did you notify the relatives that live in New Orleans of this hearing?" Judge Gray asked the case manager standing before her. It was a few months after Sankaran and Church had started observing the judge at work, and they were watching on video. Despite the upheaval caused by a global pandemic, court business continued as ever. The caseworker had petitioned to take a little girl from her parents, and Judge Gray wanted to know whether there were kin nearby who could step in, rather than handing the child to a stranger. But no relatives had shown up.

"Yes, I sent them a letter," the caseworker said.

"Wait, you just removed the child," Judge Gray pointed out, slowing the proceeding to zero in. "When did you send them a letter?"

"When I got back to the office."

Meaning after she had taken the girl, brought her to an emergency foster placement, and returned to her desk, hours later. The court then had three days to determine whether the child should be sent into the maw of the system.

"And you thought they would get the letter in time to come to this hearing?" the judge asked icily.

"Department policy is to notify all—"

"I'm not asking you about department policy," Judge Gray snapped. "I'm asking you whether you thought by mailing a letter to relatives here in New Orleans just a few days ago, you thought they would show up to this hearing."

There was silence.

"No, you don't mail them a letter," Judge Gray said, answering her own question. "When they live in New Orleans, you drive over and talk to them, tell them about the hearing, check the home out, see if they can care for this child."

The shelves in her courtroom were filled with fairy tales and picture books. A stuffed Tigger the tiger lay with its legs flopped over the judicial bench. Despite the American flag hanging behind Judge Gray and the austere portraits lining her walls, she had tried to make the room kid-friendly. But to the children who stood before her, it was still a strange and terrifying place, full of adults talking about them without explaining what was going on, making decisions about what would happen next in words the kids didn't understand. Some looked like they were trying to follow along, deciphering jargon about "reasonable efforts" and "termination of rights." But most of them just looked scared. Judge Gray would often halt proceedings to step down into the gallery and spell it all out: They were trying to decide on a safe place for him to be, she told one little boy. That might mean living away from home for a while, she said, describing an experience so disorienting and surreal to the child beside her that it felt like a bad dream.

Judge Gray had been running her court in this manner—grilling caseworkers and generally denying their petitions for foster care—for more than a decade. But the transformation of her courtroom from rubber-stamp stop on the journey to a barricade against child welfare's front door had begun long before. From the moment she stepped onto the bench in 1984, Ernestine Gray felt uneasy about the young people who appeared before her, particularly their race. New Orleans had plenty of poor white families whose kids arrived at school in dirty, ragged clothes or waited late at daycare because their parents had failed to pick them up. But these children were not the ones brought to Judge Gray for removal. In New Orleans, foster care seemed to consist almost entirely of children of color.

Born in 1946, in segregated South Carolina, Ernestine Gray had grown up keenly aware of families in need. She remembered her mother and grandmother whispering about social workers who would rifle the closets of Black women, checking for men's clothes during the early days of welfare, because no man should be living in the home of a mom presumed to be single. If the state found that a woman on welfare had a boyfriend contributing to the family income, her benefits would be cut. Those same single moms were then criticized for being too poor to properly care for their children, at which point the state took the kids.

After she joined the bench, Judge Gray saw the other end of this cycle. Children in foster care were more likely than other kids to repeat a grade in school. They were also more likely to attempt suicide. Those reunited with their families returned home more developmentally delayed than they'd been upon entering the system. In Louisiana, only half of kids who grew up in foster care graduated from high school. Sixty percent became homeless within a year of aging out. The trends were so consistent Judge Gray could hardly bring herself to use the term foster *care*. She could not shake the nagging sense that the system in which she now played a role was directly connected to America's long history of hobbling Black families, all the way back to the introduction of welfare, and the Jim Crow laws before that. All the way back to slavery.

During her first decade on the bench, Judge Gray not only failed to stanch the flow, she presided over a court deemed by the *New York Times* to be the most dysfunctional in the country. "It's medieval," said a public defender who worked there for five years before quitting in disgust. Lawyers didn't have offices in which to meet with their clients. They didn't even have telephones. At least one judge routinely asked attorneys to pray with him, requesting divine guidance before issuing a verdict. Judge Gray herself was quoted describing juvenile court as the system's stepchild. Everything about its workings suggested the opposite of "innocent 'til proven guilty," she complained to the *Times* reporter, an observation as true for parents in child-dependency cases as it was for kids accused of crime.

Despite her candor, Judge Gray was stung by the portrait that appeared in print. Then she was furious. Within weeks of the 1997 article, she began imagining ways to overhaul juvenile court. For one thing, defense lawyers and family advocates needed their own offices. For another, she was rearranging judicial assignments. Going forward, teams of judges would handle specific types of cases—one group for delinquency matters, another for petitions alleging child abuse and neglect. And the same judge would see a case all the way through to its conclusion, rather than opening the docket to whomever was on rotation.

The *Times* piece had the effect of a mirror under fluorescent lights, illuminating in stark type discomfiting aspects of Judge Gray's work that had bothered her for years. Based on what she'd seen of long-term outcomes from foster care, she wondered if it wasn't better to leave kids with their parents—even parents who could be considered negligent. All courts want to err on the side of child safety, but where judges in other parishes pursued this goal by removing children from their families, Judge Gray began to tack in a different direction. "If we're going to do worse, by golly, we should just leave them the hell alone," she told anyone who would listen. "Let them do whatever they've got to do with their families, because we're not doing any better."

The first time Judge Gray shared these thoughts publicly, she was speaking at a conference of social workers. "I think it is actually criminal that we separate children from their families because they don't have food, because their parents don't have a refrigerator. I mean, really? We're the richest country in the world," she said, standing at the lectern. The audience looked at her as if she'd lost her mind.

Was she suggesting they gamble with children's lives? colleagues asked later, their pointed questions landing like accusations.

Well, yes, Judge Gray conceded, it would be taking a chance. No one could predict what might happen to a kid left at home with a mentally unstable mom or a drug-addicted dad. But she could say with near certainty what would happen if that child grew up in foster care. To Judge Gray, this seemed by far the bigger risk.

By the early 2000s, Judge Gray was acting on these beliefs daily. When caseworkers showed up in court, arguing that a child was the victim of neglect because his home had no electricity, Judge Gray no longer waved the kid into emergency foster care. Instead, she began to drill the workers. State law said they had to address a family's problems before petitioning to remove the children—had they? Previously, this requirement was treated as a technicality. Judge Gray now used it as a cudgel.

What exactly had they done to help? Judge Gray demanded of the caseworkers before her, most of them young women, some in their first months on the job. The homes they described as dysfunctional seemed to be struggling primarily with the effects of poverty, and poverty was not the same thing as neglect, the judge pointed out. Had anyone attempted to connect the family with food stamps or subsidies to pay their electric bill? It didn't appear so. Money spent on family preservation services in Louisiana was infinitesimal compared to the budget for child removal. Nationally, only 8 percent of child welfare spending goes toward preventing foster care. Nearly ten times more goes to child removal and adoption.

Judge Gray found the hypocrisy dizzying. State officials talked about making things better for families, but they passed laws withholding financial support. Louisiana said social workers had to make reasonable efforts to address a parent's problems before removing their children, but the state doled out far more in stipends to foster families than it ever paid to care for kids at home. In a country as wealthy as the United States, how was it possible for parents to lose their children because they didn't have enough food? Couldn't the government just figure out how to feed them? Surely, that was cheaper than paying for foster care—not to mention its downstream costs in homelessness and incarceration. And if the state did decree that a child's safety necessitated removal, it was only logical to expect the government to do better than the kid's parents had. Yet the results of foster care showed that the state wasn't doing better, so what earthly justification could Judge Gray offer, as its agent, for taking a mother's children?

***

Judge Gray was cordial but wary when I contacted her. She had not enjoyed her interactions with journalists, and she was not especially keen to speak to one more. But she agreed that America's child welfare system had failed to reckon with a mountain of research showing that foster care did real harm to kids. I told her what I'd learned about brain science and attachment from psychologist Mary Dozier; how, by sundering bonds, foster care was leaving kids without the basic interpersonal skills essential for functional adulthood. I told her about Maryanne Atkins and Art Longworth in prison, about Monique and Tina struggling to get a foothold. Judge Gray said she, too, had seen how the effects of foster care could last a lifetime.

Sometimes, she'd lain awake at night, wondering about her decisions, especially in the early years when she was operating mostly on gut instinct. She worried about a mom who'd thundered, "You don't have the authority to take my kids. Only God can take my kids!" Mentally ill, Judge Gray was sure. But that didn't mean she would hurt her children. Same for a dad who'd been a stranger to his four daughters and stepped up to claim them after their mother went to prison. Judge Gray sat him down in her office for some tough talk.

"I will send these kids home with you, but I don't want to see them back here," she said.

Both cases had been a gamble, Judge Gray acknowledged. According to state law, the "health, welfare, and safety of the child" should guide every decision. But there was often "tension" between her interpretation of that standard and the opinion of caseworkers who had been inside kids' homes. Still, if they couldn't produce hard evidence

of imminent harm—even in places they insisted were "unhealthy"—
Judge Gray generally let the parents keep their kids.

What about mistakes? I asked. The cases of children who'd died
when left at home, like five-year-old Brandajah Smith, who shot herself
with a revolver in 2013. For nearly a year, Brandajah's teachers had
reported concerns that she was being sexually abused. The Louisiana Department of Children and Family Services had asked that the
kindergartener be taken into care. But under Judge Gray's orders, she
remained. When Brandajah's mother returned from the store one afternoon, her daughter, left alone, was dead from a gunshot to the head.

"Not a good feeling," Judge Gray said tersely.

She grieved for the family in such cases. She holed up in her office
to reread the files and see if there was something she'd missed. But
headline-grabbing tragedies did not shake Judge Gray's overriding
belief in the righteousness of what she was doing.

To Judge Gray, it felt worse to learn about a child harmed in foster
care, on the state's watch. There was a little girl who'd been scalded all
over her body in a foster parent's home, and a boy struck by lightning
who'd died. Their cases haunted her. She'd taken these children away
from parents who never saw them again. "We said we were going to
make things better, and we didn't," Judge Gray said.

The numbers appeared to back her up. Except for one ugly spike in
2014, data showed that kids in Orleans Parish who quickly reunited with
their families were "revictimized" no more frequently than children in
places that removed five times as many.

When discussing her views, Judge Gray often cited a nineteenth-
century poem titled, "A Fence or an Ambulance." It was a parable
about a cliffside community whose people feared falling over the edge
and landing, broken, in the valley below. What was the best answer to
this problem? Should they place an ambulance beneath the cliff to collect the bodies, or build a fence up top to prevent that fate? "If the cliff
we will fence, we might dispense with the ambulance," Judge Gray
said in a 2009 speech, quoting the verses. To her, it was a metaphor

for foster care. Rather than tackling the underlying causes of child harm—poverty, substance abuse, domestic violence, or a parent's mental illness—the U.S. government was still parking its ambulances down in the valley.

Later that year, a terrified thirteen-year-old was ushered into Orleans Parish Juvenile Court.

"What is your name?" Judge Gray asked from high on the bench.

"Kayana," said the girl, using her given name, rather than Keedy, the nickname everyone knew her by. She'd never met this stern-looking woman sitting above her, no one had explained why she was there, and she sure wasn't going to act like they were friends.

The school year had already begun, but Keedy Bradley rarely showed up. Her mother, having suffered several strokes, was in a nursing home, and her father had died years earlier, which left Keedy and her two sisters to fend for themselves. Sometimes they went to school, sometimes they didn't. But Keedy had been bewildered when a caseworker with the Department of Children and Family Services knocked at her door. She didn't know the white woman standing on her porch, and she'd been told never to open the house to strangers. The woman shouted that the department already had Keedy's younger sister. They'd picked her up at school, and now they needed Keedy to come along too. Confused by what she was hearing and terrified for her sister, Keedy opened the door.

Then came the whirlwind. A social worker rushed in and told Keedy to gather some clothes. She ushered Keedy into a car and drove her across the city to a part of town she barely knew. But Keedy's elder sister Marie, who was sixteen, had refused to get in the car. Now she was listed as a runaway.

Should we run away? Keedy and her younger sister whispered to one another at the child welfare office. They didn't understand why they'd been taken from home, or what would happen next. They heard only the word *separation.* So the girls took off, darting and weaving through New Orleans's streets, ducking behind parked cars.

They found Marie at a friend's house, and for several weeks the three sisters holed up there, afraid to go to school. If they showed their faces, the police would surely get them, Marie said. Keedy understood that being truant and running from a government office meant she had done something wrong, but she wasn't sure what it was. Anxiety shortened her breath every time she stepped outside. She scanned constantly for police, afraid of being whisked away. How long could this go on? Keedy had always planned to graduate high school, maybe even go to college.

"I think we need to turn ourselves in," she told Marie.

After listening to a caseworker narrate these events, Judge Gray stepped from behind her desk and walked down into the courtroom gallery. She seated herself on a bench next to Keedy, leaning in close, as if it was just the two of them talking, despite the lawyers, advocates, and social workers filling the room. Judge Gray explained what was about to happen: Keedy would be sent to live with someone who could care for her while her mother recuperated. But the judge would be watching. Judge Gray said she expected Keedy to go to school. She expected to see good grades. And she would be checking every month to make sure.

To Keedy, still struggling to understand what had happened to her family and why all these strangers had a say, it was just a swirl of words. But after court, Judge Gray led her to the mountain of stuffed animals she kept on a shelf in her office and told Keedy to pick whichever one she wanted. Keedy chose a stuffed bear, beginning a relationship that would shape the rest of her life.

By the time they met, in 2009, Judge Gray's early misgivings about the child welfare system had hardened into certainty. She'd spent the decade after President Clinton signed the Adoption and Safe Families Act of 1997 noting its effects. The law aimed to create stability for foster kids by more quickly terminating their parents' rights, thereby "freeing" children for adoption (a tacit acknowledgment, in Judge Gray's view, of the harm done during the limbo of foster care). But thousands of kids were never adopted. Severed from their parents, they grew up as itinerants, moving from one foster placement to the next. Those not taken in permanently by age twelve usually spent their adolescence in group homes, at which point they were deemed virtually "unadoptable." Just like Monique, in Texas.

But unlike Monique, Keedy Bradley never wished for adoption. As soon as her mother was well enough, she would leave foster care and go home. Judge Gray agreed. She refused to act as a functionary numbly authorizing paperwork, and she never severed the parental rights of Keedy's mother, who died in a hospital two years later. By that point, Keedy, at fifteen, had been separated from her little sister and shuffled through a half-dozen placements. She would live in eight foster homes before aging out during her senior year of high school.

❧❧❧❧

Judge Gray had been right about the long-estranged dad who showed up to parent his four daughters, and the mentally ill mom who got to keep her kids. None of those children appeared in juvenile court again— Judge Gray kept track—and over the next six years, between 2011 and 2017, the total number of kids in New Orleans foster care plummeted by 90 percent.

Not everyone considered this a victory. Joy Bruce, who supervised the brigade of volunteer advocates known as CASAs (for Court-Appointed Special Advocates), agreed the system was rife with problems, and she understood that Judge Gray was driven by urgency to cut the number of Black children subjected to it. She was less certain, however, about the solution. The judge seemed to be operating with no strategy for evaluating the results of her decisions, Bruce felt. No one was sure what happened to the kids Judge Gray returned home, particularly those who were turned over to relatives. Few showed up again in court, it was true. But not for one minute did Bruce believe a closed case file told the whole story of what happened behind closed doors.

Judge Gray defended herself from critics by pointing to the same trends, relying on the absence of incriminating information to prove an unknown. If you allowed Child Protective Services to monitor families, constantly looking for reasons to criticize their parenting, you were bound to find something, she said. It was just like police surveillance. Small errors of judgment that might be waved off if made by a white middle-class mom—like leaving the kids alone during a quick trip to the store—could result in a low-income Black mother never seeing her children again.

While Judge Gray piloted her one-woman campaign against foster care in New Orleans, the state of Louisiana adopted the model pioneered by Carole Shauffer and Jennifer Rodriguez at the Youth Law Center in California. They had crisscrossed the country, convincing eighty counties in ten states to stop barring contact between biological and foster parents and instead build connections between them. It led to better results for kids, they said. Scientific proof was scant. But the anecdotal evidence was persuasive enough that Florida passed a law requiring phone calls between foster and biological parents. Child psychiatrist Charles Zeanah, who'd pioneered the original studies of Romanian orphans, deemed Shauffer's Quality Parenting Initiative the best idea he'd ever seen for improving child welfare. Zeanah worked at Tulane University, essentially in Judge Gray's backyard, and while respectful of her commitment, he could not shake the same sense of unease that had concerned Joy Bruce.

There was one boy Bruce would never forget. He had been placed in foster care at eight, after his mother tried to kill him. Under Judge Gray, mother and son were reunited when the youth was seventeen. But his mother attacked again. And the kid, who had turned eighteen while home, was now too old to be taken into care. He was living on the streets, Bruce said. It was the only time she could recall Judge Gray conceding that perhaps she had made a mistake.

Beyond worrying about what was going on with youth who were never seen again, Bruce wondered if Judge Gray's tough treatment of child welfare workers was causing them to quit. Many lasted less than eighteen months on the job, and whenever one left, her duties were foisted onto those who remained. Some workers were responsible for a hundred children. They were logging twelve-hour days, six days a week, to keep up. Fewer than 20 percent said they had enough time with families to offer real help. Meanwhile, Judge Gray kept haranguing them for sloppiness.

"You're not entitled to rely on those," she chastised a young woman for presenting a family's prior run-ins with CPS as the rationale for another child removal. It was stale evidence, in Judge Gray's view, and did not meet the legal standard. "Don't come in here unless you're certain," she snapped.

Vivek Sankaran, watching these proceedings on video, was agog. Family court, in his experience, was about collaboration, not debate. Judge Gray bombarded witnesses with dozens of questions. She interrogated the logic behind their decisions, challenged the veracity of their assertions. Sometimes she reduced them to tears. At least once she chastised an intern about improper attire. The young woman was not to show up in Judge Gray's court wearing gold lamé pants again.

Despite the criticism of onlookers, as time passed Judge Gray grew only more convinced of her approach. And she kept her word to Keedy Bradley. Every month, Keedy and her latest social worker would appear in Judge Gray's court for a check-in. Each time, Judge Gray gave Keedy a book. She knew these meetings represented one of the few constants in Keedy's life. For kids in foster care, caseworkers changed routinely. Lawyers were reassigned without warning. The children shuttled between new families every year, sometimes every month. Judge Gray was frequently the only reliable figure they knew.

At each new home, chatty, outgoing Keedy would ask herself, *Am I good enough? This family could kick me out any time. Am I making them happy? Will they keep me?* She veered endlessly between worry over pleasing them and resentment at feeling like she had to.

Judge Gray tried to keep her focused on a vision for the future, on life after foster care. That meant close attention to school report cards. Judge Gray demanded to see them every quarter. This was complicated since Keedy—like Tina, Jay, and Maryanne—attended multiple high schools. The logistics did not matter to Judge Gray, who was cross with any caseworker who did not have Keedy's grades at the ready.

"I keep telling y'all, you can't plan these cases fifteen minutes before you walk into my courtroom," she'd say, shaking her head. "I guess nobody believes me."

Keedy's marks were generally good enough to escape further grilling. But she knew Judge Gray skewered caseworkers about other kids. "What makes you think this is okay?" the judge would demand, peering at a string of Ds and Fs. "If it was your child, would you accept this?"

When was Keedy's birthday? Judge Gray demanded. When was her next doctor's appointment? Her big event at school? The government had positioned itself as Keedy's parent, and a parent would know these things. As the flustered caseworker flipped frantically through her notebook, Keedy silently mouthed the answers, trying to help.

"Stop that, Keedy," Judge Gray said. "I know you know. But she needs to know, too."

Initially, Keedy dreaded these inquisitions. But as she grew older, she began to feel differently. When Keedy heard people describe the judge as "mean," she leaped to Judge Gray's defense—not because her mentor on the bench needed it, but because she wondered why holding foster care to high standards was viewed as extreme. Were expectations so low that no one considered it part of their job to know her birthday, or the last time she'd seen her little sister?

***

For many years, Judge Gray's work was unknown outside of Louisiana—until Christopher Church and Vivek Sankaran stumbled upon the numbers from Orleans Parish. Incredulous, they kept rechecking the figures. In 2011, the city had more than two hundred kids being parented by the state, which was a low rate to begin with. But six years later, as Judge Gray pushed her crusade into high gear, that number had plunged to just twenty—in a city with more than 75,000 children.

"Unprecedented," the researchers wrote. "Nothing short of revolutionary."

Church and Sankaran examined the case histories of three dozen children on Judge Gray's docket. They combed reports, searching for new abuse allegations about those she had sent home. And while they found plenty of people who disliked the judge "intensely," who believed she was relinquishing children to "families in chaos," the researchers could not get around the fact that there were fewer child fatalities in New Orleans than in parishes placing many more kids into care.

"What exists today in New Orleans is not a foster care system by any familiar standards," they wrote. Judge Gray, abiding by the letter of the law on child removal, had singlehandedly transformed child welfare in the Crescent City.

She tried, nonetheless, to maintain a low profile. Judge Gray favored austere suits beneath her judicial robes and filled her downtime by baking at home. But she was unquestionably a polarizing figure and most certainly an activist. She lobbied the legislature for better foster care policies. She convened "Judge and Teen" days at court, bringing in motivational speakers and college counselors to talk with foster youth. Keedy attended every one of them.

The judge watched with approval as Keedy enrolled at the University of New Orleans and earned her bachelor's degree in sociology. When Keedy won a summer internship at the state legislature in Baton Rouge, she reported back to Judge Gray all she was discovering about the laws that governed her life and how they had been made. Long after Keedy had aged out of foster care and become a young mother, Judge Gray kept in touch, inquiring about her baby boy's health and how he was learning his letters.

"I want for you what I'd want for my own children," she said, promising to bake Keedy one of her famous pound cakes.

***

In 2020, Judge Gray retired. She did not want to leave—there was still so much more to do. But Louisiana law mandates that most jurists stop working at seventy. So, with the world in lockdown, Judge Gray packed up her children's books and stuffed animals, her portraits of Nelson Mandela and Barack Obama. There was no party.

However, she did not go quietly. Judge Gray spent the next two years working with a team to write what she had been unable to say from the bench.

"Separating Black children from their parents in the child welfare system is intimately linked to the history of slavery in our country," reads a resolution Judge Gray presented to the American Bar Association. Her views about this connection had undergirded every decision she made on the bench. And if forced to leave the job, she would continue her work by educating the legal system.

Just as plantation overseers had wielded the threat of family separation to force compliance among slaves, America's government did the same, Judge Gray wrote. First through welfare laws, then foster care. Both had systematically crippled Black families. In twenty-four plainspoken, amply footnoted pages, the judge made her case. No euphemisms, no circumlocutions.

The document is a searing lens on history. It traces the way post–Civil War vagrancy laws made criminals of unemployed Black men, enabling their arrest and imprisonment. With their dads in jail, Black children could be legally considered orphans and "hired" by former slave owners, who kept them housed on plantations because their families could no longer support them. These "apprenticeship" arrangements were in a "child's best interests," the courts found, using language eerily close to that enshrining foster care today.

The government's underinvestment in Black families and subsequent surveillance of them had led directly to separating Black children from their parents through foster care, Judge Gray observed. And she salted her assertion with hard numbers: Black families are investigated so frequently that today more than half of all Black children interact with the child welfare system by age eighteen. Once on its radar, they are also more likely than white children to be taken away.

Even if the laws behind child welfare had been well-intended, Judge Gray added, "no profession should turn a blind eye once the consequences are clear."

After two years of dickering over her pointed references to slavery, the American Bar Association adopted Judge Gray's resolution in August 2022 and named her chair of its Judicial Division. The same month, Church and Sankaran published their paper on Judge Gray's work, framing her approach as one that offered a blueprint for juvenile courts across the country. If New Orleans's foster care rates were applied nationally, there would have been 18,211 children in care as of March 2020, they said, rather than the actual number: 415,170. The amount of suffering, disconnection, and societal cost that might be avoided was head-spinning.

Yet in the years since, Judge Gray's example has not been embraced. After she left the bench, foster care rates in Orleans Parish began to rise again, particularly in short-term removals. This is the system's front door, the place where Judge Gray had made her greatest impact. She tried to inquire about the reversal, delicately, so as not to seem like she was attempting to keep control from retirement. But she heard little response. There was, in fact, a distinct quiet around the question of building on Judge Gray's legacy.

CHAPTER 11

A Changed Man

Nearly four decades passed between the years Art Longworth roved Seattle's streets as a homeless teenager and the days when Maryanne Atkins was doing the same. During that time, more than nine million kids across the country trudged through the maze of homes and institutions that form the scaffolding of foster care. Despite the numbers and their costs, no branch of government reliably tracked the outcomes of this sprawling system until the early twenty-first century.

However, while child welfare remained mired in inertia, America was navigating a tsunami of change in juvenile justice. By 2020, legal definitions around the culpability of youth were unrecognizable. This shift, stunning in its swiftness and breadth, began in 2003, after a fourteen-year-old in Alabama beat his mother's drug dealer to death and stole the man's baseball card collection. "I am God, I've come to take your life," Evan Miller said, before bashing his victim's head with a baseball bat and burning his trailer to the ground.

Miller had been in and out of foster care most of his life. Before committing murder, he'd attempted suicide four times. Yet the eighth grader was tried as a competent adult and sentenced to life in prison. Miller's lawyers argued that the facts of his childhood had not been properly considered by the legal system, and they managed to take their case about the importance of those early years all the way to the Supreme Court. In 2012, while Miller was serving his time in a maximum-security prison, the justices ruled that all courts sentencing juveniles for homicide now must take their life circumstances into account.

Miller—sometimes described as the "children are different" decision—observed that kids are both impressionable and trapped by their dependence on adults, unable to shield themselves from "crime-producing" upbringings. They were uniquely malleable, formed by circumstances beyond their control, and it was unfair to sentence them without acknowledging this, the judges found. Reading *Miller*, I thought of Art Longworth and what he'd told me about the ways group homes and youth detention had shaped him into a kid who thought only of his own survival, who cared nothing about the harm he'd done others.

Jurisprudence evolves methodically, each decision building on those that precede it. The logic underpinning *Miller* in 2012 had been laid by two prior rulings. The first, in 2002, banned capital punishment for developmentally disabled people on the grounds of their diminished intellectual capacity. In the second, known as *Roper*, in 2005, neuroscientists had shown the high court that the same logic around disability could be applied to children, whose brain development was also deficient, particularly in the areas that control reasoning.

All of these arguments around unequal brains might have remained theoretical without technology. Through color-coded scans, judges could see for themselves that the neurobiology of adolescents was physiologically different from that of adults. And they could see that the variance was most pronounced in the parts of the brain that govern decision-making.

The court's ruling against capital punishment for youth was not merely an intellectual exercise. Between 1973 and *Roper*, America imposed the death penalty on 226 teenagers. Justice Anthony Kennedy, basing his decision in *Roper* on the biology revealed through MRIs, articulated what any parent knows intuitively: Kids have an "underdeveloped sense of responsibility," he wrote. But it wasn't irresponsibility by choice. Their neurology made them more "susceptible to negative influences." As parents also know, a child's nature is not static but fluid, changing as they grow. For this reason, it was impossible to be certain that even their most horrifying crimes indicated an "irretrievably depraved character," Justice Kennedy concluded. "From a moral standpoint, it would be misguided to equate the failings of a minor with those of an adult." Arthur Longworth was forty when this decision came down, and he read the coverage with keen interest. By then, he had been pacing prison halls for twenty years.

Neither the Supreme Court decision on the vulnerability of children nor Evan Miller's documented history of childhood abuse persuaded the courts back in Alabama. Miller's youthful pronouncements about wielding the power of life and death did not strike circuit court judge Mark Craig as boyish bravado. They were among "the most chilling" words Judge Craig said he had ever heard. "They sound like something you would see in a fictional account." In 2017, he resentenced Miller to life without parole.

***

Washington state, despite its liberal laws around recreational drug use, had long been among the more punitive places on earth. It allowed children as young as twelve to be charged as adults. It was the first state to pass a "three strikes" rule mandating lifetime imprisonment for repeat offenders—even for nonviolent crimes. And in 1984, when its voters passed an initiative abolishing parole, Washington obliterated any incentive for prison inmates to change. In 2020, only seven countries in the world had higher incarceration rates than Washington state.

There were only two allowable sentences when Art Longworth was convicted of aggravated murder in 1985: life in prison, or death by hanging or lethal injection. A psychiatrist who evaluated Longworth for capital punishment testified that, emotionally, the twenty-year-old was even younger than his age suggested. Though born bright, with "superior potential," his maturation had been so stunted by years of trauma and abuse that Longworth experienced the world like a kindergartener might, as a magical place full of mysterious forces. After this assessment, the prosecution decided not to pursue the death penalty.

During jury selection for his trial, Longworth had noticed a woman staring at him. It was annoying, this chunky middle-aged broad in a lavender pantsuit—she reminded him of his mother. He was sure he could feel hatred beaming from her eyes. But as the prosecutor began questioning this prospective juror, running through a standard checklist to probe for bias, the woman's chin began to tremble. She dabbed at her eyes. "I have one just like him at home," she said, gesturing at Longworth. "He's just a boy." In prison, Longworth would indeed add two more inches to his frame and watch his feet grow another two sizes.

The evaluating psychiatrist had described this veteran thief and practiced con as someone who saw himself as "helpless, weak, and very small," a child dressed up in his daddy's suit. But he was in no way mentally ill, the doctor said, no psychotic killing machine. Despite the savagery of his crime, Longworth was "essentially, a normal man."

I'd wondered about this from our first email exchange. In Longworth's booking photo, his face lacks the blank, impenetrable expression I'd noted on so many killers. If I'd met this kid in his white t-shirt, I would have used the word "wary." I might have assumed he was a hustler. One eye, slightly smaller than the other, appears to be focused inward, on some troubling thought. The other, staring directly at the camera, conveys suspicion. His mouth is slightly pursed. *He looks ready to do anything*, I would have thought. But in profile, with his mullet haircut and jaw jutting forward over a shallow, undeveloped chest, Art Longworth was still, quite clearly, a boy.

Who were you as a teenager? I'd asked early in our correspondence. *What kind of kid?*

He considered this a difficult question.

"Before the state got me, I can't remember a time when I wasn't scared to death," Longworth wrote back. "Later, when the state got ahold of me is when I learned to be angry. What kind of kid was I? A kid who never felt like I had anything to lose. I never believed I would live to eighteen. And when I turned eighteen, I didn't believe I'd make it to twenty-one."

Many young people facing prison anticipate with terror the idea of fending off assaults of every kind. Longworth had none of these fears. When his judge finally spoke the words "life without possibility of parole," Longworth was thinking only about returning to the jail cell where he'd stashed a razor blade. Foster care, if nothing else, had trained him on the importance of being ready—to run, or to steal, or to kill yourself and finally exert some control over your life. The idea soothed him.

But Longworth never got the chance. From court, he was ushered onto a bus with wire mesh over the windows and driven straight to state prison. Older inmates leered. *You'll never make it at Walla Walla*, one said of the maximum-security fortress where Longworth was headed, home to the death row he had only narrowly escaped. He leaned his forehead against the metal grate fracturing the world outside and thought about all the tours through juvie, and the miserable group homes, and the sound of a boy being raped. And he fantasized about smashing the laughing man's face.

⁎⁎⁎

In 2021, after Longworth had been locked away for thirty-six years, an inmate named Kurtis Monschke argued that his own youth should have been considered when he kicked a Black man to death at nineteen. Science had proven human brains continue to develop into a person's mid-twenties, Monschke pointed out, arguing that he should be resentenced in light of this fact. Washington's highest court agreed. Though Monschke, a white supremacist, had killed his victim merely to earn a pair of red shoelaces—a neo-Nazi badge of honor—the court, including four justices of color, concurred that neurobiology showed no "meaningful cognitive difference" between a youth of seventeen and someone just a few years older. Essentially, Monschke's brain had been that of a juvenile when he attacked Randall Townsend, they ruled, and he was entitled to have his sentence reviewed in light of the "transient immaturity of youth."

The *Monschke* decision made Washington the first state to extend legal protections for juveniles to people as old as twenty. Kurtis Monschke was hardly a sympathetic figure on which to base such a groundbreaking opinion. After eighteen years in prison, he was still a proud neo-Nazi, unwilling to shed any of his youthful beliefs. But for Art

Longworth, who'd murdered Cindy Nelson a month after turning twenty, the possibility of being resentenced bobbed before him like a life raft.

Longworth had petitioned for clemency once, in 2012. He was rejected, largely at the insistence of Cindy Nelson's sister, who'd urged the state to keep him locked up forever. But *Monschke* provided a new avenue. It at least offered Longworth the chance to explain how he believed foster care had shaped his life and, by extension, resulted in the end of Cindy's—things he'd had neither the words nor opportunity to express in 1985.

"I don't always think about the crime I committed, but I'm at all times conscious of it because I'm conscious of the person I killed," he wrote to me. I'd wanted to know how often he recalled Cindy's murder. Did it frame his day-to-day thinking, or had he stuffed it into a box at the back of his mind? Longworth said he'd known little about Cindy at the time and wouldn't have cared much anyway. But since then, he'd learned she was a kind person, with a mother and father so devastated by her death that they passed away soon after. "I've never been able to bring myself to believe Cindy doesn't still exist," his letter continued. "I've felt her presence many times. If it wasn't for her, I doubt I would have accomplished anything in here. When I sat down to write 'How to Kill Someone,' who do you think I wrote it for? I feel her presence most when I'm at my lowest. There have been so many times in here when I've wanted to give up. I mean, seriously, why continue to go through this? What is there to look forward to or hope for? But that's when I feel her presence strongest. I imagine her telling me, 'Don't you dare. You owe me more than this.' It's why I think she was a really good person. I've never felt her condemn me—even if that's what I deserve."

Longworth did not believe a life sentence was necessarily wrong for a crime like his. What bothered him was the word "mandatory" regarding the punishment, because it precluded any consideration of a person's circumstances leading up to that moment. Longworth found this particularly unfair for kids who had grown up in foster care.

"What I feel is significant about my situation is that I was sentenced by the same entity that raised me. . . . I feel like that's a problem," he wrote.

He knew the ghastly nature of Cindy's murder brought down a wall, making it impossible for people to care, or even to be curious about what had formed him. But he was riveted on the injustice of the state dodging any accountability. "Maybe this isn't fair of me to say—but it's what I feel—I feel like I was sentenced by my crime partner. So maybe no one who wasn't raised by the state will ever understand. But for the state not to acknowledge its role, its connection to me, has never felt honest."

***

The psychiatrist who interviewed Longworth nearly four decades earlier had commented on his tendency to view the world as a magical place. Evidence of his arrested development, the doctor said, of immaturity. But there were aspects of Longworth's story that might strike anyone as improbable. The mysterious secret bedroom at McDonald Elementary, for instance. And now another twist: The prosecutor tapped to argue against Longworth's release was also a former foster child.

Neighbors had discovered Adam Cornell at six, caring for his three younger siblings after their mother abandoned them all. Now in his late forties, Cornell had a square-cut jaw and shock of dark hair, the central casting ideal of a crusading litigator. He had been a track star in middle school, an honor student in high school, and at eighteen Cornell was crowned Youth of the Year by the Boys and Girls Clubs of America, which flew him to Washington, DC, to shake hands with President George H. W. Bush.

Despite this glittering trajectory, Cornell firmly believed that foster care could torque a psyche and create a criminal. He joked about his own "borderline attachment disorder" after living in thirteen foster homes. With each change of household, every set of new rules and pretend-siblings, Cornell lost a bit more of himself. By age eight, he hardly knew who he was. The divergence between his path and Longworth's was due almost entirely to luck, Cornell believed. In his case, it arrived in the form of a foster mom named Stella Mae Carmichael.

Widowed, twice divorced, and sixty-five years old, Stella Mae had taken in hundreds of kids by the time a caseworker brought Adam to her doorstep, and she considered it her mission to get him adopted into a permanent family. When Adam tried to hide away from other kids, Stella Mae enrolled him in choir. When he refused to get out of bed, she signed him up for Little League. "You've got to straighten up and fly right, or else no one's going to take you," Stella Mae would say. To make a family love him, Adam would have to be "the best kid," she insisted. Every baseball game was an audition, every polite handshake a bid to convince some nice couple to choose him as their son. The notion of adoption hung in front of Adam like a glowing orb, his holy grail, the prize. He and Stella Mae talked about it every day.

Within a year of moving into her home, a couple who lived nearby heard about Adam, the baseball kid. Every weekend after Little League practice, they took him bowling, or hiking, or out for a picnic. Stella Mae coached him on the meaning of these get-togethers. They were trying him on, she said, testing to see if Adam would fit into their lives, poking and prodding to make sure he really was "a good kid." Adam went along with all of it. After four months of this family pantomime, Adam's would-be dad arrived by himself one weekend. He brought Adam to a burger joint and sat him down at a table outside.

"You've probably wondered why we've been visiting with you these past few months," the man began. Adam played dumb, letting the man say what he'd been hoping to hear for two seasons. "We were thinking about adopting you. But that's not going to work out. We won't be seeing you again."

Years later, Cornell would learn that the couple believed themselves unable to get pregnant. When biology kicked in, there was no need for more weekend visits with Adam. To them, it was that simple. Stella Mae, however, was livid—as if her boy was a pet they could just return to the store! But not for one minute would she allow Adam to sulk. *You will get good grades*, she insisted. *Think of who you'll be in the future.*

Everything she said was geared toward this someday Adam-to-come. When he was eleven, another couple said they wanted him as their son. This time, Stella Mae permitted no weekend courtship. Adam packed up his small bag of clothes, her words ringing in his mind: *You've got to be a good kid, the best kid.*

He tried for a year to prove his worth—handsome, athletic, polite. He performed the role of ideal boy like an exercise regimen. And then came the verdict, handed down one spring morning in sixth grade before Adam left for school: rejected. After believing he had finally found his family, Adam would be sent back to foster care. Four decades later, he can still feel the gut punch of their words. He still calls that day the worst of his life.

"Hey, Adam! I heard that family dumped you!" a kid on the school bus shouted as they rolled past his former home a few months later, when seventh grade began. He was in a new placement, still fighting to make himself matter to someone, when a former foster kid named Arthur Longworth committed murder a few miles down the road.

Later that year, Adam's caseworker brought him to an adoption picnic at Gasworks Park in Seattle. Prospective parents were stationed at tables surrounded by balloons, piled with games and craft supplies. The children circulated among them, as if speed-dating. At one table, a man sat amid a heap of footballs and basketballs. At another was a guy who'd driven up in a Mercedes. Adam thought he must be a millionaire. Thirteen now, he was savvier than the nervous boy who'd lived with Stella Mae, and he made the rounds like a pro, silently vowing to beat out every other kid and win himself a family. He would be whomever these parents wanted. With Mercedes man, Adam played the smart kid, rattling off postal codes for every state. With sports guy, he played the jock, tossing a football. And it worked. Randy Stubbs, a high school baseball coach, finally adopted Adam Cornell.

By then, Art Longworth, just seven years older, had been sentenced to life in prison. The chasm between these two men, their common beginnings and wildly divergent ends, raised obvious questions: Why had Cornell's life turned out so much better than Longworth's? Why was he a successful public servant, rather than a killer?

Cornell felt the answer was as random and unjust as chance. It was only a fluke that his mother hadn't been using drugs while pregnant with him, unlike the months she carried his younger brother, who died in Seattle's downtown jail. And there was the luck of being white. If he had been a Black boy, or an Indigenous kid, would Stella Mae have pushed him so hard? Without her constantly nudging him to envision a future, would he have been named Youth of the Year and earned a visit to the White House to meet the president?

Three decades later, after he had gone to college, graduated law school, and become chief prosecutor of the county where Longworth dumped Cindy Nelson's body, Cornell walked into the Washington State Reformatory to confront a parallel-universe version of himself. Longworth, the kid with a seventh-grade education, had by then convinced a parade of lawmakers and philanthropists to collaborate on improving the government system that left a lost and angry teenager to the streets. Cornell, however, was there to decide what position he would take on Longworth's resentencing. He listened to his shadow self behind bars explain how the child welfare system had molded many of the criminals he lived with, how it turned children into survival machines poorly adapted to mainstream life, then locked them away.

Cornell agreed. He likened foster care to growing up on a toxic waste dump. Not every kid in that situation would develop a profoundly damaging disease, but it sure increased the odds. A childhood in foster care factored in many of the crimes that landed on his desk, Cornell believed, particularly those committed by young people. In his view, it mitigated their culpability.

I left our interview convinced the prosecutor would argue for Longworth's release. Within weeks, he recused himself from the case. Nothing about its merits had changed, Cornell insisted. But the background he shared with Longworth might raise questions about his impartiality. Someone else could handle the matter, said the prosecutor, deftly stepping away.

**

As a reporter, the sterility of modern courtrooms often struck me as incongruous, considering the chaotic lives processed within them. For Longworth's resentencing in February 2022, I chose a spot on the second row of blond wood benches in a small chamber at the Snohomish County Courthouse. I wanted to be close enough to see the expression on Longworth's face.

Though his crime had been infamous and his activism in prison a source of some renown, there were few onlookers. The courtroom felt as still as a museum archive. Nor would there be a jury for this proceeding—just Longworth, his lawyers, a prosecutor, and a judge, all of whom had been children when Longworth was locked away.

Escorted into court, his hands were shackled, both arms gripped by beefy sheriff's deputies. It was somewhat ludicrous. Longworth, the street kid, now gaunt and gray-haired, looked more like a college professor than someone who'd spent his life in institutions. Only his gait gave him away. Guided through Snohomish County's new marble-and-glass court complex, Longworth kept stumbling, unaccustomed to walking on carpet. He imagined it felt like crossing the deck of a boat lurching through ocean waves. People stared, but Longworth barely noticed. He was more interested in the ways the grimy old courthouse had changed from the place he remembered. Every room was decked out with cameras and laptops and video monitors. To him, it felt like time travel, the first moment Longworth had been seen in public since the Reagan administration.

In the back row, his sister Dawn sat huddled in a winter coat she never took off. They hadn't seen each other since the Christmas holiday in 1979, when fourteen-year-old Art visited Dawn's foster family, and he did not appear to recognize her. As he scanned the gallery with a furrowed brow, Longworth tilted his head toward his lawyer, listening carefully, then gave Dawn a stiff-armed wave, almost a salute. He pulled a pair of spectacles from the pocket of his dress shirt and peered down at the legal documents arrayed across his defense table, as if scrutinizing student papers. It felt awkward to sit in "free-people clothes," he stammered to Judge Anna Alexander as the two-day proceeding began.

The first witness was a psychiatrist who spoke to the court through a screen, over Zoom. Dr. Brian Judd had visited Longworth at Monroe prison and heard the story of his childhood, the years cycling through group homes, and the groping foster dad on whom he'd been "intermittently reliant," as the doctor put it.

Dr. Judd explained that the Centers for Disease Control had identified ten Adverse Childhood Experiences—including physical abuse, verbal humiliation, emotional neglect, sexual abuse, family disconnection, imprisonment, hunger, domestic violence, and parental substance abuse or mental illness—that could impede healthy development. Having any number above four was significant. Longworth, like many foster kids, scored a ten out of ten. Dr. Judd was not trying to cultivate sympathy. Based on his evaluation of Longworth's life before prison and the callousness of letting Cindy Nelson bleed to death alone in her car, the likelihood of another violent crime was high, he said, approximately the 92nd percentile. The cords in Longworth's neck tightened.

They eased, however, as a parade of witnesses testified on his behalf. Among the most forceful was a foster care advocate named Dawn Rains. She told Judge Alexander that while the abuse Longworth had suffered was some of the worst she'd ever heard, virtually all kids in foster care had problem behaviors. Wherever they went, at every home, in every school, they were always the new kid. Any relationships they'd held close were severed each time they moved. Chronically disconnected, they acted out in class and were routinely suspended or expelled. Many never made it past middle school. Those who ran from their placements inevitably turned to crime to survive, which landed them in locked cells at juvenile detention. Between 25 and 40 percent of young people in Washington's youth prisons had been in foster care. Only 12 percent ever earned a high school diploma. These were not permanent failures of character, Rains concluded. They were failures of our system.

A teacher who ran the University Beyond Bars, through which Longworth had finally earned a college degree, described his difficulty with a particular assignment. She'd asked her students to write an essay using metaphor to compare their parents to an object. Longworth was flummoxed. Raised by the state, he didn't know how to depict a bureaucracy as a human being.

Ross Hunter, secretary of Washington's Department of Children, Youth and Families, was the final speaker. In five years leading the agency, Hunter had shrunk foster care by 25 percent, shielding more than two thousand kids from the gauntlet of receiving homes, detention cells, and strangers that had framed Longworth's adolescence. Still, Hunter spent more mornings than he cared to count sitting at his kitchen table, reading critical incident reports about dead children who should have been removed from their families, but weren't, and kids who'd been harmed on the state's watch when they were. He was more convinced than ever that everything about foster care needed to change.

"I'm here to testify in this case because I believe we, collectively, can make the world a better place," Hunter said, standing to address Judge Alexander.

He'd been among the first visitors to attend Longworth's State-Raised Working Group in prison, and was certain Longworth could do even more good outside its walls, educating policy makers and working with kids so that they'd never end up walking the cold, cement tiers where he'd spent so many decades.

"Something thirty years ago may no longer be relevant," Hunter continued. He was referring, technically, to regulations for kinship care and how he had loosened them, allowing children to live with relatives who once would have been ruled out for any number of imperfections. But the subtext was impossible to miss. "I believe in redemption," Hunter said. "People should not be defined forever by the worst thing they have ever done."

None of these facts—neither the brutality of Longworth's childhood, nor his transformation since—salved the agony of Cindy Nelson's survivors. Her sister, Sandra Rodgers, sat alone, squeezing back tears before the proceeding had even begun. Nearly everyone in the room was there to support the former foster kid who'd tried to redeem himself, not his mostly forgotten victim. And the very traits held up as reasons to reconsider Longworth's value—his writing, his advocacy, his effort to build productive relationships—only emphasized how he had stolen Cindy's chance to do the same.

Rodgers was a social worker. She knew all about the research on brain development, the impulsivity hardwired into youth. "I mean, it's science," her daughter told me. You couldn't deny science. But science would never heal Rodgers's shattered heart, her broken family. She talked about choices, particularly those of Washington state. Longworth had been convicted of burglary at seventeen but allowed to remain on the streets. At eighteen, after an arrest for armed robbery, he was released again. Had he been locked away, Rodgers said, her sister would be alive today.

Throughout the proceeding, Longworth maintained his compo sure. But when Judge Alexander invited him to answer allegations raised by a prison informant, he was unable to contain his fury. It was about his failed bid for clemency a decade earlier. Longworth had been crushed by the denial, and he'd blamed it on a prosecutor who described him to the pardons board as chronically deceitful, constantly manipulative. The informant claimed Longworth had approached him in the prison yard afterward, suggesting that the prosecutor be assassinated. Judge Alexander now asked Longworth to respond.

The allegation was absurd, he choked out from the witness stand, his voice high-pitched and raspy, as if his throat were closing. Yes, he'd been dumbfounded when the rejection came down and disgusted with himself for daring to hope. But he was no longer a killer. Nor was he an idiot who would talk to a known informant. He leaned forward in his seat, wiping tears from his eyes. "You don't think I'm tough enough to sit this out until I die?" he asked. "I am. I can." He'd lived a diminished, locked-down life since childhood. He knew how to handle prison.

Longworth's obvious anger worried his lawyers. But toward the Rodgers family, he remained contrite. "My actions as a young person are indefensible, and I'm sorry," Longworth said. "Prison did not make me sorry. I've always been horrified by what I did."

"I think Ms. Rodgers should know that she is right," he continued. "I believe that I should have been locked up at eighteen. I needed help. I was raised to be an animal, and that's what happened."

The court broke for lunch, but no one had any appetite. In the hallway outside Judge Alexander's chambers, Longworth's sister wept—for her brother's suffering and for Cindy's family and for all the ways the true culprits, in her mind, had never answered for any of it. The lawyer in charge of collecting testimonials on Longworth's behalf did not feel much better.

"Dr. Judd's report was not good," he said, fidgeting as we stood in line at a coffee shop.

Judge Alexander had promised to render her decision immediately after the break, so I spent an hour wandering downtown Everett, trying to imagine what Longworth might be feeling, what he was doing as he sat waiting to learn if this day would become the first of a regular life.

The judge was a petite woman in her mid-forties, a daughter of Russian immigrants, who had arrived in the United States as a schoolgirl. She had a reputation for ruling in favor of unsympathetic defendants, willing to look at difficult situations from multiple angles. She'd marched into court nodding a curt hello to the lawyers but keeping her eyes averted.

She began her ruling by addressing Cindy Nelson's family.

"I heard speakers today say words like *redemption* and *second chances* and *atonement*," Judge Alexander said. No one should be allowed to tell the survivors of a murder victim to forgive or show mercy, she admonished the audience now gathered in her gallery. It was infuriating that Cindy never got to live her life, the way Longworth had. "She didn't have a chance to lead people, and she didn't have a chance to learn Spanish and Mandarin, and didn't learn to write powerfully, and love others and inspire love from new people, and she didn't have a chance to maybe one day save a life herself because Arthur Longworth took her life."

Longworth bowed his head.

Judge Alexander said she prided herself on reminding the young people who stood before her that they were more than the worst thing they'd ever done. It need not define their lives. But counseling a nineteen- or twenty-year-old was not the same as talking to a middle-aged man who had already served thirty-seven years behind bars. After two days of testimony about Longworth's journey from adolescent drifter to author and activist, Judge Alexander felt sure she understood who she was looking at. To her, Longworth's resentencing felt like a rare opportunity to travel back to the 1980s and set straight the jurist who'd deemed a grimy street kid irredeemable.

The brain of a young man "beaten and tied up and starved and raped repeatedly" was simply not the same as that of a child who'd grown up in a safe, loving home, she said. Yet, rather than embracing the "baptism of violence" that would greet him in prison, this maldeveloped youth had transformed, becoming a new person who could potentially save a life. Longworth's effect on other prisoners was obvious. She saw his attempt to change their lives as an effort to atone for his own. But he'd gone beyond that, finding ways to reach people who had the power to change the entire foster care system. That was unusual, Judge Alexander observed. "That is important."

It was conceivable that if released he might be able to do even more to prevent "the exact type of horrific tragedy that he, himself, caused the Nelson family and society as a whole," she continued. Though the previous judge missed it in 1985, Longworth had been capable of change all along, and he had proven it. "I don't have to guess at that," Judge Alexander concluded in a strong, clear voice. "He is before this court a changed man." She resentenced him to thirty years, seven fewer than he'd already served.

It was the most eloquent ruling I had ever heard, especially since much of it had been written during a lunch break.

I had imagined this moment, spinning movies in my mind of Longworth leaping from his seat and embracing his sister Dawn in the back row. I'd envisioned them walking into the February wind, free together for the first time in their lives. Instead, Longworth brushed a tear from his cheek and meekly allowed the guards to handcuff him for processing.

He would remain behind bars another two months—first at the county jail, then back across the state at maximum-security Walla Walla, where he'd begun his journey so many decades before—while lawyers and corrections officials dickered over the fine points in Judge Alexander's ruling. Finally, on a Monday afternoon in April 2022, Arthur Longworth walked out of state prison in civilian clothes.

To me, the cinematic triumph of Longworth's against-all-odds release only underscored how little had changed. The legal system might be slowly calling itself to account, but in the face of lawsuits and studies and vows of reform, foster care had undergone no such revolution. On the day Longworth walked away from his past, more than 400,000 US children were wards of the state, and half of them were headed for locked cells.

CHAPTER 12
Cottage in the Woods

On a June morning, while Tina worked through her court-ordered diversion program in Ohio and Monique trudged though community college in Texas, Maryanne was led from Washington's women's prison and driven, in shackles, to the Echo Glen Children's Center, an hour north. The youth facility had decided to take a chance on her, even though Maryanne was now twenty.

Prison wardens expected to see her back behind bars within the month. They described Maryanne in terms so dire her program manager at Echo Glen thought she was receiving some sort of Hannibal Lecter in pigtails. Listening to their warnings over the phone during Maryanne's first week, Jeanette Stephens gazed through the window of her small office and watched her newest charge outside, playing hopscotch.

Because of the pandemic, outsiders were barred from Echo Glen for a year. I received a few letters from Maryanne, talking mostly about loneliness and her sense of being constantly judged. As the eldest on campus, she chafed at the rules, the routines, even the name of her new home because it contained the word "Children's." She complained about untrustworthy cottage-mates and staff who read her journals. Often, she did nothing but hole up in her room, reading. But even in her boredom, Maryanne recognized that Echo Glen offered a kind of stability she had never known. Apart from her two-year adoption, the youth lockup represented the first time in Maryanne's life that she wasn't worried about having enough to eat.

Echo Glen had opened in 1967 as a camp-style retreat tucked into a wooded hollow forty minutes east of Seattle. At the time, it was envisioned as a place for truants and runaways. Now it housed kids convicted of armed robbery and murder. Though college-level coursework had been promised to Maryanne, Echo Glen had few college classes lined up, and the intensive therapy approved in legislation consisted of once-weekly sessions that kids could skip if they wanted. Mostly, Echo's residents plodded through worksheets geared toward K-12 students, which were meaningless to Maryanne since she had finished high school at the King County Jail. She spent a lot of time in talking circles.

I was finally allowed to visit in June 2021. We sat outside on a swinging bench set, facing each other in the sunshine. Maryanne had grown at least an inch. She was slim and tan, healthier looking than I'd ever seen her. Every few months a staffer from Echo Glen drove Maryanne into the city of Bellevue, twenty minutes away, where the state paid a technician to remove her old tattoos. *Beautiful Struggle*, once inscribed along her collarbone was gone. Her prison girlfriend's name was still visible when she pulled her hair away from her face, as was *fuck love* on her right hand. But they were fading. At Echo Glen, there were no older inmates who could claim ownership of her, and though Maryanne professed to hate therapy, she was able to talk about herself and her past in a way I'd never heard before. Less ashamed, less locked down.

In Maryanne's unit, Yakima Cottage, artwork and platitudes covered the walls of a large common area where couches were arrayed around a television. It felt more like a dorm than a prison, though the guard sitting behind a central desk determined when and for whom the doors would unlock. Two teenagers wearing the all-orange sweats of newcomers were watching an anime cartoon as I walked in. Maryanne had known nearly everyone there before, in juvie. And almost all of them had been in foster care. Her best friend, Olivia, had been running away from state placements since age eleven. When she showed up in Maryanne's cottage to serve her own short sentence at Echo Glen, Olivia brought her copy of the memoir *A Piece of Cake*, by Cupcake Brown. She and Maryanne used to read it together, sitting side-by-side on the floor in juvie, sharing the pages.

Maryanne's room was at the far end of the common area. She had decorated it with pictures of Seattle pulled off a calendar and a patchwork quilt of flowers and whales that she'd stitched herself. A star lantern dangled from the ceiling. On her bedside table stood a stack of dystopian novels. The only obvious sign of a penal institution was the bed itself—a concrete ledge with a thin mattress pad laid on top. Maryanne had tacked up a few baby pictures that showed her mother, who'd phoned once, and a snapshot of a young man from juvie whom she now considered her boyfriend. In other photos Maryanne was with Olivia, the two of them wearing mud masks and head scarves like college girls on a spa day. She walked around campus waving hello to staff across wide, rolling lawns. At Echo Glen, Maryanne was the veteran, rather than someone's trophy. Younger girls looked up to her, and she accepted the role of leader with weary grace.

"Your shirt is lit!" a plump blonde squealed, trying to curry favor.

I expected that Maryanne, who'd slept in stairwells and fed herself with stolen potato chips, would roll her eyes at such a naked expression of need. But she didn't. No longer defending against constant threat, she was able to extend a bit of kindness.

She had started writing poetry, which was her solace in detention, and she'd joined a book club. They were reading *Where the Crawdads Sing*, a novel about an abandoned girl whose mother leaves her in the care of an abusive dad. The girl grows up fending for herself in a swamp. And then she kills a man after he tries to rape her. "Some people would say he deserved it," I commented to Maryanne, who smiled in polite, if noncommittal, agreement.

Echo Glen had its problems, however. A month before Maryanne arrived, evaluators had determined that a reasonable ratio for the kind of counseling its residents needed was one therapist for every ten residents. Echo Glen had eighty-five young people on site and a single psychologist. Staff reported endless burnout, insufficient training, and constant turnover. Kids made shanks and hid them. There were lockdowns and room searches. Four boys assaulted a male nurse who was bringing their medication, then stole his keys and took off in his Ford Focus down the prison's mile-long driveway. At least one of them was serving time for murder. In the stolen car, they hit the interstate. But instead of trying to run somewhere they'd never be found, the teenagers headed straight back to Seattle. The boy convicted of murder showed up at his grandmother's house, asking for something to eat.

Despite the ongoing chaos, multiple resident escapes, and Maryanne's own history of running, at Echo Glen she attempted nothing of the sort. Hers were more quotidian difficulties. It was awkward, balancing correction with rehabilitation and the emotional needs of kids at wildly different stages. A twenty-year-old who cursed at her teacher could not be seated at a table and told to take a time-out. "I'm not five," Maryanne would snap. "Don't talk to me like I'm a baby."

In prison, she'd racked up infractions immediately, but at Echo Glen she created no such problems. Having advanced beyond the first ninety days, when newcomers had to wear orange sweats, Maryanne walked around in regular clothes for the first time in years. And when she did test the rules by getting online and emailing her boyfriend or posting to Instagram, the staff did not lock her in a room by herself. The fault was theirs, they said, for failing to set boundaries.

Still, Maryanne's rage simmered. She looked back at her younger self with zigzagging defensiveness and disgust, wincing at anything that reminded her of "what a failure" she'd been. She was particularly frustrated with the way she'd handled her criminal case. Agreeing to plead guilty had been motivated by a sixteen-year-old's wish to shut out the noise and embarrassment, get it over with and lock herself away. The alternative, fighting for herself, would have meant taking the stand to talk about being trafficked, an idea that made her nauseous. She didn't want to cry in front of jurors. She despised the idea of anyone viewing her as wounded. This was why she'd initially denied having sex with Emmanuel Gondo when Detective Duffy interviewed her at the Seattle police station—despite the glaring fact of a condom with her DNA on it at the crime scene. She realized now that the detective had been offering her a chance, a way to tell her story. But Maryanne, the panicked teenager, couldn't see that. All she could see was her shame. Even sitting in a police interrogation room under suspicion of murder, Maryanne worried about looking like a skank. Too embarrassed to admit she'd had sex with a guy who demeaned her, that she'd been pushed into doing something she didn't want to. That she'd been a victim.

Displaying that kind of vulnerability repulsed her still. It was her chief complaint about therapy at Echo Glen. Her new counselor was "this soft little woman who talks to me like a baby," said Maryanne, rocking back and forth in her chair, just as she had in court when Jessica Berliner called her a remorseless manipulator.

***

By 2023, after she'd spent three years in this quiet enclave surrounded by forest, the education and therapy programs were only modestly improved. But Maryanne had changed markedly. No longer was she the jittery girl with dark shadows around her eyes. Now Maryanne smiled, often laughed. She'd become a certified peer mediator. Sometimes she even talked by phone with her old boyfriend Montrell. He'd call while playing in the park with his three-year-old son.

"Does he treat you okay?" I asked. "Is he nice to you?"

"He is, yeah. If he wasn't, I wouldn't talk to him anymore. I can say that now."

When Maryanne was younger, you could actually see her fight-or-flight response in action. During our prison visits, she'd scanned the room constantly for threats, ready to bolt. At Echo Glen, that twitchiness calmed. Maryanne could sit with her back to a door or lie down in a room where people were coming and going, and never turn her head. She marveled at this shift, chuckling at the memory of her old self, who'd escape wherever she was by jumping out any open window. She spoke regularly to her half sister in Montana. She wondered about the woman who'd adopted her little brother and once considered adopting Maryanne too. She seemed to be trying to fit the pieces of her fractured life together, less afraid to look back.

Most striking to me was that this transformation had been generated entirely by the change in Maryanne's environment. And the relationship with Jeanette, her program manager, who scolded Maryanne
when she was petulant or inconsiderate—not in the way of a prison
guard, more like a mom.

When Maryanne began to wonder about her past, Jeanette volun-
teered to contact the Atkinses, in hopes they might send a few photos
from Maryanne's years at their home. They sent nothing and asked Jeanette never to contact them again. Same with the woman who'd adopted
Maryanne's brother. But faced with these disappointments, Maryanne
did not fly into a rage or take a swing at someone or try to cut herself,
as she once would have done. She was working on forgiveness, even if
others were not.

***

"Hey, I have something for you!" she said on my sixth visit, darting into
her bedroom and emerging with a chapbook titled *Put Some Duct Tape
On It.*

"Some poems I wrote are in there," said Maryanne, folding down
the corners of pages that held her words. The writing was part of a program called "The IF Project." As in, if there was something that someone could have said or done to change the path that led you here, what
would it have been? Maryanne and I had talked about this, many times.

"If I'd had parents—good parents," she always said. Or if she'd been
taken into foster care younger, as a baby, before the circumstances of
her childhood pushed her to the point of stealing food from other kids
in second grade and standing on a table, shrieking. Or if her adoptive
parents had been better prepared by the state for the kind of kid they
were getting. Or if, once she was out on the street, there had been a
supportive housing program like the Chelsea Foyer. "I would have had
some place to sleep at night, which was all I really wanted," she said.
Instead, Maryanne rode the light rail back and forth between Seattle
and the airport.

Now that she had a bed, food, safety, and someone—Jeanette—who believed in her, Maryanne could feel herself changing. In the room next door to her own lived a feral cat that had been abandoned as a kitten. Maryanne named her Elsa. At first, Elsa would let no one touch her. But Maryanne, despite being allergic, scooped the cat up and brought Elsa into her bedroom, clearing a space beneath the bedclothes. "She likes to lay under the covers next to me—well, I don't know if she likes it, but she stays. And she wouldn't stay if she didn't like it," Maryanne reasoned, rubbing the cat's ears. "When I first got her, she was so terrified, she wouldn't even eat. She pretty much lived under my blanket, even when I was gone. I'd come back and she'd still be under there in the little space I made so she could breathe." Elsa had since calmed enough to sleep on her own in the room next door. Maryanne showed me the cat bed she'd fashioned from a plastic drawer.

"She's come such a long way," said Maryanne, beaming. "She's just a totally different cat now, completely different. She doesn't scratch anymore."

Maryanne's empathy extended to dogs, which she trained in Echo Glen's therapy animal program. As with Elsa, talking about her canine pupils seemed to provide Maryanne a means of describing her own dawning sense of self, even if it was unconscious. "There's a dog named Hope that I really like. She's deaf, so she sounds really scary because she can't hear herself. She doesn't have a good reputation."

***

Jennifer Rodriguez, the California foster-child-turned-attorney who'd talked to me about the biology of attachment, found none of this transformation surprising when I called her to describe it. Despite the barebones staff and scattershot programing at Echo Glen, what was making the difference for Maryanne was not merely safety, but a sustained connection with an adult she could trust, her program manager Jeanette.

Their relationship was more than a soft landing for a girl who'd known little but hard edges; it was actually altering Maryanne's neurology, Rodriguez believed. "All the science tells us that adolescence is on par with—or even greater than—early childhood as a time of immense growth and opportunity, with very high returns on investment," she said. Rodriguez did not endorse prison of any kind for kids, even those who had committed murder. But a teenager like Maryanne presented enormous opportunities that had been squandered during the three years she sat in juvenile detention and jail, awaiting trial. "With a sixteen-year-old, you have this great chance."

Rodriguez felt that even a place like Echo Glen could be harmful, since it was still confinement, still part of the carceral system. The greatest harm I could see had less to do with the facility itself than the limbo it represented. Washington's Juvenile Rehabilitation to 25 law sought to address the central tension in youth crime: Should the primary aim of a court sentence be punishment or change? This legislation suggested the latter. But it went only partway. If a young person was rehabilitated in a therapeutic environment, did it make sense to send them to prison afterward? Wouldn't that reverse all the hard-won gains?

Washington was not the first state to devise a category of confinement specifically geared toward older teens and young adults. California also had held people in its Youth Authority prisons up to age twenty-five—that is, until 1996, when a twenty-four-year-old serving time for murder killed a guard in order to steal her keys, escape, and avoid being transferred to state prison on his next birthday. The guard, Ineasie Baker, had been stabbed, strangled in a supply closet, and dumped in a trash bin. Sanitation workers discovered her body two days later. The horror and subsequent outcry ended California's practice of holding twenty-somethings in youth facilities for nearly two decades.

At the time, a teenager named Frankie Guzman was serving a three-year term for armed robbery in the California Youth Authority. Today, Guzman is a lawyer with the National Center for Youth Law, and he remembers the effect of Ineasie Baker's murder. Within days, every inmate eighteen or older was rounded up and bused to state prison. The rationale, said Guzman, was that young people with sentences stretching beyond their time in a youth facility had no deterrent to committing more crimes because they had nothing to lose. Ineasie Baker's killer, for example, was already facing twenty-five years to life.

Now in his mid-forties, Guzman said he'd never known which of his fellow youth inmates were headed for prison, at least not officially. There was no obvious indicator like a different uniform or particular housing unit. But in group therapy it was easy to tell. The problem cases were almost always younger kids who had been in and out of foster care, cycling through group homes and detention with a new placement every few months. "Their attitude was 'fuck the world,'" Guzman said.

The young murderers—Baker's killer notwithstanding—were almost always better behaved.

"A big part of it was, they were just so defeated. They knew they had this dark cloud looming—that one day, they were going to go to the adult system," he said. "It seemed to weigh on them."

Even today, nearly thirty years later, the pattern held. Every month, Guzman spoke with kids in the system and observed that the ones who seemed most stable were those in for murder. The worst, those who had been in and out of foster care.

I slowed him down to make sure I'd heard correctly. Was Guzman saying there were noticeable differences in behavior between foster kids and others in lockup?

Definitely, he said.

"I remember being incarcerated with a young boy who was twelve years old, in and out of foster care. By the time he got to the Youth Authority—he was just a kid, in there with twenty- to twenty-four-year-olds—he fought like no one else." Partly, because he was smaller. But more because he'd been taught this was necessary. "Even then, I understood that he'd been processed so much that he knew what to expect at any new group home, or even just a new unit: The way you respond will determine the conditions under which you live for the remainder of your time. The young people who came from foster care were conditioned in such a way that they knew what to expect and how to respond.

Violence was the response. It had to be, or you were going to become a victim."

This sounded so much like Arthur Longworth's description of foster care in the 1970s and '80s that I was silent for a few long moments. Nothing had changed. By 2013, California again opened its youth prisons to inmates over eighteen, but only for young people whose sentences could be satisfied by their twenty-fifth birthday. They were not going to risk another Ineasie Baker.

Maryanne's counselor had never worked for the California Youth Authority. But during her twenty years at Echo Glen, she had observed similar patterns. The kids serving time for murder were the easiest to handle. Their crimes had been heat-of-the-moment, full of chaos and complexity, rather than the culmination of a steadily escalating pathology. Aside from shoplifting and charging a police officer in downtown Seattle, Maryanne herself had no criminal history before killing Emmanuel Gondo.

The most difficult resident Jeanette Stephens had ever encountered, a girl who assaulted guards and terrified other kids, was serving time for stealing a steak. And the most difficult residents of all came from foster care. They were the ones who acted like they had nothing to lose because they'd already lost everything.

This was Maryanne in the months before she committed murder.

"By fifteen, I did not care if I died. I did not give a fuck," she told me.

Echo Glen was the first place she'd begun to think seriously about what came next. And now, at twenty-three, Maryanne faced the impending reality that in two years the stability she'd found would be ripped away with a trip back to prison for another decade. She fretted about it constantly. As before, during her years in juvenile detention, birthdays brought no joy, only anxiety tinged with exasperation. All the growth that everyone praised, everything she'd accomplished—the writing, the dog training, the peer mentoring—seemed to count for nothing. Maryanne's old self-lacerating anger flared. Maybe she should get the transfer over with fast, rip off the healing bandage of Echo Glen and toss it away since prison would do the same soon enough. But the idea of adult prison clearly worried her. At Echo, Maryanne had let down her guard, easing the vigilance with which she'd navigated the world. In prison, that kind of behavior was a death sentence.

"I hope I'm not gonna get ass-fucked," she'd say.

"Maryanne!" chided Jeanette. "That is not appropriate!"

I could hardly blame her for feeling whipsawed. At Echo, every casual conversation or craft project or walk to the basketball court was intended to build confidence and motivation in kids who had none. "It's therapeutic here, just the environment," said Maryanne during one of my visits. "In prison, it's a shark tank. You fend for yourself. You can't ask anyone for help. You can't ask anyone for anything. Anything you want, you have to pay for, and if you don't have money, you don't get it."

She did, in fact, have a little money. A lawsuit filed on her behalf for being held in solitary confinement after her arrest—illegal for minors in King County—had resulted in a $20,000 settlement. In an attempt to make restitution, Maryanne had paid $10,000 to the Gondos through the state Victims Compensation fund, and she was prepared to serve every minute of her fourteen-year prison sentence for murdering Emmanuel. It was the extra five years tacked on for using a firearm that galled her, since it had been his gun.

Yet whichever way she tipped and turned the kaleidoscope of her life, Maryanne could not come up with a vision of herself as anything other than prisoner. Could not imagine herself free and doing errands, driving a car, and paying bills like a normal person. That worried her. Her heart would race and she had trouble breathing, just like the old days. But in calmer moments, after talking with Jeanette, she focused on finding new ways to explain herself to the world. Such as through the state clemency board, which sometimes heard cases brought by people serving long sentences for crimes committed when they were children.

"I know I can handle prison," Maryanne said. "But I feel like it's going backwards. That environment is just so unhealthy. There's nothing about it that's gonna make me better than I am here." We were sitting in the activities room of Yakima Cottage, amid broken exercise machines and old books. "I don't want to throw all this away. I mean, I won't throw it all away if I go back. But I know I won't get any better there."

Jeanette worried too. In prison, girls who'd previously lived at Echo Glen were addressed only by their Department of Corrections ID numbers. Sometimes, they would phone the staff at Echo just to connect with someone who knew them by name. Against that backdrop, was it any surprise Maryanne still held a painfully limited view of her future? She referred to herself as a felon, believing that was how the world would see her forever. When she daydreamed about life after confinement, she pictured herself surviving on food stamps. Her father had been a loser, she told Jeanette. So had her mother. Her sister was in and out of jail. Why should she expect any different? The rest of the world sure didn't.

Even Guzman, hardened by years in the streets and familiar with the criminal justice machine, cringed at what was coming for Maryanne. "How terrible that is!" he said. "For a young person to go to the youth prison system and focus on rehabilitation, then they're getting comfortable and acclimated to that environment and seeing the benefits. And then, at twenty-five, they're torn out of it and thrown to the wolves in an adult system that offers none of that? How would they maintain the positivity, the growth?"

Yes, I said, that's exactly my question.

When I got home from Echo Glen, I opened the chapbook Maryanne had given me. She had six poems in it. The third was titled, "What Does Nighttime Mean to Me?" It was the prompt I'd given her years before, during our first prison visit, when she'd been unable to recall a single happy memory.

Nighttime is when you can lose yourself & be yourself,

Nighttime is really just knowing I made it through the day & there's a new one coming soon.

AFTERWORD

If this book were a work of fiction, these final pages would tie up loose threads and resolve the many complex issues raised by the lives of Maryanne, Art, Sixto, Monique, Jay, and Tina. Instead, because they are real people, their stories finish in freeze-frame, questions still dangling that will take lifetimes to answer.

Monique was sure that moving out of her apartment in North Houston would be the boost she needed. Though living on her own had been a relief after all the years surrounded by other people in shelters and group homes, security at the Villa Springs development was spotty, and the place was crawling with roaches. They were in her couch, on her clothes. "They're even in my router!" Monique cried. She had been trying find a new home for three years, almost from the moment we'd met. But without a steady job or prior landlord references, it seemed nearly impossible.

On May 14, 2023, I got a text from her. *Happy mother day.*

Throughout our correspondence, whether she was regularly in touch or not, Monique always sent good wishes on Mother's Day. I gave her a call.

"Thanks for the text, are you in DC?"

The last time we'd spoken, Monique had told me about her latest gig as a youth ambassador for a national foster care conference.

"Oh, no, they let me go. It's cool, I'm used to it."

The reason, in her telling, was that she'd missed a preparation meeting held on Zoom. But she sounded disenchanted with foster care advocacy in general.

"It wasn't really working for me," Monique said.

Speaking at conferences was great because it paid $25 an hour, but she never got enough hours to keep herself afloat. She was waiting to hear about an internship with a Texas congresswoman, though she did not sound confident.

Monique had, however, found a way out of Villa Springs. She was moving to a new apartment with a boyfriend she'd met online. To get the keys, they needed $1,800, and Monique was selling everything she could. She tended to shrug off guidance from outsiders, hearing it as unhelpful criticism, so I tried to keep my questions non-challenging.

The main thing we discussed was what I'd discovered about the man she'd accused of molesting her when she was five. At the time, Monique's mother had called her a liar. No one in her family supported her claims. But I told Monique that someone of that man's age, with his unusual name, in his home state of Louisiana, had been indicted for child rape in 2021.

She let out a sigh.

"That makes me feel better, because you know, everyone said I was lying, and I started to wonder, did I misunderstand something? Overreact?"

Her doubts had been reactivated because the man was reaching out to her on social media, all friendly. She blocked him. She was moving away from the nasty roach apartment, and she was ready to start fresh, resolute as a dandelion poking through a crack in the sidewalk.

***

Tina was doing the same. After leaving the Chelsea Foyer in a whirlwind of complaints and accusations in the fall of 2022, Tina was referred to what she'd thought was another transitional-living program. It turned out to be a shelter in Brooklyn. The place had no storage bigger than a two-foot cubbyhole. What was she supposed to do with her six shopping bags full of stuff, all the blankets and dishes and clothes she'd accumulated through a year of attempted independence? At the shelter, thirty-eight women shared four bathrooms. They had to abide by a curfew, and the managers demanded that residents show their work schedules as proof of employment. *Whatthefuck*, thought Tina. *Do I always need someone in my business?*

Exhausted after carting her belongings across two boroughs to get there, Tina collapsed onto her narrow cot. But sometime in the night her eyes fluttered open. She'd sensed a change in the darkness, just like on the subway when she could feel people watching her in sleep. Tina sat up and scanned the room. Sure enough, a staffer was peeking in for bed checks—what was she, a little kid? Tina snapped on the light and grabbed her phone, scrolling for friends who might let her stay. "They checked my room!" she shouted to anyone who picked up. Within twenty-four hours she'd contacted a woman she met at a music festival. Tina could crash at her place in New Jersey, the woman said.

Their friendship disintegrated in weeks. By Christmastime, Tina was back at her mother's house in Ohio. All the old patterns continued— the screaming, the blame, the treadmill of fighting and never progressing. But Tina found a quiet apartment on the second floor of a modest single-family home an hour away, which she decorated with holiday lights. It was the first place she'd ever lived as an adult without a case manager down the hall. The rent was $600, manageable with her latest gig as a home-care aide. And the job brought out Tina's gentler side. After she'd washed their dishes and dispensed medication, Tina's elderly clients sometimes offered a little extra cash if she'd do their hair. Finally, Tina thought, she could bank some real money.

Her main goal was to save up enough for a car so she wouldn't have to keep borrowing her mother's van. She also vowed to work on her anger problems, avoiding people who upset her instead of attacking them and vanishing in a dust cloud of fury. Still, she bristled at everything—friends who'd let her down, managers who showed disrespect— pressing on wounds that never healed because, invariably, Tina wound up back in her mom's orbit.

One vestige of her old fight-or-flight ways was Tina's trail of disconnected cell numbers. Where adults in the straight world hang onto one set of digits for decades, through every kind of life change or upheaval,

Tina shed phone numbers like dead skin. She hated anything that tied her to the past.

"I did it!!!" she texted me in May 2023, with two happy face emojis above a white BMW. She'd purchased it used, and it needed repairs immediately. But Tina's new boyfriend was good with cars. By January of 2024, they had left Ohio and moved to Florida. What prompted her to go? Restlessness, wanting to start over. And one more fight with her mom, who hit her in the face on Thanksgiving. Tina framed that moment as a triumph because she didn't hit back.

***

Through all the years I worked on this book, I wondered at the relative quiet around Judge Gray's overhaul of foster care in New Orleans, the way she'd stemmed the tide of children flowing into the system, only to have her achievement met with tight silence. But in 2024, four years after she'd left the bench, a dozen attorneys filed a class action suit against the Louisiana Department of Children and Family Services that read like an aria of endorsement for Judge Gray's work shielding kids from foster care. Even the state's child welfare chief is quoted in it describing his agency as in "a death spiral."

Brought on behalf of nine foster children, the ninety-four-page complaint presents a parade of traumas told in vignette: Louisiana foster children were sleeping in hotels, hospitals, and DCFS offices. They often went weeks, if not months, without education. An investigation by the New Orleans *Advocate* found that they died in care at rates 50 percent higher than the national average.

But read another way, the suit is a chronicle of unconscionable passivity, even dereliction of duty. It tells of overburdened CPS investigators declining to take kids into care, leaving children with parents who eventually killed them. One child, a two-year-old boy, was found dead in a garbage can. Neighbors had repeatedly called authorities, alarmed by his screams.

Washington had similar problems. Determined to shrink foster care, the state had raised the bar for child removals. In the first few months afterward, eleven kids died at home.

"It's an unsolvable problem—mathematically impossible," a statistician with the federal Children's Bureau told me. No matter which direction child welfare leaned, kids were going to be harmed. After twenty years of viewing them as datapoints, the statistician was quitting—as a man in his fifties—to become a social worker and try to help.

***

The solution to foster care seemed an embodiment of the phrase *simple, not easy.* Simply provide families with stable housing, food, and medical care. That would surely cut thousands of children from the rolls who are taken away because they are hungry, cold, or homeless. It would narrow the focus of child welfare to that small subset of kids who are being outright abused. Sixto Cancel and I discussed this one afternoon in Seattle, when I asked him if he thought foster care should be abolished.

He cocked his head to the side. Abolitionists might not want to acknowledge the reality, he said, but some children will never be able to live safely at home. Sixto's preferred response was kinship care—at scale. Had he been placed with his aunt as a boy, Sixto would have grown up in an enormous extended family, rather than believing no one cared anything about him. That approach is gaining traction. In 2023, more than a third of children in foster placements were living with kin. Due in part to Sixto's advocacy, Congress passed legislation making it easier for relatives to get the kind of financial support traditionally given to strangers.

The same year, a consortium of philanthropists endorsed Sixto's vision for changing child welfare by naming Think of Us a recipient of the $47 million Audacious Prize. The five-year grant was among the largest investments ever made in a leader of color from the child welfare system.

***

Around the same time, Jay Perez-Torres was putting the final touches on his PhD, and teaching classes on criminology, victimology, and penology. He'd also won a prestigious fellowship, been recommended for further studies at Harvard University, and flown to Wales for an international conference on internet extremism. But Jay still lived in the same New York City Housing Authority apartment his defense lawyer had signed him up for at sixteen.

When he began studying criminal justice, Jay avoided anything that reminded him of those days, the wandering and fear that characterized his youth in foster care and subsequent attraction to gang life. He most certainly did not want to focus on the juvenile legal system. But in researching political extremism, Jay could not miss the parallels between terrorist groups and street gangs. Neither could he ignore certain experiences common to young people who gravitate toward these brotherhoods, and the reasons he'd been drawn to the study of organized violence in the first place. No one truly outruns their past.

Certainly not Art Longworth or Maryanne Atkins.

During his thirty-seven years in prison, Longworth had been an early riser, waking at 5 A.M. to write while his tier was quiet. He maintained the habit as a free man, though now, instead of pacing his five-by-seven cell, he walked the forty acres of Vera Kloskie's old homestead, Singing Heart Ranch. Longworth bought it while still in prison with money from the settlement he'd won against Washington state foster care.

Through the case, Longworth discovered that he'd been one among dozens of boys who'd endured the same sanctioned beatings and rapes at Kiwanis Vocational Home that drove him to flee with his blood brothers in 1980. Their escape had changed nothing. By the 1990s, daily brutalities at group homes owned by the Kiwanis had warped the lives of some forty plaintiffs. Many of them, now grown men, were in prison. Others were technically free but so broken and addicted they had to ask their lawyers for loans against future settlements so they could eat.

In the misty mornings, Longworth hiked Singing Heart's fields and forests, tracing its creeks and trees as he'd done in the woods behind his childhood home. He thought about turning the place into a haven for kids leaving foster care with nowhere to go. He wondered what Vera would think of that. He imagined her ghost watching him while he walked her rugged land—approvingly, he hoped.

Despite his settlement money, Longworth's reentry into what he called "the free world" was not smooth. His new neighbors quickly discovered Longworth's history (Google was a revelation to him), and they did not make him welcome. For all the many supporters he'd attracted as an inmate, once free Longworth felt ostracized, outcast. Years spent learning Spanish and Chinese and Buddhism behind bars had taught him nothing about the realities of property taxes or fear of people like himself. He was perplexed by family holidays and irritated by Hollywood fairy tales about prison like *The Shawshank Redemption*. For several months, he also had no job.

Ross Hunter, the politician leading Washington's child welfare agency, had assured the judge who freed Longworth that he would be employed by the state to help fix foster care. But the secretary was unable to make good. He took Longworth to lunch at a linen-tablecloth restaurant, explained the different forks and the multicourse menu. He arranged interviews over Zoom to talk about possible roles Longworth might fill. None of it went anywhere.

After eight weeks without work, Longworth, in a panic, called Dawn Rains, the advocate who'd spoken at his resentencing and described, link by link, the chain leading from foster care to juvenile detention to prison. He asked Rains if she might be able to put his experience to use as state officials had not. Within a week she'd hired him as a policy advisor on education for foster kids, particularly those who were incarcerated, like Maryanne Atkins.

Longworth plunged in with the energy of a bottle rocket uncorked. He phoned bureaucrats he'd once reviled, his voice trembling with urgency. He grilled legislators about the lack of schooling for foster kids behind bars and shook hands with the governor. At night, he lay awake and dreamed up new strategies for navigating the halls of government. *Life is good*, Longworth kept reminding himself, *life is beautiful*. He'd say it out loud, like a mantra.

He'd learned about Maryanne through me and became riveted on her case. It was like a do-over of his own. For months, he phoned lawyers, urging them to pursue a clemency plea on her behalf before the state drove Maryanne from Echo Glen back to the women's prison. The idea of her swallowed into that maw made him sick.

***

Maryanne, meanwhile, tried to ignore her looming fate and focus on education. One June afternoon she met me in front of Echo Glen's gymnasium, a bouquet of flowers in her hand. It was graduation day from cosmetology school.

This was the first time I'd ever seen her in clothes that could be called feminine. Maryanne wore a pink, bare-shouldered sheath dress and white platform sandals. Her cheeks were rouged, hair cut to chin length and elaborately braided. She was beaming.

Chairs for about fifty people were arranged facing a small podium. On one of them sat Percy Levy, from Longworth's State-Raised Working Group at the Washington Reformatory. He'd been released during the pandemic and reconnected with his old friend, as had Faraji from the State-Raised group, who also showed up for Maryanne's big moment. They made a motley crew—Longworth, arriving on a motorcycle he'd purchased the day before; Percy, who'd been incarcerated at Echo Glen as a kid and still whirled around every few minutes, anticipating punishment; and Faraji, an easygoing charmer who never removed his sunglasses—all there to support a girl they viewed as a sister because she'd grown up in foster care.

They were a far more reliable presence than Maryanne's biological family. As at her sentencing, no kin showed up. Nor did any of Maryanne's old social workers and advocates. But the investigator on her legal team had become a friend. She sat in the front row with her two toddler daughters, one of whom climbed onto Maryanne's lap during the ceremony.

"I'm grateful," Maryanne said, standing to accept an award for aptitude and using a word I'd never expected to hear when we sat across from one another in prison. Grateful to be fed, safe, and standing in new clothes. Grateful for the chance to learn a skill, and to know there were people around her who cared.

From their folding chairs in the audience, Percy, Faraji, and Longworth stood up and cheered.

***

Six months later, a room full of legislators and lobbyists at the Washington State Capitol in Olympia turned their attention toward Maryanne. She was in her usual gray t-shirt, speaking to them through a Zoom screen.

"My name is Maryanne Atkins. I just turned twenty-four years old and am currently incarcerated at the Echo Glen JR facility." The hearing had been convened by Representative Roger Goodman, a Seattle-area Democrat, to air ideas about a proposed law addressing a hole in the one that had brought Maryanne to Echo Glen. Under the current version, she would be sent back to prison for the last eleven years of her sentence with no chance to show anyone how she'd changed during the time at Echo. She read from a page of typed remarks, ticking off her life as a teenager—solitary confinement in jail, fighting in prison, and more solitary confinement as punishment. "Jail staff said it was for my protection because I was a juvenile, but it didn't feel like I was being protected, nor did it feel like they treated me as a juvenile," she said. Being in prison had been surprisingly similar to living on the streets as a foster kid, Maryanne observed. "You can't trust anybody, you're always looking over your shoulder, and you have to break rules and the law in order to survive." During her twelve months at the Washington Corrections Center for Women, Maryanne had racked up more than twenty infractions. At the Echo Glen Children's Center, she had none.

This was the whole point of the Juvenile Rehabilitation to 25 law—rehabilitation—yet it provided no forum for demonstrating that growth, no review to measure or reward it, no mechanism to determine whether prison was still a sensible punishment. In that sense, Maryanne suggested, the stated aims of JR to 25 rang a little hollow.

"We should be held accountable for the crimes we have committed—I get that. Every day I remember what my actions caused, and I am deeply remorseful," she hastened to add. But adult prison was not about rehabilitation. "The only thing you learn is how to do time."

Maryanne concluded by foreshadowing exactly what I'd feared, that the necessity of reverting to "survival mode" in prison could undo all the hard-won change—the willingness to be introspective, to show emotion, and admit fault. All she wanted was a review before returning automatically. "Please grant me the opportunity to not go back," she said. "Thank you for hearing me."

The last time I'd seen Maryanne speak to officials with power over her life had been five years earlier, at her sentencing, when she was a sobbing, red-faced teenager with no experience beyond abuse, neglect, foster care, and the streets. Raw emotion had been her only voice. Now Maryanne spoke thoughtfully. She made an argument. She fought for herself—with words.

An attorney from the Seattle Clemency Project drove out to Echo Glen to meet her a few months later. Jennifer Smith had seen Maryanne's testimony at the state capitol. She'd also received a blizzard of emails from Art Longworth urging Smith's group to represent Maryanne before the Clemency & Pardons Board, which ultimately had the ear of the governor. Smith was leery. She did not want to dangle false hope.

Yet the change in Maryanne exemplified the very reasons Smith had cofounded the clemency group. Most intriguing of all, this transformation appeared to be due entirely to the change in her environment. In light of what this implied—that a near-feral life on the street had been the foundation of Maryanne's behavior—Smith could not help wondering about the fairness of her punishment. After all, she'd been a ward of Washington state the entire time.

Smith would wait a long time to resolve the question of Maryanne Atkins. It took six months for a pro bono lawyer to accept Maryanne's case. By then, Maryanne had grown so impatient with hoping for the chance of a reprieve that she gave up and requested an early transfer back to prison. Waiting for adults to make decisions about her had framed Maryanne's entire life, and she was done with it. What was the point of sitting around Echo Glen with a bunch of teenagers when you were twenty-four years old? She told Jeanette that she was ready to go back to prison four months early, before her twenty-fifth birthday deadline. She would navigate the next twist in her case from a cell at the Washington Corrections Center for Women.

In August of 2024, we met at Echo Glen for the last time. Maryanne had packed up her room, pulling the artwork and photos off her walls. "I'm ready to go," she said. She had steeled herself.

It would be easy to view this decision as a defeat, a sign of Maryanne reverting to old impulses toward self-sabotage. But in one significant way, perhaps it is not. Maryanne's short life had given her few opportunities to demonstrate agency, rather than blindly reacting to circumstance. But there was a chance to start college if she arrived in September. Instead of waiting in limbo, passively hoping some outside force would swoop in at the eleventh hour to save her, Maryanne decided to leave with a friend who was also headed to prison. They would make the move together.

A few weeks before her departure, Maryanne returned to the tattooist who'd tried to remove her old markings. This time, she wanted to add one, a rose inked over the name of her onetime prison girlfriend. It still hadn't faded. But no longer would Maryanne be anyone's property. She was preparing for what faced her, taking care of herself the best way she knew how.

The evolution of Maryanne Atkins seemed to confirm all that I'd learned about the power of human attachment, and how the lack of it could stunt a child like a plant denied sunlight. For me, this had always been the most difficult aspect of her case, and Art Longworth's. I could never forget the people they'd obliterated, the families they'd destroyed. Legally, the fault was theirs. Yet, I was certain that if Art and Maryanne's youth in foster care had been different, Cindy Nelson and

Emmanuel Gondo would be alive today. Even Judge Ferguson alluded to a faceless entity that would never answer for the role it had played in "the enormous tragedy" of Maryanne's case. The state had forced her and Longworth and every other incarcerated foster child to account for their crimes. Would it ever do the same of its own?

ACKNOWLEDGMENTS

Every person in this book agreed to talk to me for one of two reasons, or both: They wanted to be seen, to be understood. And they wanted to change foster care. That self-interest does not minimize their generosity. To the contrary, Maryanne Atkins talked about other kids in the system the first time we met at the King County Jail. It was the main thing on her mind.

But there is risk in speaking to a writer, someone who will take your experiences and transcribe them in her own words. Seeing the most painful and confusing periods of one's life boiled down to something strangers will read is no small thing. So, to Maryanne Atkins, Arthur Longworth, Sixto Cancel, Jay Perez-Torres, and Keedy Bradley, as well as the young women I call Tina and Monique, my profound gratitude for your trust. You have done something important and brave. You were also astute editors, suggesting clarifications that made this book better.

A word of extra thanks to retired Judge Ernestine Gray, who did not seek attention from a journalist, but patiently explained the thinking behind her controversial approach to foster care. However one views her work, Judge Gray has forced a much-needed confrontation with the system.

The caseworkers, prosecutors, defense attorneys, policy analysts, and parents—both foster and biological—who spoke with me on background also deserve note. Many of them appear in this book under pseudonyms to protect their jobs. Several warrant explicit acknowledgement: The women named here as Tasha Smith and Jeanette Stephens did more than help me unravel the riddle of Maryanne—they deepened my understanding of what it means to be a parent, of any kind. Additional gratitude to: Mary Dozier, the developmental psychologist who taught me about the science of attachment; Jennifer Rodriguez and Carole Schauffer, who explained how it underpins their important reforms for recruiting and coaching foster parents; Anna Bennett, the student advocate; Adam Cornell, the foster-child-turned-prosecutor who was willing to describe some of his worst memories; Ross Hunter, secretary of Washington's Department of Children, Youth and Families, who took my innumerable calls and texts; Casey Trupin, of the Raikes Foundation, who co-represented Arthur Longworth during his resentencing and has deepened my understanding of youth homelessness; his father, Dr. Eric Trupin, who nudged my understanding of adolescent psychology; Tim Farris, the crusading lawyer who spent more than six years fighting for Washington's foster kids; and Dr. Kenneth Muscatel, who was my entry into Maryanne's case.

Twenty years ago, when I sensed this book but could not yet speak it, a well-known author told me that it takes only two people to make a book real. She meant an agent and editor who believe in the writer's vision. For *Wards of the State*, that acknowledgment is due to three people: my brilliant agent, Stephanie Rostan; Abrams's incisive and keen-eyed editorial director Jamison Stoltz; and Sarah Robbins, a young editor who recognized the importance of this story when it was merely a book proposal in a pile of other proposals and plucked it out.

I also want to hail the writer friends who have been my sounding board as I circled this project and generously read the hundreds of pages I generated before arriving at these final 244: Laura Coffey, Jennie Shortridge, Carol Smith, and Mike Lewis.

Seattle Times publisher Frank Blethen and editorial page editor Kate Riley deserve special recognition for hiring me on to the newspaper's editorial board and giving me the space to write about foster care and juvenile justice—two topics that do little to goose subscriptions—then allowing me time away to work on a book about them.

Finally, to Dan, Maiselle, Gabe, Nina, Glenn, and Ezra, who have taught me the true power of family. And lastly, to my late parents, Joyce and Gerald Rowe, who did not live to see this book published but were, in so many ways, its genesis.

NOTES

Introduction

1 **half a million kids:** "Trends in Foster Care and Adoption: FY 2005–FY 2014," U.S. Department of Health and Human Services, Administration for Children and Families, Administration on Children, Youth and Families, Children's Bureau. https://www.acf.hhs.gov/sites/default/files/documents/cb/trends_fostercare_adoption2014.pdf.

2 **to the tune of $31.4 billion a year:** Kristina Rosinsky, Megan Fischer, and Maggie Haas, "Child Welfare Financing SFY 2020: A Survey of Federal, State, and Local Expenditures," ChildTrends. https://cms.childtrends.org/wp-content/uploads/2023/04/ChildWelfareFinancingReport_ChildTrends_May2023.pdf.

40 percent of children under state guardianship are adolescents: "The AFCARS Report: Preliminary FY 2021 Estimates as of June 28, 2022 - No. 29," U.S. Department of Health and Human Services, Administration for Children and Families, Administration on Children, Youth and Families, Children's Bureau. https://www.acf.hhs.gov/sites/default/files/documents/cb/afcars-report-29.pdf.

thirty-five minutes in a shoot-out with police: Frances Robles, "How Two Middle School 'Desperados' Ended Up in a Police Shoot-Out." *New York Times*, May 12, 2022. https://www.nytimes.com/2022/05/12/us/middle-school-shootout-police.html.

a boy from the same group home had been convicted of manslaughter: "12- and 14-Year-Old Open Fire on Deputies After Breaking into Home; 1 Shooter Is Shot and Wounded," Volusia Sheriff, June 02, 2021. https://www.volusiasheriff.gov/news/volusia-county-sheriff/12-and-14-year-old-open-fire-on-deputies-after-breaking-into-home-1-shooter-is-shot-and-wounded.stml#.

swinging a knife: "An Ohio police officer was cleared in the shooting of teenager Ma'Khia Bryant," Associated Press, March 12, 2022. https://www.npr.org/2022/03/12/1086283433/police-officer-cleared-makhia-bryant-shooting.

3 **half left the system:** Mark E. Courtney, Sherri Terao, and Noel Bost, "Midwest Evaluation of the Adult Functioning of Former Foster Youth: Conditions of Youth Preparing to Leave State Care," Chapin Hall Center for Children at the University of Chicago, Feb. 22, 2004, p. 49. https://www.chapinhall.org/wp-content/uploads/Midwest-Study-Youth-Preparing-to-Leave-Care.pdf.

more than 30 percent were imprisoned for violent crime: Mark E. Courtney, Amy Dworsky, Gretchen Ruth, Tom Keller, June Havlicek, and Noel Bost, "Midwest Evaluation of the Adult Functioning of Former Foster Youth: Outcomes at Age 19," Chapin Hall Center for Children at the University of Chicago, May 2005, p. 61. https://www.chapinhall.org/wp-content/uploads/Courtney_Midwest-Evaluation-Adult-Functioning_Report_2005.pdf.

straight into homelessness: Melissa Ford Shah, Qinghua Liu, David Mancuso, David Marshall, Barbara E. M. Felver, Barbara Lucenko, and Alice Huber, "Youth at Risk of Homelessness: Identifying Key Predictive Factors Among Youth Aging Out of Foster

Care in Washington State," Report to the DSHS Children's Administration, January 2015. https://www.dshs.wa.gov/sites/default/files/rda/reports/research-7-106.pdf. Housing & Homelessness, National Foster Youth Institute. https://nfyi.org/issues /homelessness/.

3   **twice the rate of Iraq War veterans:** "Assessing the Effects of Foster Care: Mental Health Outcomes from the Casey National Alumni Study," Casey Family Programs. https:// www.casey.org/media/AlumniStudy_US_Report_MentalHealth.pdf.

"IMPROVING FAMILY FOSTER CARE: Findings from the Northwest Foster Care Alumni Study," Casey Family Programs. https://www.casey.org/media/AlumniStudies _NW_Report_FR.pdf.

more than half were living in poverty: Mark E. Courtney, Amy Dworsky, Adam Brown, Colleen Cary, Kara Love, and Vanessa Vorhies, "Midwest Evaluation of Adult functioning of Former Foster Youth: Outcomes at Age 26," Chapin Hall at the University of Chicago, 2011, p. 113. https://www.chapinhall.org/wp-content/uploads/Midwest-Eval -Outcomes-at-Age-26.pdf.

foster care causes neurological damage to children's brains: National Academies of Sciences, Engineering, and Medicine; Division of Behavioral and Social Sciences and Education; Board on Children, Youth, and Families; Committee on the Neurobiological and Socio-behavioral Science of Adolescent Development and Its Applications; E. P. Backes and R. J. Bonnie, eds., *The Promise of Adolescence: Realizing Opportunity for All Youth* (Washington, DC: National Academies Press, May 16, 2019), preface. https:// www.ncbi.nlm.nih.gov/books/NBK545480/.

Chapter 1

10   **for nearly an hour:** Seattle Police Department video and transcript of Maryanne Atkins's interview with Detective Dana Duffy, April 13, 2016.

14   **I can't be the last person who was with him:** Recording of jailhouse phone call between Maryanne Atkins and her mother.

16   **it would only "induce sympathy":** Transcript of pretrial proceedings before King County Superior Court Judge Marshall Ferguson, Nov. 29, 2018.

19   **Whenever Maryanne heard his voice:** Police report included in Maryanne Atkins case file, Washington Department of Social and Health Services.

       and hurt animals?: State's exhibit to King County Superior Court, letter and documentation provided by Mr. and Mrs. Atkins; Maryanne Atkins case file, Washington Department of Social and Health Services.

20   **"grossly different outcomes" for Black criminal suspects:** Judicial questionnaire, 31st Legislative District Democrats, Feb. 6, 2019. https://31stdistrictdemocrats.org /king-county-superior-court-judge-pos-31-judge-marshall-ferguson/.

23   **Maryanne asked to speak with a lawyer:** Seattle police routinely failed to provide detained youth with attorneys, an audit would find seven years after Maryanne Atkins's arrest. https://www.seattle.gov/documents/Departments/OIG/Audits/Youth _Access_to_Legal_Counsel_Audit.pdf.

25   **52,000 American children adopted from foster care:** "Trends in Foster Care and Adoption: FY 2010–FY 2019," U.S. Department of Health and Human Services, Administration for Children and Families, Administration on Children, Youth and Families, Children's Bureau. hhttps://www.acf.hhs.gov/sites/default/files/documents/cb/trends _fostercare_adoption_10thru19.pdf.

Chapter 2

32 **the officer blocked her path:** King County sheriff incident report 96-340483-A, included in Atkins case file with the Department of Children, Youth and Families.

33 **In West Virginia, about 12 percent:** Emily Wax-Thibodeaux, "'We are just destroying these kids': The foster children growing up inside detention centers," *Washington Post*, Dec. 30, 2019. https://www.washingtonpost.com/national/we-are-just-destroying -these-kids-the-foster-children-growing-up-inside-detention-centers/2019/12/30 /97f65f3a-eaa2-11e9-9c6d-436a0df4f31d_story.html.

In Washington state, more than 13 percent: "Missing from Care Analysis," Jan. 2019. https://www.dcyf.wa.gov/sites/default/files/pdf/reports/2019_MissingfromCare Analysis.pdf.

nearly 20 percent ran from their placements: Natasha E. Latzman, Deborah A. Gibbs, Rose Feinberg, Marianne N. Kluckman, and Sue Aboul-Hosn, "Human trafficking victimization among youth who run away from foster care," *Children and Youth Services Review* 98, March 2019, pp. 113–124. https://www.sciencedirect.com/science/article /abs/pii/S019074091830906X?via%3Dihub.

half of all foster kids report having run at least once: Natasha E. Latzman and Deborah A. Gibbs, "Examining the Link: Foster Care Runaway Episodes and Human Trafficking," Children's Bureau, Oct. 2020. https://www.acf.hhs.gov/sites/default/files /documents/opre/foster_care_runaway_human_trafficking_october_2020_508.pdf.

34 **nothing less than shocking:** Debra Boyer, PhD, "Who Pays the Price? Assessment of Youth Involvement in Prostitution in Seattle," City of Seattle Human Services Department, June 2008. https://static1.squarespace.com/static/5b71c32bec4eb7c684 a77ff4/t/5f21d74994f7832d9b15a254/1596053322562/Boyer+Who+Pays+the+Price .pdf.

35 **taken from their families in the name of safety:** Debra Boyer, PhD, "Commercially Sexually Exploited Children in Seattle/King County," StolenYouth, Nov. 2019. https://static1 .squarespace.com/static/5b71c32bec4eb7c684a77ff4/t/5dee96855704156dcb240b01 /1575917194777/Commercially+Sexually+Exploited+Children+in+King+County+201 9+Update+%28003%29.pdf.

zero in on the characteristics: Michael D. Pullman, Norene Roberts, Elizabeth M. Parker, Kelly J. Mangiaracina, Leslie Briner, Morgan Silverman, and Jeremy R. Becker, "Residential instability, running away, and juvenile detention characterizes commercially sexually exploited youth involved in Washington state's child welfare system," *Child Abuse & Neglect*, 2020. https://doi.org/10.1016/j.chiabu.2020.104423.

37 **a population it was entirely unprepared to handle:** "The foster care system was, historically, a custodial system. However, in the last twenty years, the children who have been coming into the system have been increasingly the victims of abuse, neglect, abandonment or have been harmed by prenatal or genetic injuries. As a result, the foster care system has failed to adequately transition from a system designed to provide custodial services to a system that needs to provide special services to emotionally and behaviorally disabled children." Finding of fact and conclusions of law, *Braam v. DSHS*.

37 **skyrocketed to nearly three hundred:** 2019 Annual Report, Washington State Office of the Family and Children's Ombuds. https://ofco.wa.gov/sites/default/files/2020-01 /2019_OFCO_Annual_Report_1-15-2020.pdf.

throwing off lingering memories of home life: Patrick Dowd, longtime ombuds for Washington's foster care system, focused on these "exceptional placements" in his annual report, writing: ". . . some youth become acclimated to the lifestyle and are then even harder to place, as they prefer the hotel and are no longer interested in the structure and rules of a traditional home or program. These youth have acted in a rational and adaptive manner for their circumstances, but it ultimately negatively impacts their future wellbeing."

their time in foster care will not persuade a judge: Tara Urs, "Washington's foster care system indicts itself by placing kids in hotels," Crosscut, Feb. 26, 2020. https://crosscut .com/2020/02/washingtons-foster-care-system-indicts-itself-placing-kids-hotels.

Georgia offered a $5,000 bonus: "High-needs foster kids sometimes have to sleep in hotels or offices. The pandemic made the problem worse," PBS.org, May 31, 2022. https://www.pbs.org/newshour/nation/high-needs-foster-kids-sometimes-have-to -sleep-in-hotels-or-offices-the-pandemic-made-the-problem-worse#:~:text=State%20 lawmakers%20put%20%2431.4%20million,of%20a%20hotel%20or%20office.

40   **available whenever:** Maryanne Atkins case file, Washington Department of Children, Youth and Families.

Chapter 3

44   **The country's top jailer of children:** Sarah Lippek, Starcia Ague, "The 'Becca Bill' 20 Years Later: How Washington's Truancy Laws Negatively Impact Children," Vera Institute of Justice, Dec. 15, 2015. https://modelsforchange.net/publications/842/The _Becca_Bill_20_Years_Later_How_Washingtons_Truancy_Laws_Negatively_Impact _Children.pdf.

46   **A groundbreaking lawsuit:** "Braam Lawsuit Vindicates Constitutional Rights of Foster Children in Washington State," National Center for Youth Law, Dec. 31, 2013. https:// youthlaw.org/news/braam-lawsuit-vindicates-constitutional-rights-foster-children -washington-state.

48   **That look in their eye:** Tim Farris, closing argument, Foster Care Reform Litigation.

54   **The first in a series of landmark studies:** Mark E. Courtney, Sherri Terao, and Noel Bost, "Midwest Evaluation of the Adult Functioning of Former Foster Youth: Conditions of Youth Preparing to Leave State Care," Chapin Hall Center for Children at the University of Chicago, Feb. 22, 2004, p. 49. https://www.chapinhall.org/wp-content /uploads/Midwest-Study-Youth-Preparing-to-Leave-Care.pdf.

    "Our findings call into question the wisdom of federal and state policies": Mark E. Courtney, Amy Dworsky, Gretchen Ruth, Tom Keller, June Havlicek, and Noel Bost, "Midwest Evaluation of the Adult Functioning of Former Foster Youth: Outcomes at Age 19," Chapin Hall Center for Children at the University of Chicago, May 2005, p. 49. https://www.chapinhall.org/wp-content/uploads/Courtney_Midwest-Evaluation -Adult-Functioning_Report_2005.pdf.

55   **former foster youth when they were in their mid-twenties:** Mark E. Courtney, Amy Dworsky, Adam Brown, Colleen Cary, Kara Love, and Vanessa Vorhies, "Midwest Evaluation of Adult Functioning of Former Foster Youth: Outcomes at Age 26," Chapin Hall at the University of Chicago, 2011 p. 113. https://www.chapinhall.org/wp-content /uploads/Midwest-Eval-Outcomes-at-Age-26.pdf.

55   **the first authoritative study to take a stab at it:** Joseph Doyle, "Child Protection and Adult Crime: Using investigator assignment to estimate causal effects of foster care." *Journal of Political Economy*, 2008. More recently, statisticians have disputed Doyle's cause-and-effect equation. E. Jason Baron, a professor at Duke University, analyzed 120,000 foster care investigations in Michigan with statistician Max Gross. Their paper, "Is There a Foster Care to Prison Pipeline?" was published in

2022 by the National Bureau of Economic Research. It found that foster care seemed to prevent children from involvement with crime. But it based this assertion on children who spent only a short time in the system and eventually reunited with their families.

56 **25 percent said they'd grown up as wards of the state:** Laura Bauer and Judy L. Thomas, "Throwaway Kids," *Kansas City Star*, Dec. 15, 2019. https://www.kansascity.com/news/special-reports/article238206754.html.

Put simply, foster care seemed to rewire kids' brains: *The Promise of Adolescence: Realizing Opportunity for All Youth.* National Academies of Sciences, Engineering, and Medicine, Division of Behavioral and Social Sciences and Education, 2019.

59 **The anger is your subconscious:** Arthur Longworth, "How to Kill Someone," Pen America, Nov. 21, 2017. https://pen.org/how-to-kill-someone/.

61 **did not attempt to mask its author's bewilderment:** Selections from Snohomish County Public Defender Association pretrial document used in charging negotiations. April 8, 1985.

67 **informally emancipated himself:** Hal E. Sheets, Snohomish County Public Defender Association pre-trial charging negotiations. April 8, 1985.

70 **millions of dollars funneled toward reform:** Zach Strassburger, "Crafting Complaints and Settlements in Child Welfare Litigation," *Penn Journal of Law and Social Change*, 2018. https://scholarship.law.upenn.edu/cgi/viewcontent.cgi?article=1223&context=jlasc.

74 **after his mother abandoned him:** Katherine Beckett, "About Time: How Long and Life Sentences Fuel Mass Incarceration in Washington State," Report for the ACLU of Washington, February 2020. https://lsj.washington.edu/sites/lsj/files/documents/research/05-07-20_formatted_aclu_report.pdf.

Chapter 4

78 **"idle and vicious":** Semi-Annual Report of the Chief of Police, May 1 to Oct., 31, 1849, cited in "Embryo Courtezans and Felons": New York Police Chief George W. Matsell Describes the City's Vagrant and Delinquent Children. https://historymatters.gmu.edu/d/6526/.

The Dangerous Classes of New York: Dan Scheuerman, "Lost Children: Riders on the Orphan Train," *Humanities* 28:6 (November/December 2007). https://web.archive.org/web/20180709025306/https://www.neh.gov/humanities/2007/novemberdecember/feature/lost-children-riders-the-orphan-train.

"all the ills that dirty flesh is heir to": "The Children's Aid Society: The Newsboys' Lodging Room—Its Occupants—a Speech from Paddy—A Few Stern Facts," *New York Times*, Dec. 1860. https://www.nytimes.com/1860/12/22/archives/the-childrens-aid-society-the-newsboys-lodging-roomits-occupantsa.html.

79 **a notice in one Nebraska newspaper:** Andrea Warren, *Orphan Train Rider: One Boy's True Story* (Houghton Mifflin, 1996). Excerpted in the *Washington Post*. https://www.washingtonpost.com/wp-srv/national/horizon/nov98/orphan.htm.

80 **recite a poem or a little ditty:** Scheuerman, "Lost Children."

81 **"The next thing I knew it was morning":** "Lee Nailing," National Orphan Train Complex. https://orphantraindepot.org/history/orphan-train-rider-stories/lee-nailling/.

83 **spent the next few years wandering the west:** Dennis Nicholls, "Singing Hearts on Bear Paw Creek," *River Journal*, Feb. 23, 1999.

the Home-Finding Department: Stephen O'Connor, *Orphan Trains: The Story of Charles Loring Brace and the Children He Saved and Failed* (Houghton Mifflin, 2001), excerpted in the *New York Times*. https://archive.nytimes.com/www.nytimes.com/books/first/o/oconnor-01orphan.html.

"creditable members of society": "Trains Ferried Waifs to New Lives on the Prairie," *Florida Sun-Sentinel*, Sept. 28, 1989.

Blond and blue-eyed: Joan Jacobs Brumberg, *Kansas Charley: The Boy Murderer* (New York: Penguin Books, 2003).

86   **She was wholly untaught, knew nothing of right and wrong:** "Sallie A. Watkins, "The Mary Ellen Myth: Correcting child welfare history," *Social Work*, 35:6 (1990), pp. 500–503. http://www.americanhumane.org/about-us/who-we-are/history/mary-ellen-wilson.html.

National Prison Reform Congress: Rebecca S. Trammell, "Orphan Train Myths and Legal Reality," *Modern American* 5:2 (2009). https://digitalcommons.wcl.american.edu/cgi/viewcontent.cgi?article=1023&context=tma.

87   **"utterly lacking in moral responsibility":** Kerry Drake, "Wyoming once executed a 17-year-old boy. What would be his fate today?" Wyofile, Jan. 2022. https://wyofile.com/wyo-once-executed-a-17-year-old-boy-what-would-be-his-fate-today/.

88   **"grow so rankly, or bear fruit so quickly":** G. Stanley Hall, *Adolescence: Its Psychology and its Relations to Physiology, Anthropology, Sociology, Sex, Crime, Religion and Education* (D. Appleton and Company, 1904).

89   **Nearly sixty examples of juvenile execution:** Victor L. Streib, "Death Penalty for Children: The American Experience with Capital Punishment for Crimes Committed While under Age Eighteen," *Oklahoma Law Review* 36 (1983), p. 630. https://digitalcommons.law.ou.edu/cgi/viewcontent.cgi?article=2117&context=olr.

90   **all earned under $40,000 a year:** Ji Young Kang, Jennifer Romich, Jennifer L. Hook, JoAnn Lee, and Maureen Marcenko, "Family Earnings and Transfer Income among Families Involved with Child Welfare," *Child Welfare* 97:1 (2019). https://partnersforourchildren.org/sites/default/files/2009._part_iv_baseline_parent_survey_analysis.pdf.

91   **"irreparable harm" to the "architecture" of developing brains:** Statement from the American Academy of Pediatrics Opposing Separation of Children and Parents at the Border, May 2018. https://www.aap.org/en/news-room/news-releases/aap/2018/aap-statement-opposing-separation-of-children-and-parents-at-the-border/.

consequences would extend far beyond politics: William Wan, "What Separation from Parents Does to Children," *Washington Post*, June 18, 2018.

referral to the courts for "child neglect": Linda Gordon and Felice Batlan, "Aid to Dependent Children: The Legal History," Social Welfare History Project, Virginia Commonwealth University, 2011. https://socialwelfare.library.vcu.edu/public-welfare/aid-to-dependent-children-the-legal-history/.

Laura Briggs, *Taking Children: A History of American Terror* (University of California Press, 2021).

92   **Exposed to the same environment:** "Family Assistance Plan: Hearing Before the Subcommittee on Appropriations," House of Representatives, 1961.

From providing services to intact white families: Dorothy Roberts, *Torn Apart: How the Child Welfare System Destroys Black Families—and How Abolition Can Build a Safer World* (Basic Books, 2022).

Afterward, foster care was transformed: C. Lawrence-Webb, "African American Children in the Modern Child Welfare System: A Legacy of the Flemming Rule," in *Child Welfare* (Jan–Feb 1997).

W. Robert Johnston, "Historical statistics on adoption in the United States, plus statistics on child population and welfare," Aug. 2017. https://www.johnstonsarchive.net /policy/adoptionstats.html.

more than a third of U.S. kids: Roberts, p. 37.

"Child Maltreatment 2022," annual report prepared by the Administration for Children and Families children's Bureau. https://www.acf.hhs.gov/sites/default/files /documents/cb/cm2022.pdf.

53 percent of all Black youth: Hyunil Kim, Christopher Wilderman, Melissa Jonson-Reid, and Brett Drake, "Lifetime Prevalence of Investigating Child Maltreatment Among U.S. Children." *American Journal of Public Health*, Feb. 2017. https://www.ncbi.nlm.nih.gov /pmc/articles/PMC5227926/.

Chapter 5

93 **she began to speak her feelings out loud:** Sixto Cancel, "My Only Way Out," May 2014. https://www.childrensrights.org/my-only-way-out/.

96 **more than 66,000 children were given back:** Marisa Kwiatkowski and Aleszu Bajak, "'I don't feel worthy': The intimate impact of broken adoptions in the U.S.," *USA Today*, May 19, 2022. https://www.usatoday.com/in depth/news/investigations /2022/05/19/impact-of-failed-adoption-former-adoptee-child-welfare-advocate /9727432002/?gps-source=BRNMSVCPSPXXADOPT&itm_source=usat&itm _medium=onsite-spike&itm_campaign=brokenadoptions-storytellingstudio-n&itm _content=static.

up to 25 percent of prospective adoptions fall apart: Dawn J. Post and Brian Zimmerman, "The revolving doors of family court: confronting broken adoptions." *Capital University Law Review*, 2012. https://www.clcny.org/files/118689205.pdf.

a direct contributor to the explosive rage: Developmental assessment of Maryanne Atkins by Marty Beyer, PhD, included in court exhibits.

100 **No handbags, or scarves:** Lateef Mungin, "All-male college cracks down on crossdressing," CNN, 2009. https://www.cnn.com/2009/US/10/17/college.dress.code/ ?iref=nextin#:~:text=No%20dress%2Dwearing%20is%20part,and%20walking%20 barefoot%20on%20campus.

Scott Jaschik, "What the Morehouse Man Wears," *Inside Higher Ed*, Oct. 18, 2009. https://www.insidehighered.com/news/2009/10/19/what-morehouse-man-wears.

104 **undereducated sixteen-to-twenty-four-year-olds:** "Prevalence," Youth.gov. https://youth .gov/youth-topics/opportunity-youth/prevalence.

funding from a half-dozen philanthropies: Lisa Martine Jenkins, "The Former Foster Youth Behind the White House's Foster Care Hackathon," *Imprint*, May 25, 2016. https://imprintnews.org/news-2/youth-led-nonprofit-challenges-tech-child-welfare -work-together/18309.

106 **interviewing more than two hundred former foster kids:** Sixto Cancel et al., "Aged Out: How We're Failing Youth Transitioning Out of Foster Care," Think of Us. https://www .thinkofus.org/aged-out.

Chapter 6

113 **"did not want to get involved in this situation":** P. 547 from a case file of more than 5,000 pages.

"long-term prognosis hinges": P. 1,112 of "Monique's" case file.

suspected sexual abuse: "Child Maltreatment 2001," a report of the U.S. Children's Bureau, indicates that 9.6 percent of children taken into care that year had been sexually abused. The bureau's Adoption and Foster Care Analysis Reporting System (AFCARS) indicates that 296,000 children entered foster care that year. https://www .acf.hhs.gov/sites/default/files/documents/cb/cm01.pdf and https://www.acf.hhs.gov /sites/default/files/documents/cb/afcarsreport12.pdf.

victims of neglect: "12 Years of Reporting Child Maltreatment 2001," U.S. Department of Health & Human Services, Administration for Children and Families, Administration on Children, Youth and Families, Children's Bureau. https://www.acf.hhs.gov /sites/default/files/documents/cb/cm01.pdf.

neglect underlies fully 74 percent of foster care cases: "Child Maltreatment 2022," U.S. Department of Health & Human Services, Administration for Children and Families, Administration on Children, Youth and Families, Children's Bureau. https://www.acf .hhs.gov/sites/default/files/documents/cb/cm2022.pdf.

114 ten times more on foster care payments to strangers: Roberts, p. 142.

117 the majority quit within two years: "Foster Care Worker demographics and statistics in the U.S.," Zippia. https://www.zippia.com/foster-care-worker-jobs/demographics/#.

nearly a third of the young people being raised in group homes: Sarah Fathallah and Sarah Sullivan, "Away from Home: Youth Experiences of Institutional Placements in Foster Care," Think of Us, July 2021. https://www.thinkofus.org/case-studies /away-from-home.

below average in cognitive development: Marinus H. van IJzendoorn et al., "Institutionalisation and deinstitutionalisation of children: a systematic and integrative review of evidence regarding effects on development," Lancet, June 23, 2020. https://www .thelancet.com/journals/lanpsy/article/PIIS2215-0366(19)30399-2/abstract.

123 "understanding or following directions": Case file, p. 2,446.

Chapter 7

136 "maintaining a relationship seems impossible for her": Atkins letter to Tolt Middle School, March 2014, included in State Exhibit 1.

142 "Adversity affected a very basic biological function": Mary Dozier and Kristin Bernard, *Coaching Parents of Vulnerable Infants: The Attachment and Biobehavioral Catch-Up Approach* (Guilford Press, 2019).

143 suicidal ideation increases by 68 percent: Roberts, pp. 235–236.

A child in Florida moved more than fifty times: Christopher O'Donnell and Nathaniel Lash, "Nowhere to call home: Thousands of foster children move so much they risk psychological harm," *Tampa Bay Times*, Dec. 26, 2018.

many of them in group homes: "New Federal Civil Rights Settlement Agreement Promises to Transform Broken Foster Care System and End Years of Victimization and Trauma for Kansas Children," National Center for Youth Law, July 8, 2020. https://youthlaw.org/news/new-federal-civil-rights-settlement-agreement-promises -transform-broken-foster-care-system-and.

Chapter 8

152 the voice on the other end of the line: Description of conversation in court documents seeking to remove "Tina's" robbery cases to family court.

erected in 1912 as the city morgue: "ACS Children's Center," Historical Marker Database. https://www.hmdb.org/m.asp?m=152888.

153   stored knives in their lockers: Editorial Board, "Yet another mess at ACS," *New York Post*, June 29, 2019. https://nypost.com/2019/06/29/yet-another-mess-at-acs/.

154   sometimes right in front of the Children's Center: New York Police Department report from March 31, 2020.

       "I have a knife—gimme your purse!": Robbery and assault described in court documents relevant to incident on April 19, 2020.

155   New York passed its "Raise the Age" law: "Raise the Age," Office for Justice Initiatives, New York State Unified Court System. https://ww2.nycourts.gov/ip/oji/raisetheage.shtml.

156   Handling Difficult Feelings: Description of program in CASES Court Employment Project (CEP) documents relevant to "Tina's" case.

Chapter 9

158   Congress earmarked $70 million in housing vouchers: Toni Naccarato, Megan Brophy, and Liliana Hernandez, "The Foster Youth Housing Crisis: Literature, Legislation & Looking Ahead," *Journal of Civil Rights and Economic Development* 24:2 (Fall 2008). https://scholarship.law.stjohns.edu/cgi/viewcontent.cgi?article=1039&context=jcred.

162   147,143 young people between fourteen and twenty-one: "Fostering Youth Transitions 2023: State and National Data to Drive Foster Care Advocacy," Annie E. Casey Foundation. https://assets.aecf.org/m/resourcedoc/aecf-fosteringyouth-data-2023.pdf.

164   which kinds of supportive housing worked best: Bridgette Lery, Sarah Prendergast, Annalise Loveless, and Lauren Morgan, "Supportive Housing for Young People Formerly in Foster Case: A National Scan of Programs." Urban Institute, October 2021. https://www.acf.hhs.gov/sites/default/files/documents/opre/supportive-housing-foster-oct-2021_qc.pdf.

168   "did not wish to be part of a community": Common Ground Community/Good Shepherd Services, "The Chelsea Foyer at the Christopher at Five Years: Lessons in Developing Stable Housing and Self-Sufficiency for Homeless Youth and Youth Exiting Foster Care," October 2009. https://www.issuelab.org/resources/15089/15089.pdf.

       twenty-three thousand young adults: Madelyn Freundlich, "Time for Reform: Aging Out and on Their Own," Pew Charitable Trusts. https://www.pewtrusts.org/~/media/legacy/uploadedfiles/wwwpewtrustsorg/reports/foster_care_reform/kidsarewaitingtimeforreform0307pdf.pdf.

169   The differences were striking: "Paving the Way for a More Prosperous Future for Young Adults: Results of an Outcomes Study of the Chelsea Foyer at the Christopher," April 2016. https://www.nyc.gov/assets/cidi/downloads/pdfs/foyer_brief.pdf.

170   not well suited to independent living": Common Ground Community and Good Shepherd Services, "The Chelsea Foyer at the Christopher at Five Years: Lessons in Developing Stable Housing and Self-Sufficiency for Homeless Youth and Youth Exiting Foster Care," October 2009. https://core.ac.uk/download/pdf/71361634.pdf.

Chapter 10

173   most of them left it in a matter of days: Josh Gupta-Kagan, Christopher Church, Melissa Carter, Vivek Sankaran, and Andrew Barclay. "The New Orleans Transformation: Foster Care as a Rare, Time-Limited Intervention." *Lewis & Clark Law Review* 27:2 (2023), 417–455.

175 **"No, you don't mail them a letter":** Melissa Carter, Christopher Church, and Vivek Sankaran, "A Quiet Revolution: How Judicial Discipline Essentially Eliminated Foster Care and Nearly Went Unnoticed." *Columbia Journal of Race and Law* (June 2022).

176 **Sixty percent became homeless:** Katy Rickdahl, "Meet the group of ex-Louisiana foster kids who are key players in debate around extending care." *Advocate*, Feb. 16, 2019. https://www.theadvocate.com/baton_rouge/news/article_cd6e7cb4-3185-11e9-84d3 -073002927bd6.html.

"It's medieval": Fox Butterfield, "Few Options or Safeguards in a City's Juvenile Courts," *New York Times*, July 22, 1997, https://www.nytimes.com/1997/07/22/us /few-options-or-safeguards-in-a-city-s-juvenile-courts.html.

178 **Money spent on family preservation services:** "Child Welfare Agency Spending in Louisiana in SFY 2020," ChildTrends, May 2023. https://cms.childtrends.org/wp-content /uploads/2023/05/Louisiana_SFY2020CWFS_ChildTrends_May2023.pdf.

State-by-state data shows $78 million in federal aid spent on child removal and foster care in Louisiana versus $9 million on family preservation: https://www.childtrends .org/publications/child-welfare-financing-survey-sfy2020.

family support aimed at preventing removals: "Report to Congress on State Child Welfare Expenditures," Children's Bureau 2021. https://www.acf.hhs.gov/sites/default /files/documents/cb/2021_report_to_congress_cfs101.pdf.

Nearly ten times more goes to child removal and adoption: Elizabeth Brico, "The Government Spends 10 Times More on Foster Care and Adoption Than Reuniting Families," Talk Poverty, 2019. https://talkpoverty.org/2019/08/23/government-more -foster-adoption-reuniting/index.html#:~:text=The%20federal%20government%20 spends%20almost,Needy%20Families%20(TANF)%20program.

180 **her daughter, left alone, was dead from a gunshot wound to the head:** Naomi Schaefer Riley, *No Way to Treat a Child: How the Foster Care System, Family Courts and Racial Activists Are Wrecking Young Lives* (Bombardier Books, 2021). https://nypost.com/2021 /10/09/foster-care-kids-are-at-risk-because-of-social-justice-crusaders/.

"revictimized" no more frequently: "AFCARS and the Courts: the intersection of data and practice," research of Christopher E. Church, Palmetto Family Advocacy, LLC, March 2018.

Judge Gray said in a 2009 speech: Ernestine Gray, "Judicial Viewpoints on ASFA," ABA Child Law Practice, 2009. https://isc.idaho.gov/cp/docs/Judicial%20View-points%20on%20ASFA.pdf.

184 **convincing eighty counties in ten states:** Quality Parenting Initiative, from the Youth Law Center. https://qpi4kids.org/wp-content/uploads/2022/03/QPI-Brochure -General-Information.pdf.

194 **a law requiring phone calls between foster and biological parents:** "Examination of Comfort Call Implementation," Florida Institute for Child Welfare. https://ficw.fsu .edu/Topic/WorkingWithFamilies/Project/ComfortCalls.

195 **responsible for a hundred children:** Class-action complaint filed by Robert L. Redfearn Jr. et al., April 10, 2024. https://static1.squarespace.com/static/603815c5dc93656 33e4c0830/t/6616ab4c872c8f158535b131/1712761676217/Louisiana+Complaint_4.10 .2024.pdf.

Fewer than 20 percent: Child Welfare Job Satisfaction Survey, Louisiana Department of Children and Family Services. Dec. 1, 2022. https://app.lla.state.la.us/publicreports .nsf/0/d30ce8b327892bb38625890b007621e0/$file/0000039eb.pdf?openelement& .7773098.

197 **"nothing short of revolutionary"**: Carter et al.
relinquishing children to "families in chaos": Carter et al.
"not a foster care system by any familiar standards": Carter et al.
198 **"intimately linked to the history of slavery in our country"**: Resolution of the American Bar Association Commission on Youth at Risk, August 2022.
199 **named her chair of its Judicial Division**: "Ernestine Gray named chair of ABA Judicial Division," American Bar Association, Aug. 2022. https://www.americanbar.org/news /abanews/aba-news-archives/2022/08/ernestine-gray-named-jd-chair/.
there would have been 18,211 children in care: Carter et al.

Chapter 11

200 **nine million kids across the country**: Statistics compiled by special request of the Children's Bureau, using the National Data Archive on Child Abuse & Neglect, the Adoption and Foster Care Analysis and Reporting System (AFCARS), and the Voluntary Cooperative Information System, which holds data from the years prior to 1996. The results are likely an undercount. During certain years in the 1990s, fewer than twenty states reported foster care data to the government.
"I've come to take your life": Kent Faulk, "Evan Miller, youngest person ever sentenced to life without parole in Alabama, must remain in prison," AL.com, April 27, 2021. https://www.al.com/news/2021/04/evan-miller-youngest-child-ever-sentenced-to-life -without-parole-in-alabama-must-remain-in-prison.html.
201 **America imposed the death penalty on 226 teenagers**: Victor L. Streib, "The Juvenile Death Penalty Today: Death Sentences and Executions for Juvenile Crimes, January 1, 1973–February 28, 2005," October 7, 2005. https://dpic-cdn.org/production/legacy /StreibJuvDP2005.pdf.
202 **only seven countries in the world had higher incarceration rates**: Katherine Beckett and Heather D. Evans, "About Time: How Long and Life Sentences Fuel Mass Incarceration in Washington State," ACLU of Washington, February 2020. https://lsj .washington.edu/sites/lsj/files/documents/research/05-07-20_formatted_aclu _report.pdf.
204 **No meaningful cognitive difference**: Claudia Rowe, "Washington high court charts less punitive path on juvenile justice," Crosscut, April 1, 2021. https://crosscut .com/opinion/2021/04/washington-high-court-charts-less-punitive-path-juvenile -justice.
212 **shrunk foster care by 25 percent**: United States Department of Health and Human Services, Child Welfare Outcomes State Data. https://cwoutcomes.acf.hhs.gov /cwodatasite/pdf/washington.html.

Chapter 12

219 **endless burnout, insufficient training, and constant turnover**: "Juvenile Rehabilitation Integrated Treatment Model" Legislative Report, Washington State Department of Children, Youth & Families, May 2020, p. 119.
224 **avoid being transferred to state prison on his birthday**: Douglas Haberman, "Prisoner Gets Life Term for Killing Guard," *Los Angeles Times*, Sept. 22, 2001. https://www .latimes.com/archives/la-xpm-2001-sep-22-me-48619-story.html.

Afterword

232 **"in a death spiral"**: Class-action complaint filed by Robert L. Redfearn Jr. et al., April 10, 2024. https://static1.squarespace.com/static/603815c5dc9365633e4c0830/t /6616ab4c872c8f158535b131/1712761676217/Louisiana+Complaint_4.10.2024.pdf.

they died in care at rates 50 percent higher: Andrea Gallo, "Special Report: Suffering So Young in Louisiana," Nola.com, Sept. 23, 2022. https://www.nola.com/news/suffering -so-young/collection_37ff73fc-1ff9-11ed-b105-374f67d3050f.html.

233 **naming Think of Us a recipient of the Audacious Prize**: Drew Lindsay, "Foster Care Veteran Gets $47.5 Million From Audacious Project to Redesign Child-Welfare System," *Chronicle of Philanthropy*, April 17, 2023. https://www.philanthropy.com/article/foster -care-veteran-gets-47-5-million-from-audacious-project-to-redesign-child-welfare -system.

234 **warped the lives of some forty plaintiffs**: Emily Fitzgerald, "$65.3M Settlement Reached for Victims of Alleged Abuse at Centralia Kiwanis Boys Home," *Chronicle*, Dec. 30, 2022. https://www.chronline.com/stories/653m-settlement-reached-for-victims-of -alleged-abuse-at-centralia-kiwanis-boys-home,306159.

237 **"break rules and the law in order to survive"**: Committee Schedules, Agendas, and Documents, Washington State Legislature. https://app.leg.wa.gov/committeeschedules ?eventID=2024011299#/House/31647/01-01-2024/02-29-2024/Schedule///Bill/.